Teaching Students to THINK Like SCIENTISTS

Strategies Aligned With Common Core and Next Generation Science Standards

Maria C. Grant   Douglas Fisher   Diane Lapp

D1295067

Solution Tree | Press

a division of
Solution Tree

555 North Morton Street
Bloomington, IN 47404
800.733.6786 (toll free) / 812.336.7700
FAX: 812.336.7790

email: info@solution-tree.com
solution-tree.com

Visit **go.solution-tree.com/commoncore** to find additional instructional scenarios, download the reproducibles, and access the links in this book.
Printed in the United States of America

17 16 15 14   2 3 4 5

Library of Congress Cataloging-in-Publication Data

Grant, Maria C.
 Teaching students to think like scientists : strategies aligned with common core and next generation science standards / Maria C. Grant, Douglas Fisher, Diane Lapp.
     pages cm
 Includes bibliographical references and index.
  ISBN 978-1-936765-38-6 (perfect bound) 1. Science--Study and teaching--United States. 2. Science--Study and teaching--Standards--United States. I. Title.
  Q183.3.A1G75 2014
  342.3502'1873--dc23
                    2013036618

Solution Tree
Jeffrey C. Jones, CEO
Edmund M. Ackerman, President

Solution Tree Press
President: Douglas M. Rife
Publisher: Robert D. Clouse
Editorial Director: Lesley Bolton
Managing Production Editor: Caroline Weiss
Senior Production Editor: Edward Levy
Copy Editor: Sarah Payne-Mills
Proofreader: Stephanie Koutek
Cover and Text Designer: Rian Anderson

Acknowledgments

Solution Tree Press would like to thank the following reviewers:

Jennifer Albert
Research Associate / STEM Teams
Project Director
Department of STEM Education
North Carolina State University
Raleigh, North Carolina

Lindsy Argus
University of Missouri
Columbia, Missouri

Kathy Brooks
Board of Directors
National Middle Level Science
Teachers Association
Guilford, Connecticut

Adam Devitt
PhD Candidate, Science Education
Steinhardt School of Culture,
Education, and Human Development
New York University
New York, New York

Vito Dipinto
Associate Professor, Curriculum and
Instruction
National Louis University
Wheeling, Illinois

Anita Greasor
Third-Grade Teacher
Benjamin Franklin Elementary School
Terre Haute, Indiana

Todd Hoover
Assistant Professor, Department of
Early Childhood and Adolescent
Education
Bloomsburg University of
Pennsylvania
Bloomsburg, Pennsylvania

Mary Lightbody
Assistant Professor of Science
Education, Department of Teaching
and Learning
College of Education and Human
Ecology
The Ohio State University
Newark, Ohio

Doug Llewellyn
Adjunct Professor
St. John Fisher College
Rochester, New York

Bill Metz
Science Education Consultant
Altoona, Pennsylvania

Theresa Owens
Science and Mathematics Instructor
Laurel Springs School
Charleston, South Carolina

Alison Perkins
Researcher, School of Journalism
University of Montana
Missoula, Montana

Diane Salmon
Director, National College of
Education Research
Associate Professor, Educational
Psychology
National Louis University
Chicago, Illinois

Edward L. Shaw, Jr.
Professor of Elementary Science
Education
University of South Alabama
Mobile, Alabama

Kirsten Smith
Curriculum Specialist for Science
Lincoln Public Schools
Lincoln, Nebraska

Table of Contents

Visit **go.solution-tree.com/commoncore** to find additional instructional scenarios, download the reproducibles, and access the links in this book.

Reproducible titles are in italics.

CHAPTER 3

Learning to Write Like a Scientist

CHAPTER 4

Learning to Read Like a Scientist

CHAPTER 5
Empowering Students to Think Like Scientists

APPENDIX
Reproducibles

References and Resources

Index

About the Authors

Maria Grant, EdD, is an associate professor in secondary education at California State University, Fullerton (CSUF). She has authored numerous publications centered on science literacy, formative assessment, and reading in the content areas, including articles in *Educational Leadership* and the *Journal of Adolescent and Adult Literacy*. She is coauthor with Douglas Fisher of *Reading and Writing in Science: Tools to Develop Disciplinary Literacy*.

Maria teaches courses in the credential and graduate programs at CSUF and conducts professional development with teachers at various schools across the United States. She is director of the Secondary Teacher Education Program and leads the Literacy Summer Seminar Series and the Intern Program at CSUF. Additionally, she has over two decades of public school teaching experience at the K–12 level, covering a wide array of science content, including chemistry, physics, integrated science, biological science, and earth science.

Maria earned a doctorate in education at the University of San Diego / San Diego State University joint doctoral program and a master of arts in curriculum and instruction at San Diego State University. She earned a bachelor of arts in geological sciences at the University of California, Santa Barbara.

Douglas Fisher, PhD, is a professor of educational leadership at San Diego State University and a teacher leader at Health Sciences High and Middle College. He teaches graduate courses in policy, leadership, research, and literacy. He was formerly director of professional development for the City Heights Educational Collaborative and also taught English at Hoover High School.

Douglas received an International Reading Association Celebrate Literacy Award for his work on literacy leadership. For his work as codirector of the City Heights Professional Development Schools, he received the Christa McAuliffe Award. He was also corecipient of the Farmer Award for excellence in writing from the National Council of Teachers of English for his article "Using Graphic Novels, Anime, and the Internet in an Urban High School," published in the *English Journal*.

Douglas has written numerous articles on reading and literacy, differentiated instruction, and curriculum design. He is also the author and coauthor of numerous books, including *In a Reading State of Mind, Checking for Understanding, Better Learning Through Structured Teaching, Text Complexity, Literacy 2.0, Teaching Students to Read Like Detectives, Implementing RTI With English Learners, The School Leader's Guide to English Learners*, and the *Common Core English Language Arts in a PLC at Work*™ series.

Douglas earned a bachelor's degree in communication, a master's degree in public health education, an executive master's degree in business, and a doctoral degree in multicultural education. He completed his postdoctoral study at the National Association of State Boards of Education with a focus on standards-based reforms.

Diane Lapp, EdD, is a distinguished professor of education at San Diego State University and an English teacher and literacy coach at Health Sciences High and Middle College (HSHMC). Previously, she taught elementary and middle school. Diane focuses on instruction that supports learning for a diverse range of students. Her career is founded on the idea that motivation and well-planned, guided instruction must be based on a continuous assessment of students' strengths and needs.

Throughout her career as an educator and education professor, Diane has been drawn to urban schools catering to children of poverty, who are often misunderstood, misdiagnosed, and mistreated because of the lack of communication that frequently exists between their families and teachers. Combining her two current positions, she established a high school student internship program between HSHMC and a neighborhood preK–6 school with a 95 percent population of English learners.

As an educator, she has won numerous awards and in 2005 was inducted into the International Reading Association Hall of Fame. Diane has authored, coauthored, and edited dozens of books, articles, and speeches, including *Teaching Students to Read Like Detectives: Comprehending, Analyzing, and Discussing Texts* (with Douglas Fisher and Nancy Frey); *Handbook of Research on the Teaching of the English Language Arts* (with Douglas Fisher); *Effective Instruction for English Language Learners* (with J. Jacobson and K. Johnson); *Exemplary Instruction in the*

Middle Grades: Teaching That Supports Engagement and Rigorous Learning (with B. Moss); and *Literacy Growth for Every Child: Differentiated Small-Group Instruction K–6* (with Douglas Fisher and T. D. Wolsey).

Diane earned a doctorate from Indiana University, a master's degree from Western Michigan University, and a bachelor's degree from Ohio Northern University.

To book Maria C. Grant, Douglas Fisher, or Diane Lapp for professional development, contact pd@solution-tree.com.

Introduction

Teaching elementary school students is both demanding and exciting. It involves making numerous daily decisions about curriculum, differentiation, classroom management, and assessment. You are being asked to also accommodate the demands required by both the Next Generation Science Standards (NGSS) and the Common Core State Standards (CCSS). As you prepare for this, do you sometimes feel that science teaching is one of your weaker areas, and although you invite your students to dabble in experimentation, are you unsure of how to help them augment their scientific understandings and then argue their positions? As a result of our own work in classrooms, we have realized the need to address these questions in support of our colleagues—educators like you—who are attempting to nurture rather than squelch the scientific curiosity of their students.

Teaching Students to Think Like Scientists: Strategies Aligned With Common Core and Next Generation Science Standards is a direct response to these questions. Specifically, this book shares ways to integrate science and literacy—ways that draw on many well-known instructional strategies as well as new methods to engage students in the language and practices of scientists and engineers. Science, engineering, and technology are intimately connected in real-world practices. These areas of study hold the keys to future research and development that will likely maintain and sustain progress on a global level. Cures for diseases, new devices, and novel methods for living on and protecting our planet are all dependent on a generation of young people who understand the founding principles of science, engineering, and technology. However, our workforce lacks foundational knowledge in these areas of study. The development of the Next Generation Science Standards is closely tied to this societal need (National Research Council [NRC], 2012).

Although the CCSS and the NGSS offer grade-level science and literacy goals, most teachers and parents will agree that students learn in stages that cannot be precisely associated with a given grade level. We do, however, know that when teachers offer students exciting learning challenges coupled with sound instructional practices, they will become agents for their own learning. The classroom scenarios we share in this book provide exemplars of students who, while ready at different times, are creating new science and literacy understandings.

This book is intended to help you use all that you know about teaching the English language arts to support your students in learning to read, write, and communicate about science. It is intended to help you guide students as they consider critical criteria in written, graphical, oral, or digital forms. In the 21st century, people are making decisions every day regarding which cell phone to invest in for the next couple of years, which food products to consume, or which candidate to support when going into the voting booth. They may one day need to know how to evaluate treatments for diabetes or heart disease or to make important decisions about energy use. These issues require that everyday citizens be capable of reading, analyzing, and evaluating issues in logical, strategic ways. It is through dialogue and oral language that students learn how to use data to discuss and argue an issue and come to mindful conclusions. Informed problem solving rooted in scientific inquiry thinking is the ultimate underpinning of this book.

It's a pivotal time for elementary school educators—a time of transformation and change, particularly when it comes to teaching science. Experts in the area of science education agree that science instruction should no longer consist of a series of teacher- or text-delivered facts that students memorize and recite in thought-devoid ways (Bybee, 2011; Minner, Levy, & Century, 2010; Reiser, Berland, & Kenyon, 2012). Instead, science instruction must present opportunities for students to think, talk, and write about the science they see and experience in their world. In the lesson scenarios we share, K–6 teachers implement science instruction that aligns with the CCSS for English language arts / literacy (National Governors Association Center for Best Practices [NGA] & Council of Chief State School Officers [CCSSO], 2010a) and the NGSS (www.nextgenscience.org), including the National Research Council's (NRC, 2012) foundational document, *A Framework for K–12 Science Education: Practices, Crosscutting Concepts, and Core Ideas*. (Visit **go.solution-tree.com/commoncore** to find additional scenarios, download the reproducibles, and access the links in this book.)

Throughout, we will note connections to the CCSS, NGSS, and NRC frameworks. These connections include references to the three dimensions of the NGSS:

1. The scientific and engineering practices—The NRC (2012) utilizes the term *practices* instead of the alternative term *skills*. This is intended to indicate that "engaging in scientific inquiry requires coordination of both knowledge and skill simultaneously" (p.41).

2. **Crosscutting concepts**—These include *patterns*; *cause and effect*; *scale*, *proportion*, and *quantity*; *systems* and *system models*; *energy* and *matter*; *flows*, *cycles*, and *conservation*; *structure* and *function*; and *stability* and *change*. The NRC (2012) defines crosscutting as those "concepts that bridge disciplinary boundaries, having explanatory value throughout much of science and engineering" (p. 83).

3. **Disciplinary core ideas**—These concepts were selected to provide students with an organizational framework that connects knowledge from various disciplines. Each core disciplinary idea had to meet at least two criteria (NRC, 2012), though many meet three or four. A core idea for K–12 science instruction should:

   a. Have broad importance across multiple sciences or engineering disciplines or be a key organizing principle of a single discipline

   b. Provide a key tool for understanding or investigating more complex ideas and solving problems

   c. Relate to the interests and life experiences of students or be connected to societal or personal concerns that require scientific or technological knowledge

   d. Be teachable and learnable over multiple grades at increasing levels of depth and sophistication (that is, the idea can be made accessible to younger students but is broad enough to sustain continued investigation over years)

In addition, we feature the following underpinnings of the NGSS as they play out in the teaching of grades K–6:

- Gathering and reviewing evidence
- Designing, conducting, and analyzing experiments
- Developing and presenting arguments, both in writing and orally
- Using models to gather data and make predictions by noting patterns

The emphasis on STEM (science, technology, engineering, and mathematics) learning is also woven into the lesson scenarios presented in this text.

Reading This Book

Chapter 1 suggests using all you know about teaching English language arts to support classroom science instruction. Chapters 2 through 4, on speaking and listening, writing, and reading instruction, are all structured according to an easy-to-follow protocol. We begin with "What You'll Learn in This Chapter." Then, in "What Are the Standards?" we discuss how the CCSS and the NGSS address the chapter topic. Following that, the section titled "Evidence Supporting These Standards" shares the supporting research. Finally, "Into the Classroom" offers grade-level scenarios that include implementation activities, lesson ideas, and instructional practices that mesh with standards-based science content.

The K–6 scenarios in chapters 2, 3, and 4, organized as stand-alones, provide virtual opportunities to explore real-world classroom instruction that can be adapted to your own classrooms. We also include in each of the chapters "Questions for Discussion or Reflection" that you can use to individually reflect on teaching and learning or as a way for small professional development groups to debrief and brainstorm ideas for implementation and extension. These three chapters flow from oral language to writing to reading—with the science content and engineering and science practices intertwined.

Table I.1 shows the breakdown of the scenarios in these three chapters according to grade, content area, and topic covered. Scenarios shaded in gray can be found online (at **go.solution-tree.com/commoncore**).

Table I.1. Grade, Content Area, and Topic of Lesson Scenarios in Chapters 2–4

(PS = physical sciences; LS = life sciences; ESS = earth and space sciences; ETS = engineering, technology, and application of science)

Chapter	Grade	Content	Topic
2	K	PS, ETS	Identify forces, motion, and types of interaction.
2	1	LS, ETS	Understand that plants need water, minerals, and sunlight.
2	2	PS, ETS	Understand that some changes caused by heating and cooling can be reversed and some cannot.
2	3	ESS, ETS	Explain how to solve a flooding problem.
2	4	PS	Explain how force makes objects move.
2	4	ESS, ETS	Describe how the process of weathering and erosion affect the surface of the earth.
2	4	LS	Explain how the heart functions to support blood flow.
2	5	ESS	Discuss the phases of the moon and patterns that result from the position of the sun, earth, and moon.

Chapter	Grade	Content	Topic
2	6	ESS	Explain relationships between plate boundaries and earthquakes and volcanoes.
3	K	ESS	Describe the characteristics of animals, like our pets.
3	1	PS	Explain the cause of sound.
3	2	ESS, ETS	Understand the places on Earth where water is solid and where it is liquid.
3	3	LS	Describe the life cycle of a frog.
3	4	PS	Comprehend the causes of waves.
3	5	LS	Understand the survival needs of organisms by writing a series of short paragraphs.
3	5	ESS	Conduct an inquiry-based investigation in an academic format.
3	6	ESS	Explore real-world issues of human impact on the environment.
4	K	ESS, ETS	Identify how weather changes over time.
4	1	PS, ETS	Explain how light moves through different objects.
4	2	ESS	Determine which earth processes are fast events and which are slow events.
4	3	LS	Identify common elements of the life cycle of organisms.
4	4	PS, ETS	Design and construct a device that converts energy from one form to another.
4	5	PS, ETS	Design experiments that answer questions about phase changes.
4	6	LS	Ask questions about how matter is cycled and how energy flows from living and nonliving organisms through an ecosystem.

In chapter 5, we identify and discuss effective formative assessment practices based on the scenarios in chapters 2–4. Finally, the appendix contains reproducible pages, which may also be found online (at **go.solution-tree.com /commoncore**).

Because elementary school educators are already well versed in teaching reading, writing, speaking and listening, and language, we have—like the CCSS—used these literacy processes as the foundational elements of this book. We believe that the integration of science, inquiry learning, and engineering practices coupled with these literacy processes will seem like a natural, attainable, and thoroughly fun way for young people to learn about their world. It is our hope that practicing teachers and those preparing to be teachers will implement the ideas in this text as a means to empower their students with the cognitive tools needed to explore, examine, know, and explain our natural world; generate and evaluate evidence; understand and construct scientific information; and participate productively in communicating and creating knowledge about our planet. With mental tools like these, young people can move toward a future in which they participate in an imaginative, well-connected, knowledgeable science community.

Standards Terminology

The CCSS revolve around key terms—*strands*, *anchor standards*, *domains*, *grade-specific standards*, and *grade bands*.

- **Strands:** The CCSS have four main divisions, or strands, for grades K–5 and 6–12: Reading, Writing, Speaking and Listening, and Language. Additionally, the Reading strand has two parts: Reading Standards for Literature (RL) and Reading Standards for Informational Text (RI). Foundational Skills (RF) is a third set of standards in the Reading strand for grades K–5 (see NGA & CCSSO, 2010a, pp. 15–17). The English Language Arts and Literacy in History/Social Studies, Science, and Technical Subjects standards are broken into two strands—a K–5 strand and a 6–12 strand. The literacy standards for history and social studies, science, and technical subjects have two strands—Reading (RH and RST) and Writing (WH and WST; see NGA & CCSSO, 2010a, pp. 60–66).

- **Anchor standards:** These general, cross-disciplinary expectations for college and career readiness (CCRA) are defined for each strand—Reading, Writing, Speaking and Listening, and Language—as well as the two strands in the Literacy standards. The anchor standards are numbered consecutively for each strand. For example, CCSS ELA-Literacy.CCRA.R.1 signifies college and career readiness anchor standard (CCRA), Reading strand (R), and anchor standard one (1). In this book, we use a simplified version of the standard designation; in this case, that designation is CCRA.R.1.

- **Domains:** The anchor standards are divided into specific categories for each of the ELA and literacy strands. These domains are consistent across the grades and ensure continuity as the standards increase in rigor and complexity. For example, the four domains in the Reading strand are (1) Key Ideas and Details, (2) Craft and Structure, (3) Integration of Knowledge and Ideas, and (4) Range of Reading and Level of Text Complexity (see NGA & CCSSO, 2010a, p. 10).

- **Grade-specific standards:** When people refer to the CCSS, they are likely referring to the grade-level standards. As the anchor standards are overarching expectations for an entire grade band, each grade-level standard defines what students should understand and be able to do at the end of each year. However, these standards correspond to anchor standards and domains with the similar number designations. For example, SL.3.1 signifies Speaking and Listening, grade 3, and standard one in the domain Comprehension and Collaboration. RST.6–8.1 signifies Reading strand, science, technical subjects, grade band 6–8, standard one.
- **Grade bands:** These are grade-level groupings—K–2, 3–5, 6–8, 9–10, and 11–12.

Using the K–12 Next Generation Science Standards

The National Research Council's (2012) framework for K–12 science education and the NGSS (Achieve, 2013a) identify the core ideas and practices that all students should achieve by the time they complete high school. With grade-band endpoints noted at grades 2, 5, 8, and 12, this framework defines knowledge and real-world applications that students should amass during their K–12 years in order to be scientifically literate on graduation from high school. The identification of core ideas relates to the content or concepts one should know in an area of science, while practices relate to one's *use* of those ideas.

The core ideas or concepts are drawn from the life sciences, physical sciences, earth and space sciences, and engineering and technology and from the applications or practices of these concepts as they are scaffolded across the grades. For example, in the physical sciences, the concepts involving matter and its interactions would be explored through the following eight key activities, which, according to Rodger Bybee (2011), represent an integration of scientific and engineering practices:

1. Asking questions and defining problems
2. Developing and using models
3. Planning and carrying out investigations
4. Analyzing and interpreting data

5. Using many resources from math, technology, and computational thinking

6. Constructing explanations and designing solutions

7. Engaging in argument from evidence

8. Obtaining, evaluating, and communicating findings

How would these eight practices apply to life science (LS), physical science (PS), earth and space science (ESS), and engineering and technology science (ETS)? In life science, students making real-world observations of the life cycles of frogs and butterflies could document these observations in the form of field notes and sketches. They could then design an experiment to test the questions they formulated. Another group might conduct Internet research to determine what other experts have learned from similar studies. Consider all of the knowledge that students would acquire as they explore scientific ideas through engineering practices. And consider the skills based on inquiry that students would develop through such study. Students would likely cultivate problem-solving skills that could extend into other aspects of their lives. They might hone an inquisitive, critical-thinking mindset that propels them to ask questions and seek out answers based on evidence. Along the way, they are building foundational science knowledge that will help them make personal decisions about their lives, their environment, and planet Earth.

In physical science, students might spend time observing free fall as they drop various objects (paper, tennis balls, flat pieces of cardboard, and so on) from different heights. Using their observational notes, they could work with a partner to come up with an explanation for the varying speeds of falling objects, and just like true scientists, these students could initiate ideas about air resistance and free fall. Their conjectures and wonderings could lead them to research regarding free fall in empty space (a vacuum). Then, mirroring the astronauts of *Apollo* 15, they might try to determine ways to test these ideas (visit **go.solution-tree.com /commoncore** for a YouTube video of *Apollo* 15 footage). In earth and space sciences, students learning about fossils might work in groups to correlate rocks and fossil species with geological eras. Using such data, they could forecast Earth events and determine the age of rocks, just like real geologists.

The NGSS (www.nextgenscience.org/next-generation-science-standards) may be viewed either using the disciplinary core ideas (these are the foundational concepts in physical sciences, life sciences, earth and space sciences, and engineering and technology) or by topic. The NGSS document provides a summary of the standards for elementary grades, followed by a story line and specific standards for each grade level. Handy charts that note the science and engineering practices, disciplinary core ideas, and crosscutting concepts are presented for each grade level.

The concept of *inquiry* plays a crucial role in the NGSS. The National Science Teachers Association (NSTA) adopts the National Science Education Standards' definition of inquiry as:

> the diverse ways in which scientists study the natural world and propose explanations based on the evidence derived from their work. Scientific inquiry also refers to the activities through which students develop knowledge and understanding of scientific ideas, as well as an understanding of how scientists study the natural world. (NRC, 1996, p. 23)

NSTA (2004) further elaborates on the concept of *inquiry instruction*, recommending that teachers:

- Guide students to learn how to develop scientific investigations that address questions
- Use appropriate investigative steps
- Reflect on how science is done
- Utilize data collection and analyses to change perceptions about the world
- Act in a skeptical manner when assessing science work
- Seek out explanations based on logical understandings of data

While we all can likely acknowledge that instruction founded on this kind of practice is good science instruction, the means by which to accomplish inquiry thinking and investigation are sometimes elusive. One way to approximate aspects of inquiry instruction is to apply the 5Es: *engage, explore, explain, elaborate,* and *evaluate.* We have defined the various components of the 5E model using the scientific practices of the NGSS. With this often-adopted method of teaching science, students begin with an *engage* activity—one that fosters questioning, the articulation of problems to be studied, and the use of models. The *explore* phase involves students planning and carrying out investigations. This is followed up by the *explain* part of the process. At this point, students analyze and interpret data. They may, as called for in the NGSS, use mathematical information, computer technology, and computational thinking, and they construct explanations in attempts to design solutions. When they *elaborate,* they extend the discussion of the data and perhaps develop a conclusion or evidence-based argument drawn from the data. Finally, when students *evaluate*, they make informed judgments and communicate their information.

Teachers can introduce students in the early grades to scientific concepts using pictures, diagrams, and models of animals, flowers, trees, bicycles, cars, airplanes, stars, and so on. With graduated instruction, teachers can expose upper-grade students to models with more mathematical, computational, and conceptual sophistication. The expectation for students at all grade levels is that they will be able to understand the concepts well enough to analyze and manipulate data in order to formulate explanations, propose solutions, and identify new questions to study. The concept of *inquiry instruction* will be woven through this text at all grade levels as a means to foster both independent and collaborative critical thinking. These investigations and activities do not necessarily have predetermined outcomes. Rather, in following an investigation, students examine data and draw their own conclusions.

Connecting Science Content and the CCSS Instructional Shifts

The NRC (2012) framework for science and the Common Core State Standards (NGA & CCSSO, 2010a) will be examined for common threads. The CCSS identify the essential literacy practices for grades K–12 students to become literate individuals prepared "to enter college and workforce training programs" (p. 4). The NGA and CCSSO developed the CCSS for U.S. students to foster common expectations in English language arts and literacy in history and social studies, science, and technical subjects.

Six pedagogical shifts are woven throughout the CCSS for English language arts.

1. Balancing informational and literary text: For elementary school educators, this means a move toward more nonfiction, which has previously been relegated to only a small part of the instructional time in most teachers' classrooms.

2. Building knowledge in the disciplines: This shift emphasizes building knowledge about the world through text in content-area studies.

3. Increasing text complexity: This shift underscores the requirement that students read grade-appropriate text centered on a *staircase* of instruction, gradually increasing in complexity from beginning to advanced levels. Teachers guide students to accomplish this by providing the support and time needed to focus on close reading.

4. **Using text-based answers:** This shift underscores the need for students to engage in rich, rigorous conversations rooted in evidence gleaned from text.

5. **Writing from sources:** This shift reiterates the concept that students must develop written arguments based on evidence from sources.

6. **Using academic vocabulary:** This shift notes that students should build transferable vocabulary to access grade-level complex texts. This implies an emphasis on academic terms like *hypothesize* and *subsequent*, instead of a focus solely on commonly taught technical terms (like *mitosis* or *mitochondria*, for example). To accomplish this, teachers must lead students through increasingly complex texts.

As a result of these two sets of standards, the NGSS and the CCSS, school administrators will need to mandate an increase in instructional time for teaching science that integrates science, technology, engineering, and mathematics. While this may be sound practice, many elementary school teachers who were not science majors need assistance to effectively teach science with the depth of understanding that will foster learning at the levels.

The examples shared in this book will support conversations in teachers' collaborative teams about how to design science instruction that aligns instructional practice with the requirements of the CCSS. See the Questions for Discussion or Reflection throughout the book.

Spiraling Skill Development

You'll notice as you read that many of the science topics discussed in early elementary grades (K–3) appear again in the content for upper elementary grades (4–6) in a more in-depth form. This type of spiraling is built into the CCSS and the NRC framework and the related NGSS. It is intended to foster the type of instruction that allows a student to examine foundational concepts in a more than superficial way. For instance, students might study forces and motion in K–2 by noting that objects can be pushed or pulled. By grade 5, they understand that forces on objects are exerted with a particular magnitude and in a particular direction and that they affect other aspects of motion, like velocity and acceleration. This is intended to prepare students for middle school and high school work in which they investigate Newton's laws of motion, frames of reference, and friction. With growing sophistication, a single foundational concept (for example, "a force is a push or pull") can turn into a world of understanding in which new designs for vehicles powered in alternative ways motor across our freeways and new forms of machinery gather energy sources that exceed our wildest imaginations. Invention and decision making will be in the hands of the young people sitting at the little desks in our classrooms today. Elementary educators must begin their preparation for this future.

Linking the NGSS and the CCSS

Learners examine the interdisciplinary content areas of STEM within real-world contexts by making connections among school, community, and work. While it's clear that inquiry is a foundation of all exceptional science curricula, the NRC framework calls for an extension of inquiry learning into scientific and engineering practices as a means to deepen understanding of the nature of science. The instructional examples shared in this text draw on the scientific and engineering practices as a lens through which students address content and literacy learning. It is a lens of investigation, evidence-based conclusions, and real-world applications.

Working in tandem, the NGSS and the CCSS identify the need to equip K–12 students with the skills they need to be literate in academic disciplines. This involves gaining proficiency with the language, knowledge, skills, and habits of investigation and study so that students can comprehend, communicate, and challenge text-based information. Specifically, in order to become proficient when reading an informational text, students must learn to (1) identify key ideas and details, (2) understand its structure, (3) integrate existing and new knowledge and ideas, (4) engage with texts of various levels of complexity, and (5) continue acquiring the language and content of any scientific topic. When sharing ideas through writing, they must also learn to do research in order to build on and present their knowledge (NGA & CCSSO, 2010a).

Because vocabulary knowledge is key to reading and writing informational texts, the CCSS also identify an escalation of the skills needed to acquire a working knowledge of both technical and academic language or the registers of a particular discipline. This involves teaching students how to clarify the meanings of unknown and multiple-meaning words and phrases by using context clues and determining word relationships by understanding the nuances of words and affixes (prefixes and suffixes) that lead to meaning. This is of particular importance when it comes to reading and writing informational science texts.

In essence, the CCSS, combined with the NRC framework and the NGSS, illustrate the importance for all teachers, especially science educators, of modeling and teaching students connections among science concepts, real-life issues, and the language they will meet in in-school and out-of-school experiences. While the CCSS call for teachers to address this intersection of content, language, and societal issues across content areas, this integration is unique when it comes to teaching science because of the role that inquiry plays. If a teacher is working to help students understand the influence that the ocean has on weather and the role the water cycle plays in weather patterns, she might first share information about the El Niño oscillation—a relevant, real-world phenomenon that influences weather patterns, including drought and flooding situations. Consider all of the vocabulary that needs to be taught in context of a science topic. Science is jam-packed with academic language written in a concise and direct manner. Words such as *observation* and *indication* have particular meanings when used in science. Complex structures that show cause-and-effect relationships and problem-and-solution patterns are pervasive. Words like *oscillation*, *nutrients*, and *thermocline* are critical to a full conversation on the topic.

However, while a mere definition gleaned from a dictionary might seem sufficient, the comprehension of scientific language requires more than a rote recitation from *Webster's*. An understanding of how and why warm waters pile up in the equatorial Pacific Ocean is foundational to comprehending the *oscillation* pattern. Understanding how the *thermocline* can become depressed in the eastern Pacific is essential to understanding that term. Finally, knowing that *nutrient-rich* waters increase productivity and support fisheries goes beyond the term *nutrient*.

When teachers have tools to help them identify and teach vocabulary within a content area in a deep, meaningful way, students understand the concepts and improve their reading comprehension. When students learn to recognize science language and structural patterns, they are more readily able to digest and interpret scientific ideas and, as a result, to generate their own ideas—a desired goal of any educator trying to foster critical-thinking skills.

Structure of the CCSS for ELA and Literacy

The Common Core State Standards for English language arts and literacy (NGA & CCSSO, 2010a) have three main sections: (1) grades K–5 English language arts standards, (2) grades 6–12 English language arts standards, and (3) grades 6–12 standards for literacy in history and social studies, science, and technical subjects. This book will focus on the standards for grades K–6. Additionally, three appendices accompany the CCSS: (1) Appendix A: Research Supporting Key Elements of the Standards and Glossary of Key Terms, (2) Appendix B: Text Exemplars and Sample Performance Tasks, and (3) Appendix C: Samples of Student Writing (NGA & CCSSO, 2010b, 2010c, 2010d).

Comparing Student Readiness: Kate and Marcel

The teachers we showcase in the chapter scenarios continuously observe their students' behaviors and adjust their subsequent instructional activities to promote each student's scientific language and conceptual learning. Their classrooms are filled with students, like Kate and Marcel, who come to school with a wide array of language experiences that enable additional language learning.

Seven-year-old Kate has always enjoyed learning about her environment. When she was just five, her parents took her to the local science museum, where she pulled levers, watched a tornado form, and even saw a table tennis ball hover over an air vent. The swimming lessons she's participated in since she was barely three have helped her to understand that if you want to float, you'll have to spread your arms out so they are perpendicular to your extended body; rolling up into a ball tends to make a person sink. Kate has heard the caw of a great blue heron sitting atop a nest built in the upper branches of an old eucalyptus tree that lies on the outer perimeter of the park she frequently visits. She's planted trees on Arbor Day and checked out library books about beach sand. Consider the extensive exposure to informal science that Kate has already experienced in her short life: the mechanics of a simple machine, the concept of buoyant force in water, and the real-world observation of a stately bird in its natural habitat. It's no wonder she excels in science. The technical terms and academic vocabulary she uses to discuss what she experiences, both inside and outside the classroom, are a testament to the value of background knowledge when it comes to informational learning.

In contrast, eight-year-old Marcel, who lives in an urban apartment building, has not had the opportunity to visit a museum—any museum. His daily path to and from school consists of a hurried stroll along a sidewalk to the bus stop, followed by a fifteen-minute ride in which the driver pauses at almost every corner to add new riders or release passengers to their drop-off destinations. He's seen a few cats roaming around his neighborhood, and there are trees in planters that line the sidewalks, but he's never been to the country or to the beach. Marcel's world has not allowed him to connect words to science sights, sounds, and experiences. As a matter of fact, he really doesn't have a clear understanding of what science is all about. He has a sense that it's something difficult, with lots of hard words, and that it's only suitable for "really smart people."

Consider the divergent life experiences of Kate and Marcel. Students just like them occupy thousands of chairs in classrooms across the United States. Can educators mediate the gap in knowledge that results from such contrasting life experiences? Can they offer a student like Marcel learning opportunities that will help him feel comfortable and competent when talking about science? Can they offer students like Kate ways to go deeper with content? We believe they can.

Early experiences have a deep impact on the kind of knowledge and experience students have when they meet their classroom teachers. What they already know is a base from which their school learning must grow. Science curriculum needs to be developed around core topics such as force, motion, and cell theory—topics that students investigate over time as they engage in scientific practice to extend the base of information and understanding they possess when they enter school.

In their study of high school chemistry students, Kiesha Williams, Katrina Kurtek, and Victor Sampson (2011) note four central elements of science learning: (1) self-efficacy—the beliefs a student holds about his or her own abilities; (2) interest—a student's level of concern with and curiosity about science; (3) value—how important science, scientific knowledge, and science-related activities are to a student; and (4) identity—how students view and present themselves and how others see them. They found that many students had positive attitudes relating to one or more of these elements.

Of greatest concern, however, were students who had negative attitudes, especially relating to self-efficacy and identity. As educators, we know that students, regardless of grade level, who have low self-efficacy are likely to exert low effort in the science classroom, because they think there is an inherent barrier that prevents them from learning science. These roadblocks prevent their moving forward into the curious, wondrous, and thought-provoking world of science. Instead of dooming a potentially inquisitive young person to the sidelines of science, educators must find ways to pull these learners into the fold so that they, too, may engage in scientific thinking and become conversant in science talk. Young people need to see that there are different ways to use language, depending on the need and the setting. There are times to converse casually on the playground and at home, and there are times to read, write, and talk about science in the classroom. The time to engage students is in the elementary school setting, before they develop a perspective that science is nothing more than a hurdle on the way to a diploma. This is the focus of chapter one.

CHAPTER 1

Empowering Students to Learn Scientific Practices

Think for a few minutes about all of the good teachers you've encountered in your lifetime. What qualities led you to put them in your best-teacher category? Look for the possible reasons in table 1.1, and check each statement that describes your best teachers. (Visit **go.solution-tree.com/commoncore** for a reproducible version of this table.)

Table 1.1: Characteristics of Your Best Teachers

Characteristic	
They were supportive in the way they interacted with me and other students.	
It was obvious that they cared about their students and enjoyed teaching.	
The lessons they shared were motivating.	
They provided opportunities for me to work with others in the class.	
I could see the reasons for doing what they asked.	
If I didn't get it the first time, they were willing to keep helping me.	
I had some input into the materials I used, the projects I engaged in, and the ways I responded to an assignment.	
They made the content so interesting that I continue to enjoy it and seek out related topics.	

These are some of the strengths that the best teachers have. As you can see, they interact with students, plan and implement purposeful instruction that motivates students, and are patient supporters offering additional instruction on the side to ensure that every student learns. Do you have these strengths?

As elementary school teachers, we are often very good at providing excellent purposeful instruction when we are teaching our students how to read and write.

Like most of your elementary school colleagues, you probably love to teach English language arts, and because of this, you're wonderful at sharing ideas through picturewalks, think-alouds, and guided reading groups. During these times, you teach your students to read fluently, dig deeply into a piece of literature to analyze the traits of a character, make predictions based on the clues the author gives, identify the language devices the author uses to persuade, and finally use critical thinking to evaluate, synthesize, and summarize as they compare characters and ideas across texts.

You probably also enjoy working with your students to select books for their literature circles, which you teach them to work in very productively and collaboratively. Reader's theater, dramatic play, and author's chair are most likely some of the effective routines you use to support your students' continuing language development. Interactive writing opportunities and writers' workshops, in which you teach your students how to pose ideas and persuade others while using their knowledge of language to share written reports, plays, poems, and stories, may also be very alive in your classroom. Much very well-planned learning happens every day during the English language arts block.

Is your instruction *equally* as motivating when you move into science instruction? You may be secure in saying that during science time students are engaged in very motivating activities because you are using a wonderful science kit that identifies grade-level topics and related experiments that students enjoy exploring. But you may not feel as secure teaching science as you do language arts. In order to ensure that your science time is as motivating and effective as your English language arts instruction, let's reflect on what drives your English language arts instruction and use those strengths to support your science teaching.

To begin, you have a plan and a purpose for the instruction that's being shared. Once you have identified these, you then have many ways of building the base of knowledge that students will need. This base includes the content, the language related to the content, and the skills students need to read, write, orally communicate, and study the topic or text. You continually assess to ensure that your instruction is scaffolded through the questions, prompts, and guided instruction you offer small homogeneous and heterogeneous groups. You often identify areas for inquiry that appear in your science kit. You repeatedly provide interventions until every child achieves the lesson's purpose and has amassed the knowledge needed to function both collaboratively and independently.

The collaboration that occurs as students engage in inquiry through scientific investigation is magical. Students love science and often generate many questions that springboard them to new areas of investigation. At all grades, students are very inquisitive about their world. In first grade, questions arising from an investigation of weather may include "How do weather reporters know if a storm is coming?" or "How can air have pressure?" Third graders exploring the states of matter might conclude with questions such as "Does every material on Earth fit into the category of solid, liquid, or gas?" or "Why are some materials, like seawater, made up of two types of matter: solid and liquid?" By fifth grade, students studying elements and matter often ask, "Why or how do sodium and chloride join together to form the salt that we put into our salt shakers?"

From Inquiry to Practice

Utilizing students' natural inquisitiveness, let's consider instruction designed to teach students to use the language and practices of scientists and engineers. These interrelated practices ensure that students' questions will grow in sophistication and in the understanding of how to use questions to identify possible problems for investigation. Then, students conduct an investigation that yields data or findings that through analysis catapult them into solutions, new questions, and the next problems to study. *Science inquiry* involves the development of questions and problems that can be addressed through scientific investigations. In contrast, *engineering problem solving* involves design and innovation rooted in an understanding of science concepts. While these two elements of science practice are explicitly different, they work in tandem. Teaching students to add an engineering dimension to their science questions involves envisioning a related problem and its possible resolution. Table 1.2 (page 20) has sample science and engineering questions.

If we are to help foster creative and critical-thinking skills, we must guide our students to use their science knowledge and inquiry to further their focus on engineering practices. Additionally, the NGSS call for students in elementary school to use engineering reasoning skills to address the following essential questions (Achieve, 2012):

- Grades K–2—What are different ways to solve problems and meet challenges?

- Grades 3–5—How can people work together to create better designs?

- Grade 6—How can you compare, test, and refine different solutions to problems to arrive at the best design?

As the learning and doing examples shared in table 1.2 illustrate, being able to link scientific knowledge and evidence-based explanations with engineering

Table 1.2: The Partnership of Science (Learning) and Engineering (Doing)

Grade	Science Questions "Why is . . . ?" "How is . . . ?" "What happens . . . ?"	Engineering Questions "How can . . . ?" "Are there ways . . . ?" "How could . . . ?"
K	**Life Sciences**	
	"How do some plants and animals survive in certain environments and others don't?"	"How can we enjoy swimming near coral reefs and still protect them?"
	Earth and Space Sciences	
	"How do scientists describe the weather (sunny, cloudy, rainy, warm, or otherwise)?"	"How can we tell if a large rainstorm is nearing so that we can warn people?"
	Physical Sciences	
	"How do we change how fast a toy car moves across the floor?"	"How can we design public train systems that are fast and safe?"
1	**Life Sciences**	
	"Why do certain plants and certain animals live in certain environments?"	"What can we do to help sustain the environment in areas where trees are being cut down to make paper, furniture, and other products?"
	Earth and Space Sciences	
	"How does the heat from the sun affect land, water, and air?" "Why does the moon appear differently in the sky on different days of the month?"	"How can we use what we know about how land and water heat up to help people who live near a lake or an ocean?" "How can we make new discoveries about objects that are very far away, like the moon or stars?"
	Physical Sciences	
	"How are substances affected by heating, cooling, and mixing?" "How do vibrating materials make sound?"	"Are there ways that we can use the ideas of heating, cooling, or mixing of substances to solve problems like icy roads in the winter or dried-out fields in countries with drought?" "How can we reduce noise for people who live near airports, train tracks, or freeways?"

	Science Questions	Engineering Questions
2	**Life Sciences**	
	"How does light affect the growth of a plant?"	"How could tropical plants be grown in a cold environment?"
	Earth and Space Sciences	
	"What happens, over time, when water from rain falls on rocks?"	"How can we prevent weathering of rocks on which homes are built?"
	Physical Sciences	
	"In what ways can we classify matter?"	"How can we use properties of matter to design a house that stays warm in the winter and cool in the summer?"
3	**Life Sciences**	
	"How do certain animals and plants live and grow in the tundra? In the forests? In the grasslands?"	"How can we protect the tundra? The forests? The grasslands?"
	Earth and Space Sciences	
	"How do scientists use data to predict weather?"	"How can we use weather data to help people survive severe weather conditions, like hurricanes or tornados?"
	Physical Sciences	
	"How do we describe the forces that act between two magnets placed near each other in various positions?"	"How can magnetism be used to facilitate faster, more efficient public transit systems?"
4	**Life Sciences**	
	"Why do we need kidneys to remove cellular waste from the blood?"	"How could we use an understanding of kidney function to design an artificial kidney for people with chronic kidney disease?"
	Earth and Space Sciences	
	"Why does the surface of Earth change when water, wind, and ice move over or across it?"	"How can we prevent a mountainside from weathering and eroding in a cold, wet environment?"
	Physical Sciences	
	"How does the structure of the eye allow humans to see?"	"How can we use technological advances to correct problems with vision?"

Continued➔

	Science Questions	Engineering Questions
5	**Life Sciences**	
	"How are producers and consumers related in a food chain?"	"How can we use what we know about food chains to project an ecosystem?"
	Earth and Space Sciences	
	"Why does water change form as temperature changes?"	"How can we use an understanding of the phase changes of water to help in drought-stricken countries?"
	Physical Sciences	
	"How do you test for the properties of metals like copper, silver, iron, and nickel?"	"How could you use the properties of metals (strength, conductivity, resilience, and so on) to build a new product that people can use?"
6	**Life Sciences**	
	"How are populations affected by changes in food and habitat availability?"	"How can we develop models that will help save endangered species?"
	Earth and Spaces Sciences	
	"How do we use rock data to understand tectonic motions from the past?"	"How can we use patterns in tectonic movements to predict earthquakes?"
	Physical Sciences	
	"How do digitized signals transmit data?"	"How can we use digitized signals to improve communications across the globe?"

solutions in the form of possible new products and processes means being able to do the following (Duschl, Schweingruber, & Shouse, 2007, p. 2):

1. Know, use, and interpret scientific explanations of the natural world

2. Generate and evaluate scientific evidence and explanations

3. Understand the nature and development of scientific knowledge

4. Participate productively in scientific practices and discourse

To develop these proficiencies, elementary science instruction must engage students in "scientific practice [that] involves doing something and learning something in such a way that the doing and learning cannot be separated" (Michaels, Shouse, & Schweingruber, 2008, p. 34).

Table 1.3 further considers how scientific (learning) and engineering (doing) practices might be addressed through the NRC (2012) framework. The NGSS specifically indicate that teaching and learning should address both science and engineering practices (Achieve, 2013a).

Table 1.3: Actualizing Scientific and Engineering Practices

Practice	Science (Learning)	Engineering (Doing)
Asking questions (for science) and defining problems (for engineering)	Posing questions about an observable fact or occurrence "Why is gas expensive?"	Posing questions to clarify and solve problems "What type of car could be built that would take less fuel?"
Developing and using models	Using models to explain a fact or occurrence	Using and creating models to test the truth of a hypothesis, system, or design
Planning and carrying out investigations	Identifying relevant data and variables appropriate for investigation and analysis	Identifying relevant data and variables appropriate for investigation and analysis to determine operational strengths and weaknesses under various conditions
Analyzing and interpreting data	Producing and investigating the significance of a set of data	Analyzing various sets of data to determine which offer the best solution to solving a problem under various constraints
Using mathematics and computational thinking	Using precise thinking to identify pattern and relationship correlations	Using precise thinking to create a design and to study a solution and its proposed improvements
Constructing explanations (for science) and designing solutions (for engineering)	Constructing theories that explain accounts of phenomena in our material world	Constructing solutions that best meet the identified criteria and constraints
Engaging in argument from evidence	Using reasoning and argument to explain evidence regarding a phenomenon	Using reasoning and argument to solve a problem
Obtaining, evaluating, and communicating information	Communicating findings clearly and persuasively in all forms of language	Clearly and persuasively communicating new and improved designs and technologies

Scientists and engineers in all science disciplines share a commitment to data and evidence as the foundation for developing claims about the world. As they carry out investigations and revise or extend their explanations, scientists examine, review, and evaluate their own knowledge and ideas and critique those of others through a process of argumentation. These practices have too often been underemphasized in K–12 science education (Noddings, 2006).

As the NRC (2012) states:

> Engaging in the practices of science helps students understand how scientific knowledge develops; such direct involvement gives them an appreciation of the wide range of approaches that are used to investigate, model, and explain the world. Engaging in the practices of engineering likewise helps students understand the work of engineers, as well as the links between engineering and science. (p. 42)

In tandem with integrating scientific and engineering practices, the instructional ideas we share in this book guide students to address seven crosscutting concepts of the NRC (2012) framework and NGSS (Achieve, 2013a). These are:

1. **Patterns**—Observed patterns guide organization and classification and prompt questions about relationships and the factors that influence them. For example, students will note the cycling of seasons or the symmetry of crystals and ask "why" questions. From an engineering perspective, patterns can also be noted in successful designs of devices, structures, or machines. For example, we see patterns in architectural design because certain structures, like columns or arches, are more stable or can bear more weight than other structures.

2. **Cause and effect (mechanism and explanation)**—Events have causes, sometimes simple, sometimes multifaceted. A major practice of science is investigating and explaining causal relationships and their mechanisms. For example, students might investigate the changes to a coastline as a result of sea-level changes, or they might consider the causes for a food shortage in a particular habitat. They can test these cause-and-effect mechanisms by using them to predict and explain events in new contexts.

3. **Scale, proportion, and quantity**—In considering phenomena, it is critical to recognize how changes in scale, proportion, or quantity affect a system's structure or performance. For example, students might consider scales for objects too small to be seen with the unaided eye, such

as electrons in orbit around a nucleus. They might also consider scales for objects that are very far away or for those that span great distances, such as celestial bodies in a galaxy.

4. **Systems and system models**—Defining the system under study, specifying its boundaries, and making explicit a model of that system enable the understanding and testing of ideas. For example, students might look at the respiratory system as a single entity or as a part of the human body system—either is correct. Other systems involve transfers of energy and matter, such as the relationship between predators and prey.

5. **Energy and matter (flows, cycles, and conservation)**—Tracking fluxes of energy and matter into, out of, and within systems helps one understand the systems' possibilities and limitations. For example, students might study the transfer of energy and matter from sunlight to a growing plant to an herbivore that consumes the plant. Or they might look at the transfer of energy and matter through the water cycle.

6. **Structure and function**—The shape of an object or living thing and its substructure determine many of its properties and functions. For example, students might examine car designs to see which cars are the most energy efficient, have the best aerodynamic design, and offer the most comfort. Such an analysis could help determine what structures provide the most desirable properties.

7. **Stability and change**—For both natural and built systems, conditions of stability and determinants of rates of change or evolution are critical elements of study. For example, students might look at the balanced forces acting on a pencil lying on a desk as a condition of stability. Conversely, they might consider large-scale changes, such as the erosion of a seaside cliff over several decades, as a condition of change.

These crosscutting concepts are interwoven throughout the disciplinary core ideas of physical sciences, life sciences, earth and space sciences, and engineering and technology. They are important themes that provide a context through which we can view all science and engineering studies. They act as an important dimension of the NRC framework and the NGSS by providing "common touchstones across the science disciplines and grade levels" (NRC, 2012, p. 83).

Science Literacy

The Common Core State Standards insist that the teaching of literacy and English language arts (speaking and listening, language, reading, and writing) must become an instructional responsibility of all teachers in all disciplines. Although the CCSS address each area separately, the scaffolding and bundling of these communication processes in the standards is very apparent. For example, anchor standard nine for writing (CCRA.W.9) requires that students be able to share their thinking about their reading through various forms of writing. Similarly, anchor standard four for speaking and listening (CCRA.SL.4) expects students to adapt their language to various formats that fit a variety of contexts and tasks (see NGA & CCSSO, 2010a, pp. 18, 22). These standards reflect the integration of English language arts learning that occurs in most elementary-grade classrooms: as students read, they also listen, speak, and share their ideas through writing.

Because there are many ways to ensure that such purposeful instruction occurs, making the expectations of the CCSS become a reality in classrooms rests on the insights of teachers. As an elementary teacher, you must continue to support the interdisciplinary nature of literacy learning during the elementary school years of each student's school experience. Interdisciplinary learning means that literacy instruction (speaking, listening, writing, and reading) must become essential features in the teaching and learning of mathematics, science, and social studies.

Literacy Development

Drawing on early research (Chall, 1967, 1983; Juel, 1988; Stanovich, 1980, 1986), Timothy and Cynthia Shanahan (2008) suggest three stages of literacy development: (1) basic literacy, (2) intermediate literacy, and (3) discipline literacy.

Basic Literacy

The term *basic literacy* refers to the development of K–5 foundational skills (NGA & CCSSO, 2010a, pp. 15–17) that support all reading. These skills include decoding, comprehension of print, sight-word recognition of frequently used words, and fluency routines, as well as identification of the common text types (for example, story, nonfiction, and poetry) and text structures (for example, story format and lists). These skills are developed during the elementary school years, with fluency and automaticity learned by most students in the early (K–2) elementary years (Schwanenflugel et al., 2006). Although they are still young, students in grades K–2 are able to think about the world in which they live, and as they share experiences and communicate with family and peers, they question the world around them. They pose questions such as "What makes it rain?" "Why does our cat sleep so much?" and "What makes magnets stick together?" to make sense of their world. Their outside-of-school experiences greatly influence the understandings of science they will bring to the classroom. Because of this, students in the earliest grades already exhibit a range of physical and biological scientific knowledge and language. Although their knowledge is not fully developed and often lacks cohesion, young students are definitely thinking about their world from a scientific perspective, especially as it relates to them. Effective instruction involves using their egocentricity by exploring questions such as "How are you growing and changing?" and "How is our weather different today than it was yesterday?" to expand their scientific knowledge, reasoning, and engineering.

Intermediate Literacy

As students move into the upper-elementary grades, they develop what we refer to as *intermediate literacy skills*, which support (1) recognizing, using, and understanding a larger bank of vocabulary that is inclusive of all content areas; (2) decoding multisyllable words; and (3) understanding and using a wider array of punctuation and comprehending more complex texts and structures (for example, parallel plots and problem-solution formats). It is during this time that students also become much more metacognitive. John Flavell (1979) describes metacognition as being able to think about and monitor one's own thinking; it involves having active control over one's cognitive processes while engaged in learning. When students are aware of their developing literacies, they are able to monitor and apply fix-up strategies to support their reading and writing. Their understanding of themselves as learners helps them to expand, refine, and adjust their premises by linking inextricably the *content* of science and the *process* of studying and creating new scientific solutions, questions, evidence, and theories. In other words, their developing metacognition allows them to see the relationship between scientific content and the cognitive processes by which we arrive at that content.

Discipline Literacy

As students leave elementary school, they are very involved in what we refer to as *discipline literacy*, which means using all of the literacy and language skills they have acquired to support their reading, writing, listening, and speaking within the disciplines of mathematics, science, and social science. Yet it's clear that elementary school teachers who also teach the disciplines of mathematics, science, and social studies must begin to introduce students to literacy skills within these contexts. At this stage of learning, students are able to deduce that they do not have the scientific evidence they need to come to a conclusion; they must ask more questions and continue their investigations in order to draw evidence-supported conclusions. They also develop analytic thinking as they question character motive and analyze authors' persuasive techniques. Effective teachers build analytic thinking and problem solving across disciplines and encourage students to continually weigh evidence and revise accordingly.

Supporting Discipline Literacy in Science

To be literate in science, one must be proficient at reading, writing, and talking about science concepts. This means using strategies such as predicting, visualizing, inferring, and summarizing in order to understand, interpret, and create graphs, charts, and tables that support comprehension and communication. Science literacy involves understanding scientific information, proposing and generating well-investigated evidence, reflecting and analyzing, and then persuasively sharing one's insights. But that is not all that is needed, as the following sample passage exemplifies.

> As we view from Earth, we see different phases of the moon in the sky. Because the moon orbits the Earth, we perceive various parts of the moon illuminated during different times of the month. The *sidereal* month, or average period of revolution of the moon around the Earth, is twenty-seven days, seven hours, and three minutes. At certain times in the orbit, the moon is in the new moon phase. During this phase, the side of the moon facing Earth is not illuminated. When we have a first-quarter moon, we see what appears to be half of the moon lit up. In reality, it is only a quarter of the moon that we are viewing. Similarly, when we see a full moon, we are viewing half of the moon. A third-quarter moon provides us with a view of what appears to be half the moon, but it's actually one-quarter of the moon we are seeing. We also have other terms such as *gibbous*, *waxing*, and *waning* to help us describe what we perceive of the moon as it changes position relative to Earth and the sun.

Which strategies would a fifth grader use in order to comprehend this paragraph? The student would have to connect to his or her existing topical and language bases of knowledge, infer the author's message, and visualize the sequence being discussed while synthesizing and chunking the information in order to comprehend the main ideas. Specifically the student would have to visualize the positions of the Earth, sun, and moon as described in the text. Finally, a proficient reader might chunk the text into ideas that synthesize connected sentences, such as information about the revolution of the moon, details regarding the perception of the moon given its position, and names given to phases. Our reason for sharing this paragraph about the lunar cycle is to illustrate that students need bases of knowledge to read increasingly complex texts, and this involves more than strategy instruction. Thus, in addition to teaching strategies, science instruction must include teaching the background information, language, and skills that will support comprehension of a passage.

Teachers must model how to slow down if a passage isn't making sense and how to identify the cause of the confusion by questioning oneself about the concepts, language, organizational structures, and features of the text. This modeling should happen while illustrating how to dig deeply into the passage to analyze the language (vocabulary), syntax (sentence structure), and concepts (information). Once readers can identify what is interfering with their comprehension, they can figure out the next steps. Students can learn this metacognitive thinking, which includes understanding that they are not comprehending and then analyzing next-step actions, when the teacher—the proficient reader—models it.

A skilled teacher can explain the process while modeling the reading of a science passage and supporting students as they, too, internalize interpretive and critical text-reading practices. Elementary teachers already know how to think aloud with their students; when reading science, the text may change, but the process will remain very similar. Using a strategy such as prediction may be a part of modeling, but the focus should be on teaching students to use all of their literacy skills to comprehend an actual science passage. Before beginning, it's important to analyze the passage, noting problem areas that might arise. This will include identifying concepts that may need some background building; vocabulary that must be contextually explained; text features such as headings, bullets, charts, and so on that students need to study; and repetitions, contradictions, and similarities to other texts.

Ms. Segal's Lesson on Lunar Cycles

Consider the following think-aloud conversation with third-grade teacher Stefania Segal as she builds her students' knowledge of lunar cycles while illustrating the importance of using one's literacy skills. Ms. Segal knows that an understanding of lunar cycles fits with the NGSS crosscutting concept of *patterns and cycles*—a concept that her students began working with in first and second grade (Achieve, 2013a). She builds on the background information students need in order to comprehend this text. She also holds up a pencil to model how she jots notes and makes annotations while reading to help her chunk the information.

She explains that as students read and chunk short passages, they need to keep a pencil in hand to interact with the passage by making annotations, writing informational notes and questions, and highlighting words and phrases they either enjoyed or did not understand.

She reads from the passage: "'As we view from Earth, we see different phases of the moon in the sky.'"

"Okay," she says. "I've looked up in the sky at the moon since I was very little. I know that sometimes the moon is thin and curved and other times it's full and round. Perhaps that's what the author means by the word *phases*. I'm going to highlight the word *phases* and put a question mark beside it so I can remember it and check my thinking of this word as I read more." She continues reading: "'Because the moon orbits the Earth, we perceive various parts of the moon illuminated during different times of the month.'"

She pauses again and shares some thoughts with the class. "I think I'll read that sentence one more time to be sure I didn't miss any information. Oh, yes! I see the different shapes of the moon in the sky as a month goes by. Every day, the moon looks a little different. These differences must indicate the phases. The word *illuminated* reminds me of a lightbulb. I think I'll highlight it and draw a lightbulb to remind me. I think the author is talking about how the moon looks when lit up at night." Ms. Segal reads aloud: "'The *sidereal* month, or average period of revolution of the moon around the Earth, is twenty-seven days, seven hours, and three minutes.'"

"*Sidereal month* is a new phrase for me," Ms. Segal admits. "I better highlight it too. From the sentence, it sounds like a sidereal month is how long it takes for us to see all the moon's phases as it moves around Earth one complete time. I think I'll draw a picture to help me see and remember what *sidereal* means. Now I understand the phases. Making visuals and annotations really helps my understanding."

"'At certain times in the orbit, the moon is in the new moon phase,'" Ms. Segal reads. "'During this phase, the side of the moon facing Earth is not illuminated.' That must be when we don't see the moon in the sky." She continues on: "'When we have a first-quarter moon, we see what appears to be half of the moon lit up. In reality, it is only a quarter of the moon that we are viewing.'" Ms. Segal pauses again. "Hmm. This is strange. We see what looks like half of the moon, but it's really only one-quarter of the moon. I'm a bit confused, but I'm not giving up. I need to keep reading."

She continues, "'Similarly, when we see a full moon, we are viewing half of the moon.'"

"I think I'm starting to get this now. Reading slowly and looking at the photos on this page also help me understand these phases. We only see the front side of the moon, and the moon is like a ball. That's why we are really only seeing half. We don't see the back half because it's not facing Earth. I'll make another picture."

Ms. Segal draws another picture and then continues reading. "'A third-quarter moon provides us with a view of what appears to be half the moon, but it's actually one-quarter of the moon we are seeing.'

"So the third-quarter moon is sort of like the first-quarter moon. Since we only see one side of the moon, we are only viewing one-quarter of it when we see what looks like a half-circle in the sky." Ms. Segal reads the last sentence of the passage: "'We also have other terms such as *gibbous, waxing,* and *waning* to help us describe what we perceive of the moon as it changes position relative to Earth and the sun.'

"I'm going to jot these words in a margin and look at the poster of the moon phases on the wall of the classroom. That might help me to understand these other terms." (See figure 2.8, page 68, for example.)

After this introductory modeling, Ms. Segal asks the students to use her annotations to practice analyzing the same passage. She encourages them to add their own. Then, after inviting the students to partner talk about the passage, their annotations, and the process, students share the following comments.

"Sometimes I start to read, and it's kinda hard, so I quit," says Malik. "I like chunking, 'cause it seems easier."

"Yeah," Rayyan agrees. "It doesn't seem like so much to read at once."

Andy chimes in, "I like taking a few notes."

"Me too," Raul says, "but just ones I need."

Ms. Segal steps in. "Interesting. How do the annotations help?"

Makaela notes, "They help me keep track of new words and ideas."

Andy says, "It helps me to write what's messing me up 'cause when I see what I wrote I get it better."

Science texts are complex, and students need to be taught how to read them proficiently and independently. Most students do not independently learn how to read a story; their primary-grade teachers teach them to do so. Similarly, we cannot expect our students to automatically know how to read informational texts; they must be taught how to do so. Ms. Segal's ultimate goal is to develop each student's capacity to comprehend a complex text without her providing extensive frontloading. Doing so involves teaching her students to reread a text several times and annotate it, while asking questions that push them to dig deeper and deeper to grasp the meaning.

You may have yourself experienced the need to slow down and deeply or closely read a text containing less familiar information in a course you took in high school or college. This continues to happen for many of us as we read instructions related to our smartphones, iPads, interactive websites, and any other technologies for which we may have insufficient language and background knowledge to use to scaffold our developing understandings.

Think of similar experiences in school when your teacher told you to read chapter 10 of your science text and then answer the end-of-chapter questions. Students who did well in these situations, which by the way involved no instruction, were considered to have an aptitude for learning science. Are you smiling and thinking, "What a cop-out"? Hopefully, none of your colleagues still have these antiquated opinions about learning science, mathematics, and other content information.

Effective teachers like you support students in becoming scientifically and critically literate, as well as independent readers of scientific information. They do so by teaching students to question and, from their inquiries, to develop ideas, scientific conceptions, and scientific practices that involve learning and doing science in such a way that the two cannot be separated. Building from their developing bases of information, students begin to understand explanations of science; they learn how to inquire and, from their findings, to further construct, and they learn to examine the validity of their conceptions. Such analysis requires them to reflect, modify, change, develop, and extend their ideas more fully. During this exploration, teachers need to encourage students to apply their thinking to new and different contexts. They use science practices and language to productively share and evaluate claims, investigations, and explanations. In modeling for students a process of scientific exploration that involves knowing, doing, and sharing concepts, effective elementary teachers employ such collaborative conversations, writing reports, and role plays—instructional strategies they also use to teach the English language arts.

The following chapters build on your expertise as English language arts teachers to offer insights about how to support your students in developing the language, scientific knowledge, and science and engineering practices needed to become a scientifically literate person.

CHAPTER 2

Learning to Talk Like a Scientist

Consider the amount of information we convey and receive through oral language—from offering simple directions to a lost driver to hearing a presidential inauguration speech. In each case, one person's thoughts and ideas transmit to another person through the use of words pieced together into meaningful sentences and phrases. While colloquial, informal language is perfectly acceptable for casual situations, we need precise terminology and well-crafted expressions of thought to convey academic and scholarly ideas accurately and articulately. We know that we learn everyday conversational speech on the playground and at home. The acquisition of school talk, however, requires thoughtful, well-planned instruction that targets the attainment and use of academic and domain-specific language. The goal is for students to become productive participants in conversations that center on real-world issues of information and concern. This means not only speaking about events of note but also possessing the skill of actively listening so that both argument and agreement can be part of the response.

Science discussions are often about debatable matters. Science conversation, therefore, often involves the use of evidence to establish points of discussion and will sometimes include an acknowledgment of counterarguments that the evidence refutes. Because the language of science is technical and precise, the choice of terminology is critical. Conversations about climate change, water use, nuclear power, and space exploration investigate various perspectives. To talk like scientists, students must know how to verbally cite credible resources, use appropriate terms, and incorporate concise, to-the-point phrases that include many of the common text structures (such as if/then and when/then scenarios) used in science.

Two strands of the Common Core State Standards (NGA & CCSSO, 2010a), Speaking and Listening and Language, underscore the importance of being able to use language to support information exchanges. These strands focus on ascending communication and language skill development.

What You'll Learn in This Chapter

This chapter begins with an exploration of the Common Core Speaking and Listening and Language standards and the evidence supporting them. Included next are a variety of strategies, such as shared reading, think-alouds, and language frames, for supporting students in sharing ideas in the same academic language register that teachers know well and use often. Some of these strategies are less frequently used but are very appropriate for promoting language learning and development. These include foldable flipbooks, Four Corners, glogs, discussion webs, inside/outside circles, and Picture It. Although the Reading and Writing strands and standards are introduced first in the Common Core, because learning involves the ability to understand and use language, we begin this text by focusing on the areas of speaking and listening and language. One's ability in these areas is correlated with one's knowledge of vocabulary. In fact, having an adequate vocabulary is the best predictor of school success for all students (Hart & Risley, 1995; Lesaux & Kieffer, 2010; Saville-Troike, 1984). Although these strategies are appropriate at many grade levels, we have cast each within the context of a grade-level scenario.

What Are the Standards?

The Common Core Speaking and Listening and Language anchor standards highlight the need for students to become scientifically literate communicators who question the world around them and use precise language to argue ideas gleaned from their investigations. These standards call for students to acquire interpersonal language skills, making them broadly conversant speakers and listeners. Developing such language flexibility means that students need to do more than simply share the formal presentations frequently required in classrooms. Accomplishing the intent of the Speaking and Listening standards requires that students be engaged in classroom language experiences where they:

> work together, express and listen carefully to ideas, integrate information from oral, visual, quantitative, and media sources, evaluate what they hear, use media and visual displays strategically to help achieve communicative purposes, and adapt speech to context and task. (NGA & CCSSO, 2010a, p. 8)

Additionally the Common Core Language standards note that learning to use both subject-specific language and academic or school language is a craft entailing the sharing of information according to the "'rules' of standard written and spoken English" (NGA & CCSSO, 2010a, p. 8). Although presented within different grade bands, the CCSS Speaking and Listening and Language anchor standards define what students should be able to accomplish in grades K–5 and 6–12 to become active participants in academic conversations.

Speaking and Listening Anchor Standards

When scientists seek solutions to problems in the real world, they always work in tandem with others. Research is rarely, if ever, a solo endeavor; plans for study and investigation are often formulated through discussion and implemented collaboratively, as is the presentation of results. Reflecting this reality, the Common Core anchor standards for speaking and listening consist of two domains: (1) Comprehension and Collaboration and (2) Presentation of Knowledge and Ideas. The anchor standards require students not only to convey accurate, relevant information but also to respond to ideas just as precisely. More specifically, students must be able to perform the following tasks:

Comprehension and Collaboration

1. Prepare for and participate effectively in a range of conversations and collaborations with diverse partners, building on others' ideas and expressing their own clearly and persuasively. (CCRA.SL.1)

2. Integrate and evaluate information presented in diverse media and formats, including visually, quantitatively, and orally. (CCRA.SL.2)

3. Evaluate a speaker's point of view, reasoning, and use of evidence and rhetoric. (CCRA.SL.3) (NGA & CCSSO, 2010a, p. 22)

Presentation of Knowledge and Ideas

4. Present information, findings, and supporting evidence such that listeners can follow the line of reasoning and the organization, development, and style are appropriate to task, purpose, and audience. (CCRA.SL.4)

5. Make strategic use of digital media and visual displays of data to express information and enhance understanding of presentations. (CCRA.SL.5)

6. Adapt speech to a variety of contexts and communicative tasks, demonstrating command of formal English when indicated or appropriate. (CCRA.SL.6) (NGA & CCSSO, 2010a, p. 22)

Scientists convey research, analyses of data, and evidence-based arguments through well-prepared reporting. It is incumbent on those who are scientifically literate to share what they know with friends, colleagues, and others. Moreover, we live in a world that thrives on effective global communication, and employers consistently cite communication (listening, verbal, written) as a highly sought after quality for success in the majority of professions (Hansen & Hansen, n.d.).

Language Anchor Standards

Additionally, the CCSS for language reflect the belief that language precision is the foundation for language exchanges. The standards are grouped into three domains: (1) Conventions of Standard English, (2) Knowledge of Language, and (3) Vocabulary Acquisition and Use. The first domain, Conventions of Standard English, identifies in two standards the skills that students must acquire in order to gain control over the grammar they use in spoken and written language and the mechanics that enable the sharing of written information.

Conventions of Standard English

1. Demonstrate command of the conventions of standard English grammar and usage when writing or speaking. (CCRA.L.1)

2. Demonstrate command of the conventions of standard English capitalization, punctuation, and spelling when writing. (CCRA.L.2) (NGA & CCSSO, 2010a, p. 25)

The second domain, Knowledge of Language, expresses the need for students to know language well enough to comprehend as well as share written and spoken information.

Knowledge of Language

3. Apply knowledge of language to understand how language functions in different contexts, to make effective choices for meaning or style, and to comprehend more fully when reading or listening. (CCRA.L.3) (NGA & CCSSO, 2010a, p. 25)

The third domain, Vocabulary Acquisition and Use, contains anchor standards four through six, which illustrate the power of vocabulary to support well-conveyed language exchanges.

Vocabulary Acquisition and Use

4. Determine or clarify the meaning of unknown and multiple-meaning words and phrases by using context clues, analyzing meaningful word parts, and consulting general and specialized reference materials, as appropriate. (CCRA.L.4)

5. Demonstrate understanding of figurative language, word relationships, and nuances in word meanings. (CCRA.L.5)

6. Acquire and use accurately a range of general academic and domain-specific words and phrases sufficient for reading, writing, speaking, and listening at the college and career readiness level; demonstrate independence in gathering vocabulary knowledge when encountering an unknown term important to comprehension or expression. (CCRA.L.6) (NGA & CCSSO, 2010a, p. 25)

To develop the language skills within the CCSS to engage in scientific discourse, students need to be immersed in classroom environments that promote rich experiences with aural and oral language. Although many students may choose careers outside of science, all must be scientifically aware participants in their world. Furthermore, all must be able to ask, find, or provide answers to questions resulting from their curiosity about their everyday situations.

Evidence Supporting These Standards

Opportunities for hands-on scientific learning experiences activate students' existing knowledge and encourage them to speak, clarify meanings, reword, and better understand while actively engaging with scientific language (Gibbons, 2002). Interactive language opportunities move away from the student acting as a passive recipient to teacher-asked questions that suppose one correct answer (O'Donnell, 2006; Wong-Fillmore, 1985).

Developing scientific language facility is well aligned with NGSS Science and Engineering Practices under the category of Obtaining, Evaluating, and Communicating Information (Achieve, 2013a; NRC, 2012). In these practices, students are expected to become adept at sharing scientific hypotheses, inquiry, and investigation. Specifically, this is indicated by the NGSS Science and Engineering Practices under the categories of Asking Questions and Defining Problems and Constructing Explanations and Designing Solutions (Achieve, 2013a). More specifically, the NRC (2012) framework states that students should be engaging in all of the following language-based activities: asking questions and defining problems, constructing explanations and designing solutions, engaging in arguments from evidence, and obtaining, evaluating, and communicating information. Becoming adept users of scientific language involves listening, evaluating, creating, and conveying information learned from reading, viewing, and experimenting with multiple media sources gleaned through inquiry, critical analysis, and communication.

Words used to convey scientific information take on meanings that are generally more restrictive than they are in everyday language. When a sportscaster says that an athlete running down the track has *momentum*, he likely means that the athlete is progressing well in his run. When a scientist uses that word, he is almost certainly noting that the runner has a quantifiable forward motion that can be calculated by multiplying mass and velocity. A woman describing how a new shampoo gave her hair a nice *luster* is talking in a general sense about its shininess. A jeweler may use the term *luster* to describe the way a mineral reflects light. Other precise, science-related adjectives, such as *glassy, resinous*, or *dull*, further refine the quality of luster.

Science language also involves understanding how to articulate a working hypothesis based on prior knowledge or observation. For example, an engineer who designs a new type of boat might hypothesize that it will float by citing the mass and volume of the boat material and communicating Archimedes's buoyancy principle. For students, an example of a scientific hypothesis might be that bacteria placed in a test tube will increase daily in number for a week under specific conditions of food, light, temperature, and so on. In order to study and test this hypothesis, students would need to collect daily observational data by using a spectrophotometer to measure optical density—a representation of bacterial growth. They would need to record data and plot them on a graph for analysis. The language of science also includes argumentation, which involves persuading a listener of the validity of one's ideas through data presented to support a proposed theory, model, or action (Latour, 1987; Michaels et al., 2008). When communicating in science, however, argument has a much less combative nature (Kuhn, 1991) than it does in a heated debate or discussion. For example, deliberations in the media, such as political debates or so-called discussions on reality TV, often involve raised voices and reckless name-calling. To contrast, a person making the science claim that recycling should be federally mandated to help protect the environment should support his argument with evidence. For example, he could collect data showing that the number of plastic bottles on the ground is decreasing due to increased recycling or that recycling reduces pollutants put into the atmosphere by decreasing the production of new products that instead are created from recycled material.

When teachers provide opportunities for learners to talk about content and make meaning for themselves, language sophistication becomes a reality in school

(Halliday, 1993; Krashen, 2012). Additionally, to support students in communicating or arguing like scientists, teachers must eliminate turn-taking talk (Mehan, 1979; Schegloff, 2000). Turn-taking talk precludes argumentation and hinders students from participating in respectfully argued exchanges of data-supported ideas, evidence, and explanations that convey their beliefs, how they came to this knowing, and what they are still questioning (Osborne, Erduran, Simon, & Monk, 2001). When the teacher does not mediate student talk, it becomes collaborative, productive, and purposeful argumentation that leads to possibilities for more scientific learning to occur (Eichinger, Anderson, Palincsar, & David, 1991). Instead of acting as the primary source of information, the teacher teaches students to craft an argument, tolerate differing hypotheses and theories, and be a responsible participant in their construction and presentation (Simon, Erduran, & Osborne, 2006). Engaging students in talking about science promotes their presence as agents or participants (Lemke, 1990) rather than confining them to roles as reporters who do not actually see the scientific reality they are investigating. According to William Rupley and Scott Slough (2010), the experiences that students have with science content extend, reinforce, and stimulate them to engage in deeper processing. As Richard Duschl and Jonathan Osborne (2002) state:

> A prominent, if not central, feature of the language of scientific enquiry is debate and argumentation around competing theories, methodologies, and aims. . . . Thus, developing an understanding of science and appropriating the syntactic, semantic, and pragmatic components of its language require students to engage in practicing and using its discourse. (p. 40)

Ana Taboada and Vanessa Rutherford's (2011) study of science-language acquisition for fourth-grade English learners finds that teachers do not always emphasize comprehension instruction in subject-matter classrooms and that subject-matter teachers wrongly assume that students have adequate literacy skills. These authors suggest that teachers fuse instruction by emphasizing strategy instruction, conceptual knowledge, and academic vocabulary. While this clearly sounds like a complex task, it can be effectively accomplished through well-planned lessons.

Into the Classroom

In this section, we visit exemplary classrooms to observe how effective teachers scaffold scientific learning for their students. Pay careful attention to how the students are collaborating and communicating as they talk and argue data-supported positions from their investigations and interpretations. Notice how each example promotes students' understanding of crosscutting core scientific concepts, generating scientific data, reflecting on their findings and new questions, and communicating and arguing data-supported stances. There is at least one scenario for each grade K–6 and multiple scenarios for grade 4, because by the time students reach fourth grade, many are fairly fluent readers. Learning science requires using reading skills to investigate fairly complex concepts. With this in mind, we decided to support fourth-grade teachers in teaching students to learn and use science language in ways that facilitate their talking like scientists. (Visit **go.solution -tree.com/commoncore** for two additional grade 4 scenarios.)

These lesson scenarios bundle several standards in order to illustrate that real teaching and real learning involve integrating literacy processes and standards within an instructional or learning incidence. Although the scenarios present instruction at specific grade levels, teachers can utilize these concepts, adapted appropriately, at any grade level. The questions following each scenario allow you to personally reflect on the instruction or to facilitate partner or small learning group discussions.

Mrs. Ramos's Kindergarten Class

Students in Vera Ramos's kindergarten class are just beginning to wrestle with language and print concepts. Some have come to the classroom able to read simple sentences, while others are struggling to simply sound out letters. While this variance in ability at such an early age is expected, it does challenge Mrs. Ramos, especially when she is trying to teach science concepts. To meet this challenge, she guides students through scientific investigations to build their background knowledge and develop language as a precursor to their reading about the content. As the students investigate a topic related to the NGSS concept of *pushes and pulls* and share their thinking, Mrs. Ramos is able to assess their growing understandings (Achieve, 2013a, K-PS2, p. 5). Table 2.1 shows Mrs. Ramos's lesson plan.

The NGSS guide students to examine disciplinary core ideas as topics at specific grade levels. Students move to deeper, more complex levels within the scope of core ideas as they progress in grade level. While Mrs. Ramos's students are just beginning to examine pushes and pulls, she knows that they will revisit the core idea of *forces and motion* again in third grade.

Using Background Knowledge to Hypothesize

Valerie and her classmates begin to examine pushes and pulls by tugging on strings tied around toy cars. Mrs. Ramos asks her students to talk to their table partners about why the car moves when the string is pulled. Kindergartener James

Table 2.1: Kindergarten CCSS for Speaking and Listening and Language and NGSS Lesson Plan for Physical Sciences

Crosscutting Concept	Cause and effect: Mechanism and explanation
Core Ideas	PS2.A: Forces and motion
	PS2.B: Types of interactions
	PS3.C: Relationship between energy and forces
Lesson Purpose	Understand and talk about how objects push and pull each other
Focus Strategy	Organizing ideas in foldable flipbooks

NGSS

K-PS2-1. Plan and conduct an investigation to compare the effects of different strengths or different directions of pushes and pulls on the motion of an object.

K-PS2-2. Analyze data to determine if a design solution works as intended to change the speed or direction of an object with a push or a pull.

K-2-ETS1-3. Analyze data from tests of two objects designed to solve the same problem to compare the strengths and weaknesses of how each performs.

CCSS

• Speaking and Listening standards:

SL.K.1. Participate in collaborative conversations with diverse partners about *kindergarten topics and texts* in small and larger groups.

SL.K.2. Confirm understanding of a text read aloud or information presented orally or through other media by asking and answering questions about key details and requesting clarification if something is not understood.

• Language standards:

L.K.4. Determine or clarify the meaning of unknown and multiple-meaning words and phrases based on *kindergarten reading and content.*

L.K.6. Use words and phrases acquired through conversations, reading and being read to, and responding to texts.

Source: Adapted from NGA & CCSSO, 2010a, pp. 23, 27, and Achieve, 2013a, pp. 5, 16.

thoughtfully tells Valerie, "I think the string moves the car." Listening in on this, Mrs. Ramos asks James to let go of the string and then asks why the string doesn't move the car anymore. James responds, "Maybe it's not just the string. It's the string and my hand that make the car move." Valerie adds, "James, you have to get the string and move your hand like this." She gestures to show how she pulls the string to the right to move the car in the same direction.

While the activity is simple enough, the learning can be quite profound. Students are seeing how a pull—a force in a given direction—will make an object move in that same direction. Next, Mrs. Ramos asks students to push the back of the car and then has students chat with partners about what they notice. By listening in on the partner conversations, Mrs. Ramos concludes that all students understand that the motion of the car is in the same direction as the push.

This is foundational to an understanding of force as a quantity with both magnitude (amount) and direction, and while Mrs. Ramos does not introduce that terminology to her kindergarteners, she is confident that she is preparing students to delve deeper in coming grades. She next asks the students to see if harder pushes are different from gentler pushes. James draws the car back with a great force and then pushes it forward with all his might, sending the car racing across the floor from one end to the other. Valerie then tries a gentle push—one that barely moves the car an inch. She emphatically proclaims, "Big pushes make the car go far, and little pushes have it go less." This is exactly the notion that Mrs. Ramos wants her kindergarteners to glean. In more scientific terms, she has explained that the larger the force, the greater the acceleration of the object.

Finally, to the delight of the five- and six-year-olds, Mrs. Ramos asks students to make their cars collide. She demonstrates how to do this safely so that cars do not go flying off into the air. Her modeling shows how two cars, facing each other, can be released slowly to allow for a collision. Mrs. Ramos notices out loud that her cars bounce off each other, each changing directions. Students then try to do the same. James notices that the little car moves farther than the big truck when they collide.

To Mrs. Ramos this demonstrates students' understanding that more massive objects have more momentum. It will be a long time before students use words like *momentum*, but she knows that when they do, they will be ready with appropriate background knowledge. In sum, Mrs. Ramos is satisfied that this foundational knowledge has been captured by her kindergarteners. She knows that in coming years, they will attach technical terminology and mathematical concepts to these very insights as they deepen their understanding.

Because Mrs. Ramos knows that the core idea of forces and motion will be studied again in third grade when students examine electric or magnetic interactions between two objects not in contact with each other, she will dig deeper with pushes and pulls using the attraction and repulsion actions of magnets.

As Valerie and her classmates consider magnetism as a force, Mrs. Ramos piques their curiosity by asking them to predict which objects around the room will and will not stick to a magnet. Valerie and her table partner James both predict that the paper clips on Mrs. Ramos's desk will attract a magnet. They disagree, however, on the attraction that the magnet will have for a penny. Valerie thinks that the penny will not stick, but James, believing that all shiny objects are magnetic, insists that it will. Both record their predictions in their triple-tabbed foldable flipbooks, which will ultimately be glued into their science journals. Students use the flipbooks to draw, illustrate, and write their ideas (figure 2.1).

What Pulls?	What Pushes Away?	What Does Neither?
Paper clips	Two magnets with an S	Pennies
Staples		Wood blocks
Metal legs of desks	Two magnets with an N	Rocks
Whiteboard		Paperweight
Gray rock		Yellow rock

Figure 2.1: Triple-tabbed foldable flipbook.

Students in the class make predictions about a row of staples, wood blocks, metal legs of desks, the whiteboard, a few rocks, a paperweight, and other magnets on the table in the back of the classroom. Both James, who believes that shiny objects are magnetic, and Valerie use their background knowledge to sort through ideas. Valerie remembers seeing her teacher stick letters on the whiteboard. She recalls seeing a small black rectangle on the back of each letter. She wonders if the whiteboard is magnetic and if the black rectangle on each letter might have been a magnet. It is clear from the student conversations and from the diligent effort put toward completing the foldable flipbook that students are engaged in the task.

Conducting Investigations

Both Valerie and James eagerly begin moving around the room with their small magnet, holding it to every object about which they made a prediction. The staples are pulled to the magnet, as are the paper clips. Surprisingly, the dullish gray rock sitting on Mrs. Ramos's desk also pulls the magnet, but the yellow rock does not. As Valerie suspects, the whiteboard attracts the magnet, affirming her prediction that the black rectangles are magnets. When the penny does not draw the magnet, James abandons his prediction that everything shiny is magnetic. The gray rock is magnetic, and it is just about the dullest object they tested.

Teacher Modeling

Mrs. Ramos then passes out a pencil and six ring-shaped ceramic magnets to each pair of students. Modeling how to determine which poles attract and which repel, Mrs. Ramos holds two ceramic rings near each other. She flips one, while holding the other stationary until she feels the magnets pushing apart, and states, "These two magnets *repel* each other. I can tell because I feel them pushing apart." Then she flips one of the magnets again so that the two pull together. "Now they *attract* each other," she explains. She then directs the students to slip the magnetic rings onto the pencil into an arrangement in which two side-by-side magnets *repel* each other. She notes focused concentration, broken only by gasps of delight, around the room as the rings of magnets "float" on the pencils in an almost magical way.

Posing a Theory

The students in Mrs. Ramos's class know, however, that there will be a scientific explanation to clarify this seeming mystery of magnetism. Prepared by their newly built background knowledge and augmented vocabulary, they expand their conceptions of the terms *repel* and *attract* by learning that some materials are magnetic and some aren't. Mrs. Ramos presents a shared reading from the trade book *What Magnets Can Do* (Fowler, 2005). Holding up page three, she reads, "Why are these nails sticking to this bar?"

Students listen attentively, responding periodically when Mrs. Ramos intersperses other text-dependent questions for the class intended to tie the classroom activity to the reading. When she shares a picture of an electromagnet lifting an old car in a junkyard, she asks students, "How can this machine lift the car? What must the car be made of?"

David replies, "I think this machine is a big magnet. I see the word *magnet* below the picture. That's a clue."

Marley adds, "The car must have a lot of metal in it. The bumper looks like metal, and remember, the paper clips look like metal, too. They were attracted to the magnets in the classroom."

Mrs. Ramos praises both students for using text clues to support their responses, acknowledging that David used clues in the book to correctly identify the electromagnet as a big machine with magnetic properties and that Marley noticed the car had parts that looked like the material of the paper clips.

Both students were drawing on the text, previous instruction, and their personal learning to decipher science concepts from their reading. Clearly, Mrs.

Ramos's strategy to support the construction of essential background knowledge and to build vocabulary acts to successfully support language expansion. Students were able to listen, think about the read-aloud, and converse using the language of science.

The disciplinary core idea for Mrs. Ramos's lesson on forces and motion was examined in several ways within the structure of the class. Students engaged in an investigation of how different amounts of pushes and pulls can have different strengths and directions. They learned that objects can come together or collide and that there is a connection between a bigger push and greater speed. They also were introduced to noncontact pushes and pulls. The activity conducted with magnets, while intriguing for kindergarteners, could be expanded and augmented to support third graders' more in-depth study of forces and motion (Achieve, 2013a, p. 18). To use this activity for third graders, a focus on the distance between magnets and the orientation of the magnets could be added to the investigation. Additionally, the concept of a force having size and direction could be introduced.

Questions for Discussion or Reflection

1. Mrs. Ramos was creating a climate that invited accountable or academic talk (Resnick, 1995) or high levels of classroom discourse as students communicated (listened and spoke) during partner talk and whole-class discussions. Academic or accountable talk occurs as teachers provide experiences that encourage students to listen with a purpose, think about what they are hearing, and then use academic language to articulate and share their response. Remember, if they are going to engage in accountable talk, they must have something to talk about. What scientific experiences do you provide students that promote the need for accountable talk and involve comparing and contrasting ideas, asking questions, and describing scientific phenomena?

2. Consider the magnet investigation in Mrs. Ramos's class. How might your students use a foldable flipbook to investigate science concepts in the classroom? What science concepts would they be investigating?

3. What resources and experiences would you need to integrate into your instruction to build background knowledge for your lessons?

4. Which grade-level NGSS and CCSS does your instruction address?

Ms. Andrews's First-Grade Class

Breanne Andrews's first graders are studying plants, including what plants need to grow and how they survive. This connects to NGSS disciplinary core ideas Structure and Function (LS1A); Growth and Development of Organisms (LS1B); and Information Processing (LS1D). In simpler terms, this means that by the end of first grade, students should understand that plants have external parts that help them survive and grow (roots, stems, leaves, flowers, and fruit); adult plants can have young plants; and plants respond to external inputs, including air, water, soil, minerals, and light, which they need to grow. Table 2.2 demonstrates Ms. Andrews's lesson plan.

In the next lesson, Ms. Andrews's students will investigate the structure and function of plants, while also participating in information processing that looks at how they respond to external outputs, such as sunlight.

Building a Base of Knowledge

Ms. Andrews's first graders discover that plants have varying needs for nutrients and light. To help augment their understanding, the students grow beans from seeds in Styrofoam cups. While this is a common first-grade activity, Ms. Andrews doesn't stop with the hands-on experience of seeing a seed sprout and grow into a plant. She deepens her students' understanding by offering a different read-aloud every day for a week. Students hear Ms. Andrews enthusiastically articulate the words from *How a Seed Grows* (Jordan, 1960). They are enthralled by her animated reading of *From Seed to Plant* (Gibbons, 1993). They listen closely to every word of *Jack's Garden*, by Henry Cole (1997). After extending the students' body of knowledge and providing the real-world experience of nurturing a seed to grow into a mature plant, Ms. Andrews reads the book *Plants and the Environment* (Boothroyd, 2007). As a part of the shared reading, she shares the section titled "We Need Forests":

- Wood is used for fuel, paper, furniture, and homes.
- Trees help make oxygen. Oxygen is a gas in the air. All animals need oxygen to breathe.
- Millions of plants and animals live in forests.
- Roots hold soil in place so the rain doesn't wash it away.
- People enjoy camping and hiking in forests. (Boothroyd, 2007, p. 21)

Table 2.2: First-Grade CCSS for Speaking and Listening and NGSS Lesson Plan on Life Science

Crosscutting Concept	Patterns and structure and function
Core Ideas	Structure and function
	Growth and development of organisms
	Information processing
Lesson Purpose	Understand and discuss how plants need water, minerals, and sunlight to grow and live
Focus Strategy	Arguing positions using Four Corners

NGSS

LS1-1. Use materials to design a solution to a human problem by mimicking how plants and/or animals use their external parts to help them survive, grow, and meet their needs.

LS3-1. Make observations to construct an evidence-based account that young plants and animals are like, but not exactly like, their parents.

K-2-ETS1-1. Ask questions, make observations, and gather information about a situation people want to change to define a simple problem that can be solved through the development of a new or improved object or tool.

K-2-ETS1-3. Analyze data from tests of two objects designed to solve the same problem to compare the strengths and weaknesses of how each performs.

CCSS

• Speaking and Listening standards:

SL.1.1. Participate in collaborative conversations with diverse partners about *grade 1 topics and texts* with peers and adults in small and larger groups.

    a. Follow agreed-on rules for discussions (for example, listening to others with care, speaking one at a time about the topics and texts under discussion).

    b. Build on others' talk in conversations by responding to the comments of others through multiple exchanges.

    c. Ask questions to clear up any confusion about the topics and texts under discussion.

SL.1.2. Ask and answer questions about key details in text read aloud or information presented orally or through other media.

• Language standard:

L.1.6. Use words and phrases acquired through conversations, reading and being read to, and responding to texts, including using frequently occurring conjunctions to signal simple relationships (for example, *because*).

Source: Adapted from NGA & CCSSO, 2010a, pp. 23, 27, and Achieve, 2013a, pp. 10, 16.

After much discussion, Ms. Andrews asks her students to think about all the information they learned about plants in the books they shared. Together they recall the following: plants need food, air, and water to grow; plants grow from seeds and develop roots, stems, fruits, and leaves; and plants help put oxygen in the environment.

Using Text-Based Data to Support Argumentation

Ms. Andrews then asks her students to consider the amount and type of care that the bean seeds need to develop into plants. She tells them that they will have the chance to defend their thinking. She explains that this is what scientists do—they use facts to argue a position or theory.

Using a strategy known as Four Corners, Ms. Andrews points to the four corners of the classroom, where she has posted four signs: (1) Strongly Agree, (2) Agree, (3) Disagree, and (4) Strongly Disagree. She explains that she will make a statement and then students will go to the corner of the room with the sign that best fits their viewpoint regarding the statement. She models with an easy-to-follow example.

"Here's a science statement," she tells the class. "'Endangered animals should be kept in zoos.' I am going to the Agree corner because I think that this statement, based on what I have learned, is most like what I think. Once at the Agree corner, I'll discuss why I *agree* that endangered animals should be kept in zoos. I could tell the other students in the Agree corner that endangered animals are animals that might not exist on our planet for very long, because there are no longer many of them here. Sometimes this is because people have taken over their environment where they live, and sometimes it's because they lose their food source. We need to protect them, and zoos can help with this. Perhaps another student, like Jose, might go to the Strongly Disagree corner. Jose might explain that animals have the right to be in their natural habitat—places where they were born. Neither of these opinions is actually right or wrong; however, both are based on an understanding of science."

After modeling, Ms. Andrews shares three photos with the students (figures 2.2, 2.3, and 2.4). The first photo shows a pot set in full sunlight, the second shows a pot in the shade, and the last shows a pot sitting in a darkened room.

Ms. Andrews asks students, "Do you think bean seeds need lots of sunlight, or can they sprout with just a little bit of sunshine or even with none at all? Let's list some ideas from our readings. I'll write your ideas on the board."

Figure 2.2: A bean plant in full sunlight.

Figure 2.3: A bean plant in partial sunlight.

Figure 2.4: A bean plant in the shade.

Miguel notes, "In the text *From Seed to Plant* by Gail Gibbons we read that plants use sunlight to make food."

Daniel adds, "I've seen a plant grow in the shady part of my backyard and in my house."

Cesar wonders, "Maybe even when it's shady, some sunshine gets to the plant."

Maddie says, "Plants need oxygen. They can get that indoors or outdoors."

After working with students to build background knowledge and vocabulary awareness, Ms. Andrews poses this statement: "Plants can grow without sunlight." Some students move instantly to a particular corner, while others think first and then proceed to the location that matches their views.

Ms. Andrews then asks students to talk with others in their corner about their opinions. She listens in to monitor progress.

Shannon tells the others in the Strongly Disagree corner, "Plants can't make food without sunlight. They need food to grow."

Shawn chimes in, "Remember in the plants book it says that we get oxygen to breathe from trees and plants. We need plants to be outside in sunlight so the oxygen gets into the air."

Over in the Agree corner, students are talking about the possibility that plants can grow without sunlight.

Marcus notes, "I think you can use special lamps to grow plants inside. They can grow without sunlight."

Shayla thinks aloud, "Maybe they just need a little sun every day." A few other students, like Shayla, begin to reconsider their corner choice based on the conversations and a review of their own experiences. Ms. Andrews allows such students to move themselves to other corners that better fit with their emerging views on the topic.

As students discuss the issue, Ms. Andrews notes who uses information from the books, discussions, hands-on activities, and demonstrations. She also identifies who needs more support and offers cues, prompts, and even direct explanation when needed. She reminds Janette, who isn't sure how to explain why she *strongly disagrees* with the statement, that she can use evidence from the books she read and from the class discussion to support her opinion. Janette then states that two of the books talk about how important sunlight is to a bean plant's growth.

After the activity, Ms. Andrews discusses the need for plants to have sunlight to make food. She reviews several pages in the read-aloud books. She concludes by sharing a synopsis, in first-grade-friendly language, of an article in *Scientific American* about researchers who have been experimenting to create plants that can grow without sunlight and have had some success (Leutwyler, 2001).

Retesting a Theory

Following this activity, Ms. Andrews's students conduct an experiment in which each group of three students plants bean seeds in pots. Two groups put their pots outside in an area that is always sunny. Two groups put their pots in an area that gets about four hours of sunshine per day. Finally, two groups put their pots in the classroom closet. All six groups water their pots daily and record drawings of any changes they notice over the course of two weeks. After conducting their individual experiments, the students share their drawings and ideas. To conclude this study, Ms. Andrews repeats the Four Corners activity with the same statement: "Plants can grow without sunlight." This time, more students confidently and quickly choose a corner that represents their opinion. Conversations are based on background knowledge gleaned from readings and discussions, as well as from understandings garnered from the bean seed experiment.

Ms. Andrews often employs Four Corners to engage students in stating their views. Even first graders like to make their opinions known. In science, opinions—or viewpoints—need to be founded in well-supported knowledge. However, not all issues have a clear-cut *correct* perspective. There are many controversial issues in science, including the use of cloning, genetically modified foods, reclaimed water, and stem cell research. Students' opinions should be rooted in some understanding of the issue at hand. Ms. Andrews believes that if students, even as young as first grade, have opportunities to build background knowledge while learning topical vocabulary in order to talk about an issue, they will be able to verbally express opinions on complex science topics using content knowledge and language.

Questions for Discussion or Reflection

1. Notice how Ms. Andrews created conversational situations that enabled students to practice using language to inform, reason, persuade, argue a position, and promote their propositions while using text-based information. What situations in your classroom promote students using scientific language to make and communicate inferences and judgments about information they're learning?

2. What science issues might be suitable for a Four Corners activity in your classroom?

3. Students need to see how an expert supports an opinion with evidence. How will you model this skill for students? Try it, and invite a colleague to help you reflect on how well you accomplished your purpose.

4. Which grade-level NGSS and CCSS does your instruction address?

Within the context of this lesson, Ms. Andrews's students use text-based evidence and real-world experiences to defend their opinions. This draws on aspects of learning addressed in both the NGSS and the CCSS. In several cases, students note the use of plant structures in order to defend their ideas. They use their experience of growing plants to formulate their thoughts. They are also exposed to the concept that not all science ideas have one right answer. Quite the contrary—science is a dynamic and fluid field of study with concepts and ideas rooted in experimentation, evidence, data collection, and deep analysis. While these concepts are presented at a foundational level, they will be fleshed out to a greater degree as students progress from first all the way up to twelfth grade.

Mr. Joseph's Second-Grade Class

Second-grade teacher Marshall Joseph wants his students to explore changes in matter through observations of how heating and cooling affect different materials. He approaches this topic by first allowing students to explore properties of matter and then permitting them to see how changing temperature can sometimes cause permanent changes and other times can cause reversible changes. This lesson is intended to build foundations for future studies when students explore the differences between chemical and physical changes. Table 2.3 shows Mr. Joseph's lesson plan.

Using Properties to Describe Materials

Upon entering the classroom, Mr. Joseph's students are delighted to find an array of materials, including a small block of metal, an apple, a rubber band, a sponge, a square of sandpaper, a cup of water, and a cube of ice in a Ziploc bag, lying across the desks. Mr. Joseph next distributes a note guide that has all of the items listed in a column. Next to the column is a space to record observations for each item (figure 2.5, page 54; a reproducible version of this figure can be found at **go.solution-tree.com/commoncore**). Mr. Joseph holds up a baseball-sized rock and tells students to listen in as he makes observations.

Closely looking at the rock, Mr. Joseph begins by noting its various colors. "I see white, black, gray, reddish brown, and even a few pink grains. This rock is multicolored. That means it's many different colors. Some materials are one color, like the red ball on my desk." Mr. Joseph proceeds to discuss the rock's texture. "This rock feels bumpy when I run my fingers across it. That tells me that it has a rough texture." Walking over to his desk to pick up the ball, Mr. Joseph adds, "The ball has a smooth texture." Mr. Joseph next shows how he determines hardness, elasticity, and other characteristics, such as shape. He then asks students to work with a partner to observe all the items on their desks. They are instructed to talk to their partners and then to record observational data in the Characteristics column of the note guide.

When Sammy asks Jennifer if she thinks ice is elastic or not, she replies, "You can't stretch ice. It always stays the same—a square, unless it melts. I don't think it's elastic. The rubber band is stretchy. That's elastic." Conversations that involve discussion and debate ensue till all students are finished describing their materials.

Table 2.3: Second-Grade CCSS for Speaking and Listening and Language and NGSS Lesson Plan on Physical Sciences

Crosscutting Concept	Patterns, cause and effect, and energy and matter
Core Ideas	Structure and properties of matter Chemical reactions
Lesson Purpose	Understand and discuss how some changes caused by heating and cooling can be reversed and some cannot
Focus Strategy	Organize evidence-based information into an oral argument
NGSS	
PS1.A: Structure and Properties of Matter. Different kinds of matter exist and many of them can be either solid or liquid, depending on temperature. Matter can be described and classified by its observable properties. (2-PS1-1) PS1.B: Chemical Reactions. Heating or cooling a substance may cause changes that can be observed. Sometimes these changes are reversible, and sometimes they are not. K-2-ETS1-2. Develop a simple sketch, drawing, or physical model to illustrate how the shape of an object helps it function as needed to solve a given problem.	
CCSS	
• Speaking and Listening standards: SL.2.1. Participate in collaborative conversations with diverse partners about *grade 2 topics and texts* with peers and adults in small and larger groups. SL.2.6. Produce complete sentences when appropriate to task and situation in order to provide requested detail or clarification.	
• Language standards: L.2.3. Use knowledge of language and its conventions when writing, speaking, reading, or listening. L.2.6. Use words and phrases acquired through conversations, reading and being read to, and responding to texts, including using adjectives and adverbs to describe.	

Source: Adapted from NGA & CCSSO, 2010a, pp. 23, 27, and Achieve, 2013a, pp. 13, 16.

Material	Characteristics
Block of metal	Color: Smooth or Rough: Hard or Soft: Elastic or Inelastic: Other:
Apple	Color: Smooth or Rough: Hard or Soft: Elastic or Inelastic: Other:
Rubber band	Color: Smooth or Rough: Hard or Soft: Elastic or Inelastic: Other:
Sponge	Color: Smooth or Rough: Hard or Soft: Elastic or Inelastic: Other:
Sandpaper	Color: Smooth or Rough: Hard or Soft: Elastic or Inelastic: Other:
Water	Color: Smooth or Rough: Hard or Soft: Elastic or Inelastic: Other:
Ice	Color: Smooth or Rough: Hard or Soft: Elastic or Inelastic: Other:

Figure 2.5: Form to record data for observed objects.

Guiding Students to Construct an Argument With Evidence

Once students have sufficiently observed all objects, Mr. Joseph asks them to visit four stations he has set up around the room. He strategically arranges his groups so that they are heterogeneous. For example, he places two English learners with two students who are enthusiastic about science and have deeper background knowledge. He then adds one student who is a little fearful of learning science to the group.

Students visiting the first station are instructed to put on goggles. They find a pot of water simmering on a hot plate. Mr. Joseph monitors this station and makes sure that the students are at least three feet away from the hot plate. On days when he has a paraprofessional in the classroom, he will often employ the support of that person to monitor stations where safety is critical.

On the backside of their note guides, students are instructed to draw a picture of what they observe. Second grader Alia sketches a picture of the pot with lines representing steam coming from the water's surface. At another station, students find a block of ice melting in a bowl. Christiana draws a square with water spilling out from the bottom. At another station, students compare a leaf that was put in the freezer overnight with a leaf that is fresh. After students make sketches and accompanying notes for all stations, they return to their seats. Mr. Joseph then puts the following question on the whiteboard: "Can all changes to matter be reversed?"

He next walks across the front of the classroom, turns, and walks back to his starting point, explaining, "I walked to one end of the classroom, then I reversed my direction. That means I went back to where I originally started. When you reverse a change in matter, the matter is going back to its original state." He next asks students to discuss this question: "After we change water into ice, can we reverse the change?" Christiana tells her partner Maxwell, "Yes, we can. At station two, we saw the ice melting. It can go back to water." After students discuss this question, Mr. Joseph asks them if they think the frozen leaf could be returned to the same state as the fresh leaf. Then in a moment of drama, Mr. Joseph lights a safety match. After a few seconds, he blows it out and asks students to observe the burnt wooden stick, while offering the partner-talk prompt, "Can we reverse the change to this match? Can we make it like a new match?" MaryAnn emphatically tells her partner, "No, once you burn something, you can't change it back. I don't think you can reverse everything." Her partner, Miguel, agrees.

After exhibiting a cooked egg and melted butter, Mr. Joseph asks his students to talk to partners so that they can come to an agreement about their response to the initial question, "Can all changes to matter be reversed?" He also provides students with two academic sentence frames to use for their discussion. "One partner," begins Mr. Joseph, "must use this sentence frame: 'I believe that changes are/are not always reversible, because . . .'" He continues: "The other partner must then say, 'I agree/disagree with you, because . . .'" These sentence frames are posted on the document camera for all to clearly see.

Mr. Joseph listens in as Miguel begins: "I believe changes are not always reversible because the burned paper would stay burned. It can't be new again." His partner, MaryAnn, agrees. "Yeah, I agree with you because the egg is the same. If you cook it, you can't make it a new chicken egg."

Mr. Joseph is satisfied that students understand the importance of using evidence to state an opinion and that they are becoming familiar with the use of academic language to be used when stating their views. This is the first step in moving toward the construction of an argument based on evidence.

Questions for Discussion or Reflection

1. Mr. Joseph provided students with evidence that they could use to support a science-based opinion. What kinds of experiences will you provide to students to help them organize their ideas so that they can state an opinion based on data?

2. Typically students in second grade do not have the academic language used to state an opinion based on evidence. How will you offer students opportunities to talk to each other using appropriate academic language? What language supports will you provide?

3. What resources and experiences would you need to integrate into your instruction to build content knowledge for your lessons?

4. Which grade-level NGSS and CCSS does your instruction address?

Ms. Lopez's Third-Grade Class

Alison Lopez believes that even in third grade, students can use their ingenuity and sense of inventiveness to create solutions to real-world problems. When students study weather and climate and address the Next Generation Science Standard that calls for them to make a claim about the merit of a design solution that reduces the impact of a weather-related hazard (3-ESS3-1), she has them work collaboratively to research and then brainstorm potential solutions given a realistic scenario, such as the following: "There is a river in a town. The river flows near homes. In winter it snows. The river floods when the snow melts. People of the town want to protect the land and the homes. They are asking you to share your ideas at a town meeting on Friday." Table 2.4 shows Ms. Lopez's lesson plan for studying weather and climate.

Table 2.4: Third-Grade CCSS for Speaking and Listening and Language and NGSS Lesson Plan on Physical Sciences

Crosscutting Concept	Patterns and cause and effect
Core Ideas	Weather and climate Natural hazards
Lesson Purpose	Understand how to solve a flooding problem caused by snow melting
Focus Strategy	Using a model to solve an environmental problem caused by a weather-related hazard

NGSS

3-ESS3-1. Make a claim about the merit of a design solution that reduces the impacts of a weather-related hazard.

3-5-ETS1-3. Plan and carry out fair tests in which variables are controlled and failure points are considered to identify aspects of a model or prototype that can be improved.

CCSS

• Speaking and Listening standards:

SL.3.4. Report on a topic or text, tell a story, or recount an experience with appropriate facts and relevant, descriptive details, speaking clearly at an understandable pace.

SL.3.6. Speak in complete sentences when appropriate to task and situation in order to provide requested detail or clarification.

• Language standards:

L.3.3. Use knowledge of language and its conventions when writing, speaking, reading, or listening.

    a. Choose words and phrases for effect.

    b. Recognize and observe differences between the conventions of spoken and written standard English.

Source: Adapted from NGA & CCSSO, 2010a, pp. 24, 29, and Achieve, 2013a, p. 21.

Challenging Students With a Weather-Related Hazard

Because students aren't always familiar with the weather phenomena that cause such environmental hazards, Ms. Lopez spends time familiarizing students with forms of precipitation, including rain, snow, hail, and sleet. While some students have experienced these forms of water falling from the atmosphere, not all have. She shares photos of each type of precipitation and even lets students watch video clips of falling snow and listen to audio of rain falling. Because students are being asked to brainstorm solutions to the problems of flooding, lightning, and severe winds, she also shares how the land and people can be affected by heavy rains and by melting snow. She shows pictures of rivers overflowing and lightning striking a tree. She shows a roof being blown off a building.

When some students express surprise that this can occur, Ms. Lopez tells them that they have the ability to solve problems that might be caused by too much precipitation in one location over a relatively short period of time. She then distributes five dishwashing basins to table groups (approximately one foot square by one-half foot depth) throughout the classroom. She pours fine sand into each basin and asks students to work with their partners to make a long riverbed using their fingers.

She models how to do this by putting her basin under the document camera, then pushing her finger into the sand to draw a line that stretches from one end of the basin to the other. Students all do the same within table groups. Ms. Lopez gives each group four Lego™ blocks and tells students, "These are your houses. You can place them in your basin wherever you would like."

She next asks each group to place a one-inch square block under one end of the basin to tilt it up. When all basins are set up, Ms. Lopez provides each group with a 100 ml beaker full of water and directs students to slowly pour the water into their finger-traced "river." Students watch as the water goes down the river to the end of the basin. Ms. Lopez next tells students to pour more water and to think about how they could protect the Lego homes. Third grader Jennifer and her group use sand to build up a barrier between the homes and the river. Yusef and his team put pencils along the riverbank. Betty suggests that her group pull the houses out to put more sand under the homes to make a mountain on which the houses can reside. Ms. Lopez encourages students to try out different solutions.

Making Claims About the Merits of a Design Solution

Once each group has a plan for protecting the river and the homes, Ms. Lopez asks the students to summarize their group's plan by drawing a sketch and writing at least three sentences to explain why the plan will work. Ms. Lopez provides students with this writing and speaking and listening prompt:

1. Draw your idea.

2. Write about your idea.

a. Your first sentence should describe your solution.

b. Your second sentence should explain how your solution helps the people living in the town.

c. Your third sentence should explain how the problem of flooding will be solved.

4. Read your plan to your group.

5. Listen when your group members read their sentences.

Questions for Discussion or Reflection

1. Ms. Lopez allowed students to experiment with simple equipment that can be used to model a problem and determine a solution. What materials might you utilize to model a real-world weather-related problem, like damage caused by high winds or lightning strikes on tall buildings?

2. How would you have students consider multiple solutions to weather-related problems?

3. Ms. Lopez shared photos, video, and audio so that students could see and hear various types of precipitation in advance of discussing flooding caused by snowmelt. What foundational content knowledge might students need to discuss other weather phenomena (wind, acid rain, and so on)?

4. Which grade-level NGSS and CCSS does your instruction address?

Betty's sketch shows a mound of sand with four buildings on top. Her summary is as follows: "We built a mountain and put the houses on top. People can drive down the mountain in their cars. When snow melts it will not go up to the houses because they are high up."

All students share their written interpretation of their group's ideas. They also listen to the statements written by the others in their group. Through this activity, students visualize a solution, build a model, and tackle a real-world problem that is a worldwide concern. Flooding happens across the globe. Ultimately, students are starting to do the work of engineers by building solutions to science-related environmental issues. They both express their understanding of science content and show their application of engineering practices.

Mr. Davis's Fourth-Grade Class

Fourth graders in Stephen Davis's class address NGSS 4-ESS2-1: "Make observations and/or measurements to provide evidence of the effects of weathering or the rate of erosion by water, ice, wind, or vegetation" (Achieve, 2013a, p. 26). To illustrate the differences among the concepts *weathering*, *erosion*, and *deposition*, Mr. Davis employs videos from Discovery Education (http://streaming .discoveryeducation.com), conducts demonstrations, and has students read carefully selected texts. Table 2.5 shows Mr. Davis's lesson plan.

Observing and Hypothesizing

To share information about *weathering*, the breaking or wearing down of rocks, Mr. Davis has students put a piece of chalk in a beaker of water and another piece in a beaker of vinegar. He then asks them to observe both beakers for ten minutes. Students record observations and discuss the differences between the two beakers. Mr. Davis then explains that chalk is made of calcium carbonate, just like the rock limestone. Calcium carbonate reacts with acids, like vinegar. Mr. Davis adds that when rocks react with solutions like acids, including acid rain, and break down, the process is called *chemical weathering*. Mr. Davis refers to the posted words, such as *acid rain*, *chemical weathering*, and *mechanical weathering*, hanging on the prominent word wall on the side of the classroom. To illustrate the difference between *chemical* and *mechanical weathering*, Mr. Davis passes out a cracker to each student. He asks his students to place the crackers in their mouths but tells them not to chew.

Denise announces, with a full mouth, "It's dissolving!" He tells students to chew and swallow. He then asks students to share with a partner how letting the cracker dissolve in their mouths might have been like chemical weathering.

Candace tells Mikey, "The chalk broke up just like the cracker broke up in my mouth. I think the chemicals in my mouth are dissolving the cracker." Mikey adds, "I think I remember that last year we talked about how saliva in your mouth dissolves food, just like how vinegar dissolves chalk."

Next, Mr. Davis tells students that when they chew the cracker, they are mechanically—or physically with their teeth—breaking down the cracker. "Just as your teeth can break down the cracker, wind, rain, snow, waves, or freezing water can break down a rock. This is called *mechanical weathering*," he tells the class. He then shares a photo of pounding ocean waves mechanically breaking down rocks (figure 2.6, page 62).

Table 2.5: Fourth-Grade CCSS for Speaking and Listening and Language and NGSS Lesson Plan on Earth and Space Sciences

Crosscutting Concept	Earth's systems
Core Idea	The roles of water in Earth's surface processes
Lesson Purpose	Understand and discuss how the processes of weathering and erosion affect the surface of the Earth
Focus Strategy	Chunking texts to support science reading and using discussion webs to streamline information sharing Thinking aloud to model how to read and think about information in the text

NGSS

4-ESS2-1. Make observations and/or measurements to provide evidence of the effects of weathering or the rate of erosion by water, ice, wind, or vegetation.

3-5-ETS1-2. Generate and compare multiple possible solutions to a problem based on how well each is likely to meet the criteria and constraints of the problem.

CCSS

• Speaking and Listening standards:

SL.4.1. Engage effectively in a range of collaborative discussions (one-on-one, in groups, and teacher-led) with diverse partners on *grade 4 topics and texts*, building on others' ideas and expressing their own clearly.

    a. Come to discussions prepared, having read or studied required material; explicitly draw on that preparation and other information known about the topic to explore ideas under discussion.

    b. Follow agreed-on rules for discussions and carry out assigned roles.

    c. Pose and respond to specific questions to clarify or follow up on information, and make comments that contribute to the discussion and link to the remarks of others.

    d. Review the key ideas expressed and explain their own ideas and understanding in light of the discussion.

SL.4.2. Paraphrase portions of a text read aloud or information presented in diverse media and formats, including visually, quantitatively, and orally.

SL.4.4. Report on a topic or text, tell a story, or recount an experience in an organized manner, using appropriate facts and relevant, descriptive details to support main ideas or themes; speak clearly at an understandable pace.

Continued➜

- Language standards:

  L.4.1. Demonstrate command of the conventions of standard English grammar and usage when writing or speaking.

  L.4.3. Use knowledge of language and its conventions when writing, speaking, reading, or listening.

  L.4.6. Acquire and use accurately grade-appropriate general academic and domain-specific words and phrases, including those that signal precise actions, emotions, or states of being (such as *quizzed*, *whined*, *stammered*) and those that are basic to a particular topic (such as *wildlife*, *conservation*, and *endangered* when discussing animal preservation).

Source: Adapted from NGA & CCSSO, 2010a, pp. 24, 28, 29, and Achieve, 2013a pp. 23, 26, 32.

Figure 2.6: Mechanical weathering of rocks.

Continuing with the discussion, Mr. Davis asks students to think about what happens when rain, wind, snow, or waves break down rocks and to discuss this with their partners. "Where does the broken rock material go?" he asks them.

Vinny tells his partner, Kareena, "I think the rain or snow washes away broken rock particles. Or maybe the waves take them out to the middle of the ocean." Kareena adds, "I wonder if sand is from broken rocks?"

Next, Mr. Davis asks the students to describe where the chewed cracker particles went when they swallowed. Kareena, recalling a term from third grade, states, "The particles went down my *esophagus*." Hearing this, Mr. Davis asks Kareena to share her statement with the class. He then adds, "*Erosion* is when broken rock particles are moved from one place to another. The particles are transported."

Joe questions cautiously, "Is that like how the cracker particles traveled from our mouths to our stomachs? That must be how erosion and swallowing the cracker are alike!" Mr. Davis compliments Joe on his insightful comment and then continues by saying: "Joe mentioned that the cracker particles traveled to our stomach. That's where they were deposited, at least for a little while. Later, the cracker will break down even more. We'll talk about that part in another lesson. For now, let's think about the cracker now sitting in our stomach. This is like the ocean waves carrying the rock particles out to sea where they come to rest at the bottom of the ocean. When particles come to rest after being eroded, we call that *deposition*. Particles are deposited, or laid down, when there is not enough energy for them to be transported, or moved, any further."

Mr. Davis often follows a scientific word or phrase with student-friendly terminology to ensure students understand. He also invites them to initiate original ways to share their scientific findings. His teaching was based on a belief that students need to understand the functional uses of language, since as Michael Halliday (1961) and Carolyn Temple Adger, Catherine Snow, and Donna Christian (2002) have suggested, language evolves as humans interact with their world.

Modeling How to Read Scientific Information

To further augment this lesson, Mr. Davis asks his students to read and discuss a text on related material. This time, he chooses a real-world issue that connects to the discussion on weathering, erosion, and deposition. He provides a letter that a man in India wrote and published in the *New York Times* (Kapur, 2010). (Visit **go.solution-tree.com/commoncore** to read the full article, which discusses the devastating effects of wave and tidal erosion on the village of Chinnamudaliarchavadi.)

Mr. Davis admits eagerly that he doesn't know the correct way to pronounce the name of the village and adds that this is OK, since he can still read the article and determine the main ideas. He can learn the correct pronunciation later. This is a way for Mr. Davis to strategically share that a proficient reader doesn't allow long, unfamiliar words to block or intimidate his or her understanding. He can "read around" them and decipher main ideas and core meaning. As usual, Mr. Davis models and thinks aloud about how to read and think about the structure and language within the first paragraph of the text (see chapters 3 and 4 for more on *think-alouds*). He also shows how he uses a pencil to annotate and make notes in the margin to document key ideas and questions that arise while reading. Then he rereads the paragraph to more deeply explore the content.

Chunking Sentences to Support Comprehension

Mr. Davis shows students how to break complex sentences down into component parts. To do this, he uses the following sample sentence: "In 2004, as fishermen sorted through the day's catch, the Asian tsunami roared through the village, destroying huts and boats." Mr. Davis lists the individual sentence parts: (1) fishermen sorted through the catch, (2) the tsunami roared through the village, and (3) the tsunami destroyed huts and boats. Mr. Davis uses this method of sentence (conceptual) chunking to help students tackle difficult-to-read sentences. After students develop proficiency in sentence chunking, they can more facilely approach complex sentences. As this occurs, Mr. Davis removes the chunking scaffold and allows students to more fluidly move through a sentence. He next asks his students to read the remainder of the text with a pencil in hand.

Mr. Davis knows that this article, like so many texts in science, raises more questions than answers. Building on this element of science texts, he incorporates a discussion web (Alvermann, 1991) into his lesson (figure 2.7). Using a discussion web helps students identify opposing viewpoints as they quickly visualize the key elements of an issue. This organizational tool promotes discussions as students first identify ideas of argument, then critically evaluate these opposing positions, and finally make text-supported conclusions.

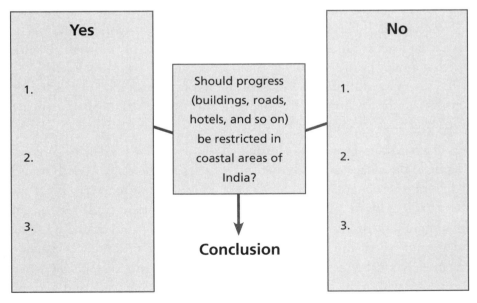

Figure 2.7: Sample discussion web.

Mr. Davis poses a question for students: "Should progress (buildings, roads, hotels, and so on) be restricted in coastal areas of India?" He adds, "Be sure to consider what you know about weathering, erosion, and deposition, and include the information you learned in the article." He then shares a five-step protocol for the discussion web conversation.

1. Reread the *New York Times* article (Kapur, 2010).

2. Discuss it with your partner by determining reasons for encouraging and permitting progress (buildings, roads, hotels, and so on) and record these in the "Yes" box. Be sure to support your thinking and talking with facts from what you're reading.

3. Continue your discussion by considering reasons for restricting progress and record these in the "No" box.

4. With your partner, come to a conclusion and record your ideas in the "Conclusion" box.

5. Prepare to share your concluding ideas with the class.

Mr. Davis is able to identify students who need more help by listening to student discussions. For instance, when Marvin tells his partner, Wilson, that he is confused when the article mentions global warming, Mr. Davis intervenes: "Global warming is when the atmosphere heats up due to the burning of fossil fuels, like gas and coal. Scientists see that sea level is rising because the polar ice is melting due to warmer atmospheric temperatures—air temperatures. The rising sea level affects the coastal regions. Take a look at this section in the textbook. It discusses global warming and rising sea level."

Realizing that he hasn't formally discussed global warming with the whole class, Mr. Davis jots down a reminder to himself: "Remember to do a think-aloud of the book *Our Choice: A Plan to Solve the Climate Crisis* (Gore, 2012)—just the part about sea level rising."

In science, students will encounter challenging language, including unfamiliar terminology. Teaching them to persist and persevere when reading is a powerful skill—one that they will carry with them in their essential tool kit from elementary school to college. Students need to be empowered to draw on their own resources when encountering new words and concepts. Additionally, an understanding that some texts provide answers to questions, others raise and provoke questions, and some do both is essential to science learners.

Questions for Discussion or Reflection

1. Mr. Davis modeled for his students how he reads and interrogates a text, because he believes that learning to read a text initially involves teacher support. This practice is described in much more detail in chapter 4 (page 125). What questions do you have about reading science texts? Compile a list, and then read chapter 4 closely for additional information.

2. In the classroom scenario, students connected vocabulary terms, such as *mechanical* and *chemical weathering*, to dissolving and chewing a cracker. How might you help your students acquire new vocabulary?

3. Mr. Davis used a discussion web to guide students to investigate a real-world problem through conversation. How might you utilize a discussion web in your classroom? What science topics would your students study?

4. Which grade-level NGSS and CCSS does your instruction address?

Mr. Martinez's Fifth-Grade Class

When Lucien joined Javier Martinez's fifth-grade class, he knew very little about the moon's appearance during the four-week lunar cycle. To help students like Lucien build the knowledge that is needed to talk about the moon's phases, Mr. Martinez uses a wide array of tools. One such tool is a shared think-aloud reading of *The Moon Book* (Gibbons, 1998). When using this strategy, he clearly articulates words like *phases* and *lunar* as he reads. Table 2.6 shows Mr. Martinez's lesson plan.

Pausing from reading, Mr. Martinez moves to a poster located near the left side of the classroom (figure 2.8, page 68). The poster shows the phases of the moon in *The Moon Book* plus some additional ones, like the waxing and waning crescent and the waxing and waning gibbous. Mr. Martinez studies the poster as he articulates his thoughts: "There sure are a lot of new names for different phases of the moon," he says. "I'm glad some are listed in the text, and others are on this chart. I'm not sure I can remember all of these right now, but I do want to understand why we see the moon differently when we stare upward at night. I did notice that last night it was almost full. I wonder how it will look tomorrow night or next week?"

Table 2.6: Fifth-Grade CCSS for Speaking and Listening and Language and NGSS Lesson Plan for Earth and Space Sciences

Crosscutting Concept	Patterns
Core Idea	Earth's place in the universe
Lesson Purpose	Understand and discuss the phases of the moon, patterns that result from the position of the sun, Earth, and moon
Focus Strategy	Using think-alouds and creating glogs to share ideas

NGSS

5-ESS1-2. Represent data in graphical displays to reveal patterns of daily changes in length and direction of shadows, day and night, and the seasonal appearance of some stars in the night sky.

[handwritten margin note: no moon patterns for MS]

CCSS

- Speaking and Listening standards:

SL.5.1. Engage effectively in a range of collaborative discussions (one-on-one, in groups, and teacher-led) with diverse partners on *grade 5 topics and texts*, building on others' ideas and expressing their own clearly.

  a. Come to discussions prepared, having read or studied required material; explicitly draw on that preparation and other information known about the topic to explore ideas under discussion.

  b. Follow agreed-upon rules for discussions and carry out assigned roles.

  c. Pose and respond to specific questions by making comments that contribute to the discussion and elaborate on the remarks of others.

  d. Review the key ideas expressed and draw conclusions in light of information and knowledge gained from the discussions.

SL.5.4. Report on a topic or text or present an opinion, sequencing ideas logically and using appropriate facts and relevant, descriptive details to support main ideas or themes; speak clearly at an understandable pace.

SL.5.5. Include multimedia components (e.g., graphics, sound) and visual displays in presentations when appropriate to enhance the development of main ideas or themes.

SL.5.6. Adapt speech to a variety of contexts and tasks, using formal English when appropriate to task and situation.

- Language standards:

L.5.1. Demonstrate command of the conventions of standard English grammar and usage when writing or speaking.

L.5.6. Acquire and use accurately grade-appropriate general academic and domain-specific words and phrases, including those that signal contrast, addition, and other logical relationships (e.g., *however, although, nevertheless, similarly, moreover, in addition*).

Source: Adapted from NGA & CCSSO, 2010a, pp. 24, 28, 29, and Achieve, 2013a, p. 31

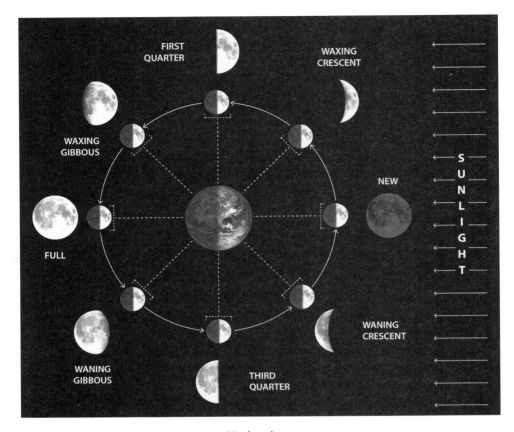

Source: David Rose, moonconnection.com. Used with permission.
Figure 2.8: Moon phases.

Exploring Multiple Sources and Infusing Vocabulary

Mr. Martinez is strategically showing students how he familiarizes himself with new ideas by looking at all kinds of materials, from books to posters. He also demonstrates that when he doesn't know or understand something—in this case, the terms on the poster—he does know how to get information by wondering, questioning, drawing on personal experiences, and reading. For example, "I did notice that last night the moon was almost full. I wonder how it will look tomorrow night or next week."

Mr. Martinez also strategically decides when to infuse vocabulary instruction. Introducing the terms *lunar* and *phases* during the instruction, he builds understanding within the contextual framework. Specifically, students see pictures in their book, hear the teacher read and think about the moon, and are introduced to new scientific terms.

Continuing, Mr. Martinez says, "I see from the poster that the moon goes around Earth. I think that's called orbiting. I remember that from *The Moon Book*, which we just read. I also see that there are sun rays shining from the right side of this poster. This must represent the sun. I know that the sun is too large and too far away to fit on the poster. I think that's why rays are used to show that it's there. I wonder if we see the moon because the sun is lighting it up? If I were standing on Earth here [*Mr. Martinez points to where he would be standing on Earth viewing the moon*], I would be looking at the side of the moon that is not facing the sun. I can see from the poster label that this is a new moon. I think a new moon looks dark in the sky because the lighted side is not facing Earth."

Demonstrating Problem Solving

Mr. Martinez intentionally shows how he uses problem solving when looking at the poster. He ignores confusing elements (such as the various names of the phases, which are unfamiliar), and he focuses on the visual elements that help him make sense of the poster, saying, "I also see that there are sun rays shining from the right side of this poster." Additionally, Mr. Martinez makes a concerted effort to use academic language. He purposefully uses the term *represent*, an academic word commonly used in science. As he notes that the sun is too large and far away to fit on the poster, he suggests the meaning of *represent*, saying, "I think that's why rays are used to show that it's there."

While this read-aloud is a subtle way of sharing with students how to figure out new information when given a text, poster, or other form of media, it is a critical element of the learning process, from modeling to practice to independent problem solving and critical thinking. Mr. Martinez knows that students like Lucien, who lack rich science experiences, can draw on classroom materials. Instead of telling Marcel the information, Mr. Martinez wants to show him how he can independently find information. This information equips him to continue his scientific investigations long after he leaves fifth grade.

In order to further help Lucien and his classmates build more background knowledge on the moon, Mr. Martinez shows them how to make a glog—an interactive online poster—that includes information about the moon using Glogster (http://edu.glogster.com). Mr. Martinez starts with a blank page to which he adds a background design and some photos of the moon. He decides to upload two videos about the moon using SchoolTube (www.schooltube.com), which is accessible through Glogster. After he completes his glog, Mr. Martinez reviews his interactive online poster by studying each image and by watching the videos he uploaded (see figure 2.9).

Mr. Martinez tells students, "I can click on the brown tag, labeled *The Moon*, which is a link, and it takes me to a NASA photo of a full moon. The caption of the photo says that this was taken by Expedition 5's crew members. Expedition 5 must be a space mission with astronauts. Now I'm going to watch this video clip. [*He clicks on the video and views it.*] I see the various phases of the moon, just like the ones I read about in *The Moon Book*—new moon, first quarter, full moon, and last quarter."

Figure 2.9: Mr. Martinez's moon glog.

After examining and discussing all parts of the poster, Mr. Martinez groups his students in pairs and asks partners to create their own moon glog. As his students begin to explore the videos and a few links to websites that he has bookmarked, Mr. Martinez moves around the room, listening in on student conversations. Lucien and his partner determine which phase of the moon correlates with a given moon image at a NASA website. (Visit **go.solution -tree.com/commoncore** to access the links in this book.) Seeing that the boys are struggling with identifying moon phases, Mr. Martinez walks over to the moon phase poster tacked to the wall and points to the image labeled *first quarter*. The boys compare the poster image with the photo on the website and agree that it is a first-quarter moon. Mr. Martinez intentionally directs their attention to the appropriate image on the wall poster in order to offer a *cue* to scaffold their understanding. Both boys decide that this is a good website to put onto their glog.

Well-chosen texts, online videos, images, and other forms of media are effective ways to help bolster background knowledge. This, in turn, facilitates oral language development, because students now have the background information required to have a conversation. Believing that students can build a base of knowledge as they explore multiple sources, Mr. Martinez finds innovative ways to engage and motivate students to independence as they amass and share new understandings.

Synthesizing ideas from multiple resources requires practice before expertise is attained. When a teacher asks students in elementary school to incorporate images, videos, and audio podcasts, along with more standard texts, into a format that conveys ideas about a topic, students come to see these resources as valuable pieces of an assemblage of information. In our technology-infused world, students will need to develop a wide range of literacy skills—skills that allow them to analyze photos, listen to science experts in video or audio form, and draw conclusions from observed data. Being literate in science means you can read, write, listen, and speak about a wide array of media and resources.

Questions for Discussion or Reflection

1. Mr. Martinez used multiple sources to share scientific language with his students and modeled how to investigate a wide array of sources. What would your wish list of Internet and text sources to expose students to a wide array of scientific language look like? How might students engage with these sources in your classroom?

2. Mr. Martinez modeled how he thinks and talks about a visual resource (the moon poster). What visual resources might you use to model how to talk about and utilize visual aids?

3. How could you incorporate the glog strategy into your instruction?

4. Which grade-level NGSS and CCSS does your instruction address?

Ms. Gardner's Sixth-Grade Class

In Sharon Gardner's sixth-grade class, science is a time of the day when questions, investigations, and inquiry reign. Ms. Gardner knows that simple ideas can percolate, build, and then grow into full-fledged scientific studies if the initial ideas are nurtured through collaborative, collegial small-group conversations. How does Ms. Gardner promote these in-depth conversations? Table 2.7 (page 72) shows Ms. Gardner's lesson plan.

Understanding the power conversation as a means to share, validate, expand, and revise ideas, Ms. Gardner provides opportunities for students to engage in collaborative conversations with classmates as a way to expand their scientific understandings.

Table 2.7: Sixth-Grade CCSS for Speaking and Listening and Language and NGSS Lesson Plan on Earth and Space Sciences

Crosscutting Concept	Systems and system models
Core Idea	Earth's systems: Plate tectonics and large-scale system interactions
Lesson Purpose	Understand and discuss the relationship between plate boundaries and the occurrences of earthquakes and volcanoes
Focus Strategy	Using Picture It to promote discussion

NGSS

MS-ESS2-2. Construct an explanation based on evidence for how geoscience processes have changed Earth's surface at varying times and spatial scales.

MS-ETS1-3. Analyze data from tests to determine similarities and differences among several design solutions to identify the best characteristics of each that can be combined into a new solution to better meet the criteria for success.

CCSS

- Speaking and Listening standards:

SL.6.1. Engage effectively in a range of collaborative discussions (one-on-one, in groups, and teacher-led) with diverse partners on *grade 6 topics, texts, and issues*, building on others' ideas and expressing their own clearly.

     a. Come to discussions prepared, having read or studied required material; explicitly draw on that preparation by referring to evidence on the topic, text, or issue to probe and reflect on ideas under discussion.

     b. Follow rules for collegial discussions, set specific goals and deadlines, and define individual roles as needed.

     c. Pose and respond to specific questions with elaboration and detail by making comments that contribute to the topic, text, or issue under discussion.

     d. Review the key ideas expressed and demonstrate understanding of multiple perspectives through reflection and paraphrasing.

SL.6.2. Interpret information presented in diverse media and formats (for example, visually, quantitatively, or orally) and explain how it contributes to a topic, text, or issue under study.

SL.6.3. Delineate a speaker's argument and specific claims, distinguishing claims that are supported by reasons and evidence from claims that are not.

SL.6.4. Present claims and findings, sequencing ideas logically and using pertinent descriptions, facts, and details to accentuate main ideas or themes; use appropriate eye contact, adequate volume, and clear pronunciation.

SL.6.6. Adapt speech to a variety of contexts and tasks, demonstrating command of formal English when indicated or appropriate.

- Language standards:

L.6.1. Demonstrate command of the conventions of standard English grammar and usage when writing or speaking.

  a. Ensure that pronouns are in the proper case (subjective, objective, and possessive).

  b. Use intensive pronouns (for example, *myself* or *ourselves*).

  c. Recognize and correct inappropriate shifts in pronoun number and person.

  d. Recognize and correct vague pronouns (such as ones with unclear or ambiguous antecedents).

  e. Recognize variations from standard English in their own and others' writing and speaking, and identify and use strategies to improve expression in conventional language.

L.6.2. Demonstrate command of the conventions of standard English capitalization, punctuation, and spelling when writing.

  a. Use punctuation (commas, parentheses, dashes) to set off nonrestrictive or parenthetical elements.

  b. Spell correctly.

L.6.3. Use knowledge of language and its conventions when writing, speaking, reading, or listening.

  a. Vary sentence patterns for meaning, reader/listener interest, and style.

  b. Maintain consistency in style and tone.

Source: Adapted from NGA & CCSSO, 2010a, pp. 49, 52, and Achieve, 2013a, pp. 31, 58, 63.

Supporting Collaborative Conversations

One of Ms. Gardner's favorite tools to support collaborative conversations is Picture It, which involves the use of pictures or photos that students discuss and question. For this lesson, Ms. Gardner wants her students to recognize that mountain ranges, deep ocean trenches, earthquakes, and volcanoes occur in patterns—a concept that relates to the NGSS topic *Earth's interior processes* (Achieve, 2013a, p. 58). To help them build this knowledge, Ms. Gardner shares two pictures with students: a tectonic plate map that shows convergent, divergent, and transform boundaries (figure 2.10, page 74) and a map showing patterns of volcanoes and earthquakes (figure 2.11, page 74). Visit **go.solution-tree.com/commoncore** to see color versions of these maps. She asks students to respond to the following two prompts in teacher-created groups of three: (1) What similarities do you notice between these two maps? and (2) What are two questions that you might ask about these maps?

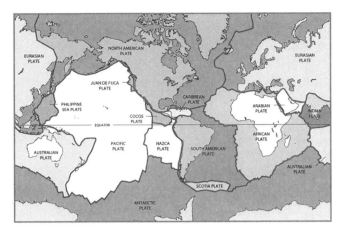

Source: *Map courtesy of the U.S. Geological Survey, 1997.*

Figure 2.10: Tectonic plate map.

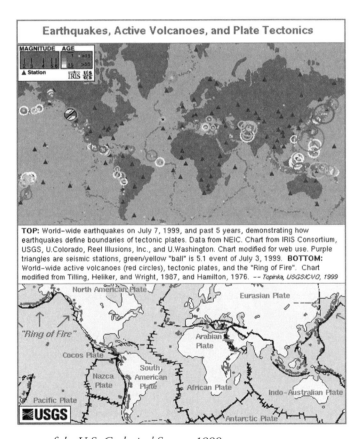

Source: *Maps courtesy of the U.S. Geological Survey, 1999.*

Figure 2.11: Earthquakes and active volcanoes map based on plate tectonics.

In response, Maddie, Moriah, and Ashlyn begin to talk about the two maps. Moriah recalls that convergent boundaries are those in which tectonic plates come together. "Remember when we learned about subduction zones, where an oceanic plate dives under a continental plate? That's where you have a really deep trench." Maddie adds, "Yeah, there's also that boundary where two continental plates come together. What's that called?"

Ashlyn responds, "Well, I don't know what it's called, but the Himalayas are found at that kind of a boundary."

To pull the group together, Ms. Gardner, who's been listening in on the conversation, redirects the students: "How do these boundaries you've been so accurately describing from the first map compare to information on the second map?" The students study both maps. Then Moriah thinks aloud: "Well, I see that the earthquakes seem to be at the same places as the convergent boundaries." After a few seconds, she adds, "Actually, the earthquakes are at the same places as all boundaries—convergent, divergent, and transform. That's strange. I wonder why."

Maddie jumps in. "Moriah, there's one of our questions: 'Why are the earthquakes at the plate boundaries?'" Ashlyn adds, "And here's another question, 'Why are volcanoes at the boundaries?' We need to know more about volcanoes to know why, I think."

Satisfied with this group's progress, Ms. Gardner notes the students are doing the following: (1) accurately using newly learned content language (*convergent*, *divergent*, and *transform*), (2) making logical connections between what they know and what they are observing, and (3) asking relevant questions they can research or investigate to find the answers. In essence, students are talking and behaving like real-world scientists!

Supporting Further Investigation to Test Predictions

The next step after students prepare their questions is to encourage groups to act like engineers to determine and test ways to answer their questions. Maddie, Moriah, and Ashlyn's questions may lead them to online research using the library's digital database of articles and relevant media. Researchers have already addressed the questions that Maddie and her group are asking and continue to ask in geologic studies, so it is likely that through their group study, the students will learn more about the density of oceanic plates compared to continental plates and will come to understand why oceanic plates slide underneath continental plates. They'll learn about how the subducting plates may melt, causing magma to rise to the surface to create a volcanic eruption. They'll also read about the pressure that occurs during subduction and how earthquakes may result. Ms. Gardner's intentional plan is to (1) prompt students to review scientific materials, especially visual materials like the maps, within the structure of a collaborative small group; (2) guide students to share ideas using content language; (3) invite research questions; and (4) have students work with partners to find ways to answer their questions. Throughout this process, Ms. Gardner monitors student groups. She adjusts her instruction or mediates for a struggling group and guides a group to dig deeper to extend learning. She determines her next steps by observing students' conversations, using the language of the content. She knows that opportunities for student talk are also opportunities for teacher progress monitoring and a chance for the teacher to appropriately adjust and personalize instruction.

Questions for Discussion or Reflection

1. As illustrated in Ms. Gardner's classroom, making data-supported predictions is an essential feature in a scientific investigation. Her students identified future questions to study through observations they were making. How might this practice apply to a scientific investigation you're planning at your grade level?

2. How could you use Picture It to guide students to compose real-world science questions?

3. What questions might students investigate? What resources would you provide to help them dig deeper?

4. Which grade-level NGSS and CCSS does your instruction address?

Oral Language Is Foundational

In each classroom scenario presented in this chapter, the teacher models the synergistic and reciprocal relationship between language and scientific knowledge. The very intentional instruction of the teachers is based on a continuous assessment of students' developing understanding of language form and function. Subsequent instructional tasks provide opportunities for students to try on language as they inquire, predict, describe, explain, validate, present, and discuss scientific concepts. These teachers very purposely design instruction that supports their students in developing the mindset of a scientist who can engage, explore, explain, elaborate, evaluate, and communicate scientific wonderings and findings. Doing so artfully addresses the intentions of the CCSS for speaking and listening by allowing students to build their capacities for academic science conversations.

CHAPTER 3

Learning to Write Like a Scientist

The old saying "A picture is worth a thousand words" is at the heart of writing instruction, because to become an expert writer, one must be exposed to writing through the texts he or she hears, reads, talks about, and attempts to craft. According to the CCSS, "Students need to learn to use writing as a way of offering and supporting opinions, demonstrating understanding of the subjects they are studying, and conveying real and imagined experiences and events" (NGA & CCSSO, 2010a, p. 18). Instruction designed to support students as writers must remain a priority if we expect them to learn to write texts that inform, entertain, explain, and argue information.

The results of the National Assessment of Educational Progress (NAEP, 2011b; National Assessment Governing Board [NAGB], 2012; National Center for Education Statistics [NCES], 2012), which measures the writing proficiencies of U.S. students, amplify this need for very intentional writing instruction. Of the 24,100 eighth graders and 28,100 twelfth graders who completed the assessment, representing both public and private schools, only 3 percent at each grade level performed at the advanced or superior level, and only 24 percent at both grade levels performed at the proficient level. These findings indicate that the majority of students in each of these grades—54 percent of eighth graders and 52 percent of twelfth graders—performed at a basic level, suggesting they have only a partial mastery of the prerequisite skills and knowledge needed to perform as proficient writers. These data send an alert to teachers in grades K–6 that greater attention must be placed on purposeful writing instruction that ensures students will leave their elementary school years knowing how to write well across the disciplines. At least 20 percent of students at both grades performed at a below-basic level, indicating that they have much less than a partial mastery of the skills and knowledge needed to share ideas and information through writing. These data further indicate that the majority of eighth and twelfth graders are not proficient at sharing their thinking through written statements that persuade, explain, and convey information.

Future NAEP results for grades 8 and 12 will be compared with the 2011 results to provide information on achievement trends over time. It is important to note that because the 2011 assessment used a computer-based word-processing format with new assessment elements of writing, the 2011 results cannot be compared with previous NAEP writing assessments.

While fourth graders were not assessed in 2007, the NAEP gave them a pilot test of writing in 2012, and fourth graders will be included in the regular administration of future NAEP assessments (NAGB, 2012). Although their future scores also cannot be compared to previous assessment data, fourth graders' 1998 and 2002 assessments evidenced gains. This does not mean that teaching fourth-grade students to write is a done deal, since data from the 2002 assessment reveal that less than one in three fourth graders scored at or above the proficient level (National Writing Project, 2003). The data indicate that greater attention needs to be directed toward the teaching of writing in grades K–12.

What You'll Learn in This Chapter

This chapter looks at the Common Core Writing standards and then explores ways to support students in sharing their written ideas, including strategies like think-alouds, language (phrase and sentence) frames, Venn diagrams, semantic feature analysis, graphic organizers, author's chair, timed writings, and video explorations. In addition to revisiting these, we share some less-used strategies, including collaborative and argumentative guidesheets, RAFTs, and Frayer word cards. Although these are appropriate at many grade levels, we have cast each within the context of a grade-level scenario in which a teacher is using the strategy specifically to address the CCSS Writing standards.

The instructional examples in this chapter also reflect the sentiments of the National Writing Project (2003):

> Writing is the process by which we learn how to convey our ideas, to use our powers of observation, and to persuade others about our viewpoints. In addition to emphasizing classroom practices shown to improve student writing, we must continue to place value on the practice of writing itself. If writing occurred in every classroom every day, student achievement across content areas would reach new heights for all. A much higher percentage of our young people should be able to write at the proficient level; and all our young people

should be able to write at the basic level. To accomplish this, we need a profound commitment to writing in our schools along with support for teachers from organizations like the National Writing Project. (p. 2)

Notice how this description of the writing process parallels the mandates for proficient science writing documented in the research—a need for writers to *establish detailed associations among evidence, warrants, claims, and reflective commentary* (Yore, Hand, & Florence, 2004). The scenarios invite you to peek inside the classrooms of expert science teachers to see how they guide students to write like scientists.

What Are the Standards?

The Common Core State Standards (NGA & CCSSO, 2010a) require students to write well across the content areas and grades. The CCSS identify ten broad Writing anchor standards that remain constant throughout grades K–12 and emphasize the specific writing skills students should develop by the time they complete grade 12. More specific grade-level standards that correspond by number to each anchor standard identify a performance progression of skills and understandings that students should be developing as they move through the grades. Developing sophistication in all facets of language use supports one's strength as a writer.

The Writing anchor standards fall under four domains. The first, Text Types and Purposes, involves learning to write many types of texts for many purposes. Standards in the second domain, Production and Distribution of Writing, emphasize writing well-organized and well-edited texts that align with a specific purpose and engage writers in collaboration with others. Research to Build and Present Knowledge—domain three—calls for using one's writing abilities to amass a base of topical knowledge as a result of recalling information and organizing, analyzing, and interpreting additional information gained from reading widely. Standards within domain four, Range of Writing, emphasize applying one's abilities as a writer to produce texts of varying length and type, across content areas, that clearly address audience and purpose. These four domains are more explicitly shared in the following ten Writing anchor standards.

Text Types and Purposes

1. Write arguments to support claims in an analysis of substantive topics or texts, using valid reasoning and relevant and sufficient evidence. (CCRA.W.1) (NGA & CCSSO, 2010a, p. 18)

Although often not referred to as writing an argument, learning to convey an argument begins early, as the kindergarten Writing standard one notes:

> Use a combination of drawing, dictating, and writing to compose opinion pieces in which they tell a reader the topic or the name of the book they are writing about and state an opinion or preference about the topic or book (e.g., *My favorite book is . . .*). (W.K.1) (NGA & CCSSO, 2010a, p. 19)

By third grade, students should be able to write opinion pieces on topics or texts and support a point of view with reasons (W.3.1).

By grade 6, students should be able to write and support an argument with clear reasons and relevant evidence (W.6.1).

Notice that anchor standards two and three address writing many different types of genres for different purposes.

2. Write informative/explanatory texts to examine and convey complex ideas and information clearly and accurately through the effective selection, organization, and analysis of content. (CCRA.W.2)

3. Write narratives to develop real or imagined experiences or events using effective technique, well-chosen details, and well-structured event sequences. (CCRA.W.3) (NGA & CCSSO, 2010a, p. 18)

Anchor standards four through six call for students to have the skills to share clear and coherent thinking by publishing writing via many outlets.

Production and Distribution of Writing

4. Produce clear and coherent writing in which the development, organization, and style are appropriate to task, purpose, and audience. (CCRA.W.4)

5. Develop and strengthen writing as needed by planning, revising, editing, rewriting, or trying a new approach. (CCRA.W.5)

6. Use technology, including the Internet, to produce and publish writing and to interact and collaborate with others. (CCRA.W.6) (NGA & CCSSO, 2010a, p. 18)

Anchor standards seven through ten identify the importance of supporting one's written premises with data and of building stamina as a writer.

Research to Build and Present Knowledge

7. Conduct short as well as more sustained research projects based on focused questions, demonstrating understanding of the subject under investigation. (CCRA.W.7)

8. Gather relevant information from multiple print and digital sources, assess the credibility and accuracy of each source, and integrate the information while avoiding plagiarism. (CCRA.W.8)

9. Draw evidence from literary or informational texts to support analysis, reflection, and research. (CCRA.W.9) (NGA & CCSSO, 2010a, p. 18)

Range of Writing

10. Write routinely over extended time frames (time for research, reflection, and revision) and shorter time frames (a single sitting or a day or two) for a range of tasks, purposes, and audiences. (CCRA.W.10) (NGA & CCSSO, 2010a, p. 18)

When reflecting on these standards with the backdrop of the NAEP data discussed earlier in this chapter, it becomes apparent that there is a major gap between the CCSS writing expectations of K–12 students and their current performance. To accomplish these standards, students in their early school years will need to be taught how to write multiple types of texts for many audiences and purposes and to use their writing skills to promote their continued learning within each content area. Becoming a skilled writer of scientific information involves learning to deeply think about phenomena in one's world and then knowing how to document ideas and plans for investigation, utilize resources, collect and analyze data, develop evidence-based arguments, and use models to predict patterns and gather data. These practices, concluding discoveries, and next questions often occur during collaboration with peers. Classrooms promoting scientific practice must provide environments that encourage these opportunities for collaboration and discovery.

Evidence Supporting These Standards

Did you notice that Writing anchor standard ten calls for writing often, for various amounts of time, and in many contexts? This is very significant, since the first-ever computer-based writing assessment presented students with multimedia prompts, including video or audio segments, newspaper articles, and real-world data, and asked them to complete two thirty-minute tasks, each measuring one of three communicative purposes: to persuade, explain, or convey experience

(NAEP, 2011b). Previous writing assessments have not looked at student writing using multimedia options or given a variety of communication purposes. Students used laptops to communicate their responses, which allowed access to spell checking and a thesaurus. Those students who used a computer more frequently to edit their writing scored higher than students who did not, and those who wrote four to five pages a week for English language arts homework scored higher than those who wrote fewer pages. This does not necessarily suggest that homework requirements should be increased; however, it does suggest that students who engage in the act of writing become better at it, especially when it is coupled with explicit, engaging writing instruction (Saddler & Graham, 2005). Additionally, students who are more familiar with word processing and using associated editing elements may have an unfair advantage because of this familiarity. Additionally, the NAEP writing assessments and the CCSS, which emphasize the importance of students being taught to use a range of technologies to write and collaborate about writing, suggest that writing instruction must become even more purposeful and engage students in writing tasks that involve the use of technology or word-processing skills. Again there will be a disadvantage for schools and students who do not have frequent or sufficient access to these materials (Gilbert & Graham, 2010) because they will be unsure of how to use them. Being assessed via the computer is a requisite skill that will be needed by students, who in 2014–2015 will be completing computer-based CCSS assessments designed by the Partnership for Assessment of Readiness for College and Careers (PARCC) and the Smarter Balanced Assessment Consortium (SBAC), which are two of the four government-funded consortia developing common assessments. (Refer to www.parconline.org and www.smarterbalanced.org for more information.)

Teachers as Writers

Despite the fact that engaging students in writing is critical to their learning to write and to addressing the skills in the CCSS, Jennifer Gilbert and Steve Graham's (2010) national survey of elementary teachers finds that students in grades 4–5 spend only twenty-five minutes per day in writing activities and about fifteen minutes on daily writing instruction. In a previous national survey, teachers of younger students, in grades 1 and 3, reveal that they teach writing for at least thirty minutes per day and engage students in writing-related activities for at least one hour per day (Cutler & Graham, 2008).

Students cannot learn to write well if they are not taught the skills or given opportunities to write. Limited time may be allocated for writing instruction because many teachers and preservice teachers feel that they have not been well prepared to teach writing (Gilbert & Graham, 2010; Lapp, Fisher, & Wolsey,

2012). Many lack confidence in their own writing, have had limited professional development to support their knowledge of ways to teach writing, and perceive that they do not have enough classroom time to teach writing (Street & Stang, 2008). When teachers learn how to better teach writing, their perceptions of themselves as writers improve and so does the writing of their students (Lapp & Flood, 1985). Continuing self-reflection and professional development significantly affect the performance of teachers as teachers of writing.

Writing Processes

The Common Core Writing standards highlight the thinking processes of writers as they prepare to write, craft the actual text, and reflect on and distribute their writing. These align with the early work of Donald M. Murray (1972), who suggests that writing should be viewed as a process of discovery rather than an end product. The process begins with prewriting, during which the writer identifies the topic, audience, and format. The process continues with the writer writing the first draft and then rewriting or editing every segment of the piece. Murray encourages teachers to step aside and permit writers to take the lead at this stage in crafting and revising personally selected topics. Linda Flower and John Hayes (1981), building on the work of Murray (1972), also note that writers engage in a process of deep thinking as they plan, draft, revise, edit, and rewrite. However, they suggest that this process occurs recursively rather than linearly with the writer entering and cycling through all the phases, often more than once, as he or she writes. By viewing writing as a process of thinking deeply, we realize the personal nature of writing and come to understand that people may need to spend different amounts of time with each phase. Less proficient writers, for example, need more time to revise and edit. When students are taught to think through the process, the quality of their writing increases (Rijlaarsdam & van den Bergh, 2006). This involves promoting their ownership as writers and teaching them how to recursively engage in each stage of the process.

Science writers write for various purposes. At times, they write in a concise, academic manner to explain, analyze, and draw conclusions about data. At other times, they write in a less formal journal-like style to record comments or flesh out thoughts, ideas, and observations. Sometimes science writers write to explain real-world science to the public, as in a magazine, in a newspaper, or on a blog. Science writers often enter the process at different stages. For instance, a blogger may need to research a topic in order to develop an understanding of an issue, like the consumption of genetically modified foods or the need to restrict carbon dioxide emissions. He or she might use bullet points or rough sentences during this prewriting stage that will later be reconstituted to form a first draft. The blogger might reread the first draft for clarity and revise before posting. On the other hand, many bloggers follow the rules of proper grammar while composing in a less formal and less academic style.

Consider, however, an author who wishes to compose an analysis and conclusion for a formal lab write-up. In this case, the writing needs to be concise and to the point, with terms that are precise, technical, and academic in nature. Because science lab writing is devoid of flowery explanations and descriptive adjectives, it typically incorporates topical language that gets right to the point. Such composing might involve prewriting followed by multiple revisions. During each revision, the author rethinks his or her ideas and refines the language. The degree to which a writer engages in the stages of writing depends on his or her background knowledge and need to rethink the text while composing.

When students are writing, it's incumbent on the teacher to determine when they have attained enough insight through the rewriting process that they can move toward a final version. This, of course, requires ongoing assessment through student monitoring.

Writing Scaffolds

Susanna Benko (2012) identifies a number of scaffolds that teachers can employ to support very individualized writing development. These include the following:

- Using multiple models to teach writing skills—This of course seems very reasonable when you consider that it is difficult to write a poem or a research report if one has never read or heard one. A novice student writing a conclusion to a lab report would need to see an exemplar that shows how concise, topical language is used to reference data and state explanations. This student would also benefit from hearing the teacher explain how he composed the writing (for example, thinking aloud about the composition process). A student documenting observation notes for the first time while out in the field would benefit from seeing an expert, like the teacher, model how to create tables, concept maps, and other organizational tools so that the student can later reread and reference his own notes. This is also true of writing a scientific thesis or a resulting theory.

- Structuring lessons so students can integrate old and new learning— Prior knowledge of a topic and experience writing in a particular genre certainly influence the amount of time needed to familiarize oneself with the structure and audience.

- Ensuring that tasks are appropriately challenging while providing opportunities for student ownership—As teachers expose students to laboratory writing, journal notes, and writing for the public—types of scientific writing—these genres or styles of writing will become less challenging and more natural.

- Sharing simplified versions of a task as a stepping-stone to the next part—When teaching students how to write a succinct and thoughtful science report, a teacher might share a completed template that includes questions to ask; tests to conduct; observations to make; claims, counterclaims, and evidence to analyze; and reflective thoughts to conclude.

- Providing formative feedback to direct and redirect students' attention to task features so that they may accomplish the intended purposes—Although formative assessment is usually done by the teacher, an added feature should be to acquaint students with the process of formatively assessing their own writing by comparing it to the intended purpose, which in science could be to argue a claim or share procedures to retest a hypothesis. Doing so allows students to self-assess by asking questions about both the content and the format and to gain immediate insights about themselves as writers and how their writing can be strengthened.

- Individualizing the instruction to accommodate learning and performance differences—While accommodating differences can occur in the instruction provided and the types of performance that are expected, there should be no difference in the bases of knowledge to which all students in a classroom are exposed. Science learning occurs around big ideas and themes. Instruction that links concepts across the disciplines of science promote inquiry that over time scaffolds understanding. Concepts most familiar in elementary classrooms include such topics as the following:

  - Human impacts on Earth's systems
  - How weather occurs and the climate patterns we see over time
  - The structures of animal and plant parts needed for survival and how they function
  - Patterns that can be observed, described, and predicted for Earth, as a planet in the solar system

Structured questioning guided by the teacher about these concepts ensures that everyone is learning the identified scientific concepts.

Based on these scaffolds, there is an obvious need to design explicit instruction that supports students' learning to write well. The question remains, How does this type of instruction look in general and, specifically, for science? Hope Gerde, Gary Bingham, and Barbara Wasik (2012) reiterate Benko's (2012) scaffolds and add, among other guidelines, the following:

- Providing models for various science texts

- Encouraging students to read their own writing

- Allowing students to incorporate predictions, observations, and summaries

- Engaging students in collaborative conversations

- Incorporating technology to support writing

Sandra Abell (2006) notes that writing in science classrooms should draw on prior knowledge about the informational content as well as the writing genre or format for sharing information and should also (1) serve as a scaffold to learning, (2) foster new learning, (3) consolidate and review ideas, and (4) reformulate and extend knowledge. Brian Hand, Vaughan Prain, Chris Lawrence, and Larry Yore (1999) clarify that scientific literacy involves understanding *the nature of science*. The National Science Teachers Association (2000) states that "science is characterized by the systematic gathering of information through various forms of direct and indirect observations and the testing of this information by methods including, but not limited to, experimentation." Hand et al. (1999) further add that scientific literacy involves the possession of a working knowledge of the function of reasoning and interpretive beliefs, which are the subjective meanings that people attach to ideas based on how they interact with the world. John Kirkman (2005) explains that science writing includes simple, varied sentences and an effective use of subclauses to provide clarification and support comprehension. The nature of science remains an element of the National Research Council (2012) framework and a foundational underpinning of inquiry instruction.

Given these discipline-specific features of science writing, it's clear that the most effective means by which students can move toward competency is to have opportunities to practice academic science writing, to study models and exemplars of science writing, and to receive formative feedback that guides them to progress and gain skill.

Into the Classroom

We know that reading, writing, and speaking go hand in hand. Growth in one of these areas supports growth in the others. It is, however, not enough for a teacher to simply believe that reading and speaking about content will help students learn to write scientifically. In actuality, students need models, opportunities to practice, feedback, and an effective teacher who provides purposeful instruction designed to teach students to write many genres for many purposes in all content areas. Science writing is concise and evidence driven and often follows particular formats. It involves tasks of language and instruction integrated into inquiry activities (Yore, 2000).

The following scenarios take us inside classrooms that illustrate the extensive learning that can occur when science and literacy instruction address purposeful standards-based goals. There is one scenario for each grade K–6 and two for grade 5, because it is here that students are becoming more abstract thinkers better able to distinguish different properties of matter and how these properties affect and interact with each other and the world in which they live. Students are more readily able to take on the task of clarifying and elaborating on their thinking about science through their writing. (Visit **go.solution-tree.com/commoncore** for an additional grade 5 scenario.)

Mrs. Ruiz's Kindergarten Class

Concepcion Ruiz wants her students to notice the animals in the world around them so that they can note characteristics that allow animals to live in particular environments. She also wants students to try out tools that will help make patterns and relationships evident so they can proceed with documenting such relationships in the form of writing. Table 3.1 (page 88) shows how she accomplishes this.

Examining the Concepts and Language

After reading *About Pets* (McKay, 2002), Mrs. Ruiz and her students talk about all the pets they own or wish they owned. This is Mrs. Ruiz's way of approaching the NGSS related to the relationship between the needs of different plants or animals (including humans) and the places they live (K-ESCS3-1; Achieve, 2013a, p. 6). To help facilitate an understanding of this standard, Mrs. Ruiz first wants students to identify characteristics of animals. With this understanding, she will then move them toward recognition of suitable environments for particular organisms. She makes a list of the students' animals on a chart for students to refer to later when classifying their animals and writing. This chart will ultimately include a list of the animals' characteristics, such as feathers, fur, scales, live birth, egg-laying, and so on. Such a chart is called a semantic feature analysis (figure 3.1, page 90). These charts can provide a quick assessment of what the students know about a subject. (A blank version of figure 3.1 can be found in reproducible form on page 210 and online.)

Table 3.1: Kindergarten CCSS for Writing and NGSS Lesson Plan on Life Sciences

Crosscutting Concepts	Patterns, cause and effect, system and system models
Core Ideas	Organization for matter and energy flow in organisms
Lesson Purpose	Identify the characteristics of animals, like our pets
Focus Strategy	Word cards and sentence frames
NGSS	
K-ESS3-1. Use a model to represent the relationship between the needs of different plants or animals (including humans) and the places they live.	
CCSS	
• Writing standards: W.K.2. Use a combination of drawing, dictating, and writing to compose informative/explanatory texts in which they name what they are writing about and supply some information about the topic. W.K.5. With guidance and support from adults, respond to questions and suggestions from peers and add details to strengthen writing as needed. W.K.8. With guidance and support from adults, recall information from experiences or gather information from provided sources to answer a question.	

Source: Adapted from NGA & CCSSO, 2010a, p. 19, and Achieve, 2013a, p. 6.

Scientists often look for *patterns* and *cause-and-effect* relationships in nature. Noticing that animals with scales often live in water environments and those with fur or hair or lungs usually live on land environments is key to seeing these relationships. Instead of telling students this information, Mrs. Ruiz is allowing students to discover and see these patterns themselves. The semantic feature analysis is a clear and detailed tool for recording—just as real-world scientists do—the kind of data that will allow such relationships to become evident.

Mrs. Ruiz also uses word cards to model academic language use for her students. The word cards are simply index cards with selected academic terms, like *prediction* and *hypothesis*, written in clear lettering. These are terms that students might choose to insert in a sentence frame. Young students as well as English learners will benefit from the use of word cards that provide academic word options to insert into a sentence frame. For example, in a science lesson, Mrs. Ruiz provides the following sentence frame and word option (noted in parentheses): "I am making this _____ because I've seen puddles of water evaporate after the sun comes out" (*prediction*).

As students develop knowledge and language, she provides several words and then encourages the students to select the one that best completes the sentence. For example, for the previous sentence frame, Mrs. Ruiz initially provides only one word card (*prediction*). As students' knowledge of academic words increases, she provides options (*prediction* or *hypothesis*, for instance). This allows students to choose from among viable options so that they can say precisely what they mean. Another example: "According to my _____, tomorrow we will see a full moon in the sky" (*data*, *findings*, or *results*).

Modeling to Expand Learning

Depending on students' language facility with the topic, teachers also often use word cards and phrases and language frames to support their use of academic phraseology. Mrs. Ruiz asks students to draw a picture of their pet or their ideal pet. Then she asks them to think about something interesting they could share about their pet. She draws a picture of her own cat, Bunny. Next she shares two sentence frames and models how to complete them. She emphasizes that she first shares her thoughts orally and then writes the information in the following sentence frames: "This is a picture of _____" and "An interesting fact about _____ is that _____."

Mrs. Ruiz holds up her drawing and says, "This is a picture of my pet cat, whose name is Bunny. An interesting fact about Bunny is that I got her at Easter, so I gave her an Easter pet name." The students think this is very funny and ask many questions about Bunny. Mrs. Ruiz promises to bring a real picture the next day. She continues, "Now that I have told you this information, I can write it." She then completes the sentence frames.

After the students draw, she invites them to partner share their drawings and share information about their pets. Once they chat, she asks them to use the frames to write the information in two sentences. When finished, the students share with a new partner. Mrs. Ruiz sometimes uses an author's chair, which invites a writer to sit in a special chair to share his or her writing with the class.

Moving to Independence

Mrs. Ruiz always invites the students to share their ideas orally before they write. She believes that an oral draft should always be the first draft of writing, because it supports developing the thesis and organization of what will be shared

Pet	Has feathers	Has fur or hair	Has scales	Gives birth to live babies	Lays eggs	Drinks milk from mother	Has lungs to breathe	Lives on land	Lives in water	Warm-blooded	Cold-blooded
Dog		X		X		X	X	X		X	
Fish			X		X				X		X
Snake			X		X		X	X			X
Bird	X				X		X	X		X	

Figure 3.1: Sample semantic feature analysis.

in the written draft. She encourages the listener to ask questions that push the speaker's thinking about details and sequence and support the writer's future written draft. At the conclusion of the lesson, Mrs. Ruiz invites the students to bring pictures of their actual pets.

When the students return to the topic of pets the next day, Mrs. Ruiz begins with a reading of *Animal Classification* (P. Goodman, 2004). Her purpose is to support students' understanding that their pets could be classified in various ways—for example, as having feathers, fur, or scales, or as birds, mammals, or fish. Building on their previous writing, she creates the following sentence frame to support them in developing conversations and writing about their pet classifications: "My pet _____ named _____ has _____."

Together, Mrs. Ruiz and her students first classify the pets into categories— those with fins, feathers, fur, and scales. Using the chart Mrs. Ruiz started yesterday, the students regroup the pets. Using sentence frame three, Mrs. Ruiz models, "My pet cat named Bunny has fur."

The students follow with partner talk about the characteristic of their pets. Then they complete sentence frame three, which they share with a new partner.

Next, Mrs. Ruiz and the students learn more about classifications through the Kid's Corner animal classification website (www.sheppardsoftware.com). (Visit **go.solution-tree.com/commoncore** to access this and other links mentioned in this book.)

The class returns to the semantic feature analysis chart (figure 3.1, page 90) and adds additional animal characteristics. Mrs. Ruiz models again how to think about and complete a fourth sentence frame. Showing the students the frame "My pet _____ can be classified as a _____, because _____," she says, "My pet cat can be classified as a mammal, because she is warm-blooded and gives birth to live babies."

The student partners continue to talk about the characteristics of their pets. When finished, Mrs. Ruiz encourages them to write about at least two of the distinguishing characteristics. Then, they share with a new partner. Mrs. Ruiz models how to glue their four sentences onto a colored sheet of paper and add a heading. Figure 3.2 shows Ricky's paragraph about his pet, Buddy.

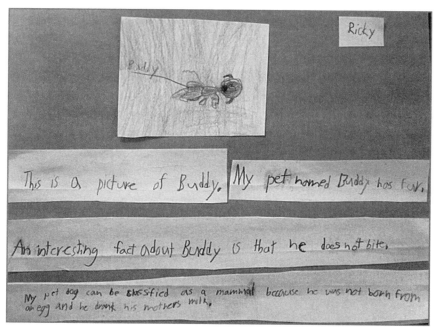

Figure 3.2: Ricky writes about his pet, Buddy.

Questions for Discussion or Reflection

1. Mrs. Ruiz is using word, phrase, sentence, and paragraph frames that support discussing and writing science information. In chapter 2, the teachers used sentence frames to support students in learning to convey spoken academic information. How might you create a supportive atmosphere that would encourage your students to use these frames in a collaborative manner, one that promotes their preparation for writing and for sharing their thoughts through writing?

2. Now that you've built an atmosphere that supports students orally sharing their scientific ideas, what sentence frames will you use to support informational talking and writing?

3. How can sentence frames be used to guide students to include supporting evidence for statements or claims that they make?

4. Which grade-level NGSS and CCSS does your instruction address?

Ms. Burnett's First-Grade Class

Sandra Burnett is introducing the topic of *waves* to her first-grade students. Like other core areas of study, waves will be covered in consecutive grades, up through twelfth grade. In first grade, students may learn about sound or light waves. In fourth grade, they will likely study the structure of waves, including wavelength, wave height, and amplitude. In later years, they'll cover seismic waves and wave speed. For now, however, the foundational concept that *sound is produced by vibrations* is the area of focus (Achieve, 2013a, p. 9). Table 3.2 demonstrates Ms. Burnett's lesson plan.

Young students are naturally curious about noise and sound. They enjoy banging pots together, plucking strings on toy guitars, and even pounding on tables with little fists or open hands. For first graders to take this natural inquisitiveness one step further as they look at what causes sound is, of course, a logical progression. In this class scenario, Ms. Burnett moves students from the entertainment of sound making to deep processing about sound production.

Examining the Concepts and Language

Because Ms. Burnett is preparing her students to write complete sentences using key science words, she decides to use a graphic organizer that consists of a folded sheet of colored paper to help her five- and six-year-olds acquire the

Table 3.2: First-Grade CCSS for Writing and NGSS Lesson Plan on Physical Sciences

Crosscutting Concept	Cause and effect
Core Ideas	Wave properties
Lesson purpose	Understand the causes of sound
Focus Strategy	Organizing ideas in folded graphic organizer
NGSS	
1-PS4-1. Plan and conduct investigations to provide evidence that vibrating materials can make sound and that sound can make materials vibrate.	
CCSS	
• Writing standards: W.1.7. Participate in shared research and writing projects (e.g., explore a number of "how-to" books on a given topic and use them to write a sequence of instructions). W.1.8. With guidance and support from adults, recall information from experiences or gather information from provided sources to answer a question.	

Source: Adapted from NGA & CCSSO, 2010a, p. 19, and Achieve, 2013a, p. 9.

needed vocabulary to begin science writing. Science writing is characterized by complex academic and topical vocabulary set among sophisticated text structure. Ms. Burnett knows that from an early age, students need to see that writing in science requires particular terms used to express precise meaning. The use of the graphic organizer to support vocabulary and writing is intended to help students begin the process of strategic, specific word choice to convey intended meaning.

Modeling to Expand Learning

Ms. Burnett instructs all students to follow her lead by writing the word *sound* at the top left of the folded paper. She then models how a visual can help them to understand this term. On her folded paper, just below the word, she sketches an ear. Ms. Burnett also strikes a tuning fork with a rubber mallet and asks students to listen for sound. She next shakes a bell that produces a high-pitched ringing tone. Before the bell stops ringing, she shows students its underside, where the clapper hits the bell to generate the sound. Finally, she takes a pencil and taps her desk in rhythmic form, again reminding students to listen.

Following this display of rings, tones, and drumming, Ms. Burnett asks the students to each turn to a designated partner to discuss what caused the sounds.

As she listens in to monitor student understanding, she hears Jennika tell Harry, "One thing hits something to make the sound."

Harry adds, "Yeah, like the bell."

After listening to partner conversations for a few minutes, Ms. Burnett asks her students to write a word or draw a picture in the space below the word *sound* to tell something about sound. Jennika draws a picture of the clapper hitting the side of the bell. Harry writes the word *bang*. On the other side of the paper, Ms. Burnett asks students to write the word *wave*. She then shows them an animation of a sound wave moving through a coiled spring from the Physics Classroom website (www.physicsclassroom.com), telling students that sound always has to move through something like air or water or even through rocks.

She pauses again to allow students to talk to partners about how they think sound moves away from the bell so that they can hear it.

Shawn tells Andrew, "The sound moved through the room." While Ms. Burnett clearly realizes that Shawn is not making the connection that sound requires a medium, she notes that he does understand that sound moves from where it originates outward to other places. Assessments like this offer insights about a student's understanding that help teachers to plan subsequent lessons and determine what immediate guided instruction can be offered that will propel a student's learning. In this case, Ms. Burnett strikes a tuning fork in air, in a beaker of water, and on a rock to help clarify the need for a medium. While doing so she says to Shawn, "Do you think sound can travel through the water? Can it travel through the rock?"

Thinking for a moment, Shawn replies, "The sound is different in the water. In the water it splashes, and I hear the splash noise. The rock has a different noise." Pausing, he cautiously adds, "I think sound can go through water and through rock. I heard the noise." Satisfied that Shawn is discovering that sound travels through different mediums, Ms. Burnett encourages him by saying, "I think you're doing a very nice job of noticing sound coming from the water and from the rock when each are struck with the tuning fork. You're thinking like a real scientist!"

Tomorrow she may even pull out the school's vacuum pump and bell jar and place a ringing alarm clock under it. Students would then see that they couldn't hear the sound, since there is no air—no medium—inside the bell jar.

Moving to Independence

Ms. Burnett next asks students to write a word or draw a picture that shows an aspect of the word *wave*. Shawn draws springs moving from the tuning fork.

Ms. Burnett again makes a note—this time to remind herself to ask Shawn what the springs show, just to clarify his current comprehension of the concepts. She wants to know if the springs are representing sound waves or if Shawn is drawing actual springs. Ms. Burnett knows that, in science, students can sometimes confuse images meant to *represent a concept* with the object of the image. The springs represent the movement of sound through a medium, like air or water.

Noticing that students seem to have a grasp of the concept of sound, she asks each student to choose from an array of sound makers she provides, including a triangle, an assortment of horns, bongo drums, a toy keyboard, and a stack of kazoos. Each student takes an instrument and practices making sounds. To conclude the lesson, Ms. Burnett asks students to draw a picture of the sound maker they chose. She tells them that their investigations and the pictures they are crafting as illustrations of sound makers represent the start of the reports they are writing about sound. (See figure 3.3 for a sample completed student graphic organizer.)

Figure 3.3: Sample first-grade folded-paper graphic organizer.

Ms. Burnett provides her first graders with opportunities to hear, see, talk about, and write about sound. When students are allowed to engage in focused observations and subsequent conversations supported by guided instruction (for example, What causes the sound?), they are employing the use of science skills (through observation) and science processing (through conversation). Students are then guided to document their thinking on the graphic organizer in the form of a word, sentence, or picture—just as scientists in the field would do. They are being introduced to the notion that scientists investigate, document, and convey information through many formats.

Questions for Discussion or Reflection

1. As with Ms. Burnett's lesson, writing doesn't happen without some initial thinking and planning. In this instance, she introduces a graphic organizer. What other types of organizing structures might you use to help your students initially collect and expand their ideas as they conduct a scientific investigation?

2. Ms. Burnett tells her students that their pictures represent the start of their reports about sound. How can images be used to support writing for students in kindergarten and first grade?

3. How will you support deep content learning and prewriting skills for younger elementary students?

4. Which grade-level NGSS and CCSS does your instruction address?

Ms. Nguyen's Second-Grade Class

Deena Nguyen wants to ensure that students know how to obtain and interpret information using science resources. When addressing the Next Generation Science Standard that asks students to obtain information to identify where water is found on Earth and verify that it can be solid or liquid (2-ESS2-3; Achieve, 2013a, p. 15), she provides potential resources and then asks students to assemble ideas based on their understanding of the data. Table 3.3 shows Ms. Nguyen's lesson plan.

Examining the Concepts and Language

Naima's sense of the size and scope of the Earth is limited by her life experiences. She's spent all of her eight years on this planet living in the same neighborhood, walking the same sidewalks, and shopping at the local grocery store with her parents. The idea that planet Earth is a large oblate spheroid (the Earth is flattened at the poles and bulges at the equator) is far from her mind. While the concept that water exists in different states is somewhat familiar—she's seen ice in her water glass and lives near a small aquatic lake—she is not aware that the

Table 3.3: Second-Grade CCSS for Writing and NGSS Lesson Plan on Life Sciences

Crosscutting Concepts	Patterns and stability and change
Core Ideas	The roles of water in Earth's surface processes
Lesson Purpose	Understand locations on Earth where water is solid and where it is liquid
Focus Strategy	Generative sentences
NGSS	
2-ESS2-3. Obtain information to identify where water is found on Earth and that it can be solid or liquid. K-2-ETS1-2. Develop a simple sketch, drawing, or physical model to illustrate how the shape of an object helps it function as needed to solve a given problem.	
CCSS	
• Writing standards: W.2.2. Write informative/explanatory texts in which they introduce a topic, use facts and definitions to develop points, and provide a concluding statement or section. W.2.8. Recall information from experiences or gather information from provided sources to answer a question.	

Source: Adapted from NGA & CCSSO, 2010a, p. 19, and Achieve, 2013a, pp. 15, 16.

various states of water on Earth may be linked to seasonal changes in temperature, latitude, or weather conditions. Ms. Nguyen wants Naima and her classmates to begin to make connections between the state of water and its location on Earth. To facilitate this, she asks students to work with their table groups. She has four students per group who will work collaboratively to document the correlation between states of water and location. To ensure that all students really do have an understanding that water can be found in different phases, Ms. Nguyen places paper cups with ice chips on each group's desks. She also places cups of water on the desks. She then asks students to describe the contents of each cup and to share their ideas with their groups. Chad tells Naima that the ice is cold and the water is "regular" temperature. Hearing this comment, Ms. Nguyen asks Chad to explain "regular" temperature.

Chad clarifies: "It's the temperature here—not too hot, not too cold." Ms. Nguyen adds, "We sometimes call that room temperature." Prompting more thought, she asks the class if water can be really cold.

Naima emphatically says, "Yes, it can be really cold, like water with ice."

Still moving the students deeper, Ms. Nguyen questions, "What happens when water gets very cold, like when you put water in the ice tray in the freezer?" Chad, making a connection to popsicles, replies, "When I made popsicles in the freezer, it was like water at first, then it froze."

Affirming Chad's connection, Ms. Nguyen adds, "Yes, your popsicles were made from liquid that froze. Your popsicle started in a liquid state, like water, and then changed to a solid state, like our ice chips, as the temperature dropped in the cold freezer. Water can change from a liquid to a solid." Now that students are focused on two states of water (they'll learn about water vapor in the future), Ms. Nguyen begins the investigative piece of the activity.

Modeling to Expand Learning

She next provides students with a map that shows bodies of water, glaciers, and ice caps. She also provides a map that shows average February temperatures across Earth. Ms. Nguyen reminds students that the map is a flat, two-dimensional representation of the oblate sphere we live on. To do this, she wraps the map around a globe in her classroom to physically illustrate that parts of the Earth are distorted when laid out on flat paper for us to view. When Shanti asks why we don't just use globes all the time, she replies that maps are easy to carry and slip into a notebook or bag, and we can easily access them on the Internet.

Next, students are asked to fold a sheet of pale, pink-colored paper in half. They then are guided to fold the half-folded paper in half again. To finish off the graphic organizer preparation, students follow Ms. Nguyen's lead and fold over one of the corners—the one that is actually in the middle of the paper. This last fold creates a triangle in the middle of the paper. When students unfold the paper, they have a foldable with four quadrants with a rhombus shape in the middle (Zike, 2013) (figure 3.4).

Ms. Nguyen models the next step using the document camera to project the maps. She strategically thinks aloud for all to hear, "First, I'm going to find one location on the map that is really cold, around 10 °C or lower." Searching the temperature map, she settles on Greenland as a really cold location. Then she looks at the maps showing water in various states. "It looks like this location, Greenland, is covered in ice. I'm going to write this down on my foldable in the upper right corner." Ms. Nguyen writes, "Greenland, -16 °C, ice." Next, she identifies a place that is warmer. She picks North Africa and notes that the temperature is about 20 °C. She then looks to see if there is a body of water near that location. She finds Lake Chad and notes that it is in the *water* state. Next, she tells students that they should each also locate two places on the map, record the temperature, and note if

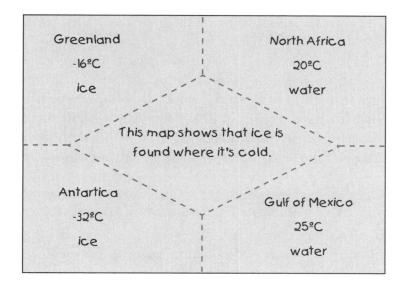

Figure 3.4: Chad's completed foldable.

they would find water or ice there (liquid or solid water). Once the students have recorded their own data, she asks them to share in their groups. As each student shares, the others record the data in a different corner of the foldable.

Moving to Independence

Once all data have been recorded, Ms. Nguyen invites students to observe anything about temperature and the location of ice on Earth. Sammy shouts out, "Ice is where it's cold on Earth."

"Yes, Sammy. Now I want you all to write your ideas about water, ice, and location on Earth in the middle of the foldable. I'd like you to make your sentence using this phrase: 'The maps show that . . .'"

Chad writes, "The maps show that ice is found where it's cold."

Naima writes, "The maps show that when the temperature is cold, water on Earth freezes."

Satisfied that the appropriate, accurate sentences students generated indicate their understandings, Ms. Nguyen adds, "I'd like you to write one more sentence. This time you'll need to use the words *states* and *water*."

Chad immediately scribbles the sentence, "Water is in different states."

Naima, taking more time to think, writes, "Ice and water are two states on Earth."

Students generate their own sentences using criteria offered by Ms. Nguyen, who intentionally includes academic language in her criteria along with topical language. She wants her students to become accustomed to integrating both aspects of science writing. Through this lesson, the students in Ms. Nguyen's class are drawing on the sophisticated science skills of observation, analysis, and identification of patterns. They do this by correlating map information in a way that always recognizes patterns. Additionally, they learn ways to document their science thinking using a construction of academic and domain-specific language.

Questions for Discussion or Reflection

1. Ms. Nguyen allows students to work in a collaborative group to collect and interpret data. What kinds of opportunities will you create for students to share and discuss data?

2. The recognition of patterns in nature is an essential science skill. What other patterns can you identify in science? How might you encourage students to identify these patterns?

3. Documenting data and then writing about data is a part of science investigation. Ms. Nguyen has students record and interpret their data in a graphic organizer by generating sentences that have particular language criteria. What generative sentences will you use to get students to write about data?

4. Which grade-level NGSS and CCSS does your instruction address?

Mr. Lancer's Third-Grade Class

Often in science students must view an issue or topic of study from a particular perspective, or from more than one perspective, in order to gain a complete and in-depth understanding. The strategy RAFT supports students in writing from a designated perspective to a particular audience, in a determined format. Table 3.4 demonstrates Nate Lancer's third-grade lesson plan.

Science writers compose all types of writing, from informal blogs to very academic articles for peer-reviewed journals. Young writers in grades K–5 need opportunities to engage in a wide array of writing formats. Often in science, students must also view an issue or topic of study from a particular perspective or from more than one perspective in order to gain a complete and in-depth understanding. The RAFT strategy supports students in writing from a designated perspective to a particular audience and in the creation of both formal and informal writing tasks.

Table 3.4: Third-Grade CCSS for Writing and NGSS Lesson Plan on Life Sciences

Crosscutting Concept	Structure and function	
Core Ideas	From molecules to organisms: structures and processes—growth and development	
Lesson Purpose	Examine the life cycle of a frog	
Focus Strategy	RAFT	
NGSS 3-LS1-1. Develop models to describe that organisms have unique and diverse life cycles but all have in common birth, growth, reproduction, and death.		
CCCS • Writing standards: W.3.2. Write informative and explanatory texts to examine a topic and convey ideas and information clearly. W.3.8. Recall information from experiences or gather information from print and digital sources; take brief notes on sources and sort evidence into provided categories.		

Source: Adapted from NGA & CCSSO, 2010a, pp. 20–21, and Achieve, 2013a, p. 20.

Examining the Concepts and Language

In Mr. Lancer's third-grade classroom, students express their understanding of science using perspective writing. Specifically, they write about a topic from a given point of view. As they learn about life cycles of animals through read-alouds, shared readings, video clips, discussions, and visual aids, they negotiate meaning for themselves and organize ideas through writing. Students are addressing the Next Generation Science Standard that requires students to "develop models to describe that organisms have unique and diverse life cycles but all have in common birth, growth, reproduction, and death" (3-LS1-1; Achieve, 2013a, p. 20).

Modeling to Expand Learning

When Mr. Lancer asks his students to write about the life cycle of a frog, he doesn't simply ask them to write a paragraph. Instead, he shares a RAFT (Santa & Havens, 1995) with an example.

R	**Role:** Who is the writer?
A	**Audience:** To whom is the writer writing?
F	**Format:** What format does the writer use?
T	**Topic:** What are you writing about?

Mr. Lancer explains, "When I write, I am thinking like a tadpole who is writing an email to another tadpole friend. I want to tell my tadpole friend about how I will change as I become a frog."

Mr. Lancer writes the RAFT as follows.

R	A tadpole
A	Another tadpole friend
F	Email
T	How I'm going to change into a frog

Moving to Independence

After Mr. Lancer shares his example, the students create their RAFTs using information from their reading. Tori writes the following RAFT.

> Hi Jimy. You ar my tadpole frend. I was a egg first. Now I am a tadpole like you. Soon I will grow legs. I will get a tail to. Then I will be a frog and I can jump out of the watr. By Jimy.

Teachers can vary the format of a RAFT to meet student needs. Cartoons, pictures, bumper stickers, and lists might be more suitable for kindergarteners and first graders, while older students might compose diary entries and formal reports. RAFTs are also effective ways for students at all grade levels to write from a particular perspective—from the viewpoint of the cloud or the rock, as figure 3.5 shows. They also become insightful assessment tools for teachers wishing to check for understanding.

Students need to build stamina to write for long periods of time. They can also benefit from short, more frequent writing assignments. Because of this, teachers need to provide tools for both extended and brief writing tasks. RAFT is a flexible tool that can be developed to support both types of writing.

Grade		Physical Sciences	Life Sciences	Earth and Space Sciences
Kindergarten				
	R	Bicycle	Seed	Cloud
	A	Little boy or girl	Dirt	Weather reporter
	F	Cartoon	Letter	Map
	T	How to go faster and slower	How I will grow	Where I'm going to be tomorrow
First Grade				
	R	Stuffed bear	Squirrel	Daylight
	A	Boy or girl	Tree	Earth
	F	Picture	Letter	Diagram
	T	How light helps find me in the dark	What I need from you	How I change during the day
Second Grade				
	R	Iron nail	Caterpillar	Rock
	A	A block of wood	Tree branch	Geologist
	F	Bumper sticker	Story	Field report
	T	My best properties	How I'll change	How I'm moving during an earthquake
Third Grade				
	R	Car	Turtle	The sky
	A	Owner	Zookeeper	Weather reporter
	F	Memo	Journal entry	Picture book
	T	Why I need gas	Why I have a shell	How I change within a month

Figure 3.5: Possible RAFTs for students in grades K–6.   Continued➔

Grade		Physical Sciences	Life Sciences	Earth and Space Sciences
Fourth Grade				
	R	Electricity	Earthworm	Granite
	A	Lightbulb	Soil	River
	F	Schematic diagram	Email message	Diary entry
	T	What I need to send you energy	How I'll add nutrients to you	The day you broke me apart
Fifth Grade				
	R	Oxygen	Blood cell	Fog
	A	Periodic table	Human body	Earth
	F	Element diagram	Flowchart	Letter
	T	What I'm composed of	How I move through you	How I formed overnight
Sixth grade				
	R	Oxygen atom	Prokaryote	Oceanic plate
	A	Two hydrogen atoms	Eukaryote	Continental plate
	F	Conference call	Venn diagram	Blog entry
	T	Our strong bond	How we're different	How I'm melting for you

Questions for Discussion or Reflection

1. Sometimes students have a difficult time getting their writing started because they can't find their voices. RAFTs are very motivating for many students. How does using a RAFT combat the no-voice problem?

2. In science, we often need to examine an issue from various vantage points. RAFTs help facilitate such an exploration. What science topics at your grade level could best be learned from an exploration via RAFTs?

3. What RAFTs would work well with science concepts you are planning to teach? Create a RAFT that you could use to teach a science lesson that includes writing. Share with a colleague or partner.

4. Which grade-level NGSS and CCSS does your instruction address?

Mr. Bernstein's Fourth-Grade Class

Table 3.5 demonstrates Larry Bernstein's lesson plan on waves and their characteristics, leading to the writing of an informational paragraph.

Table 3.5: Fourth-Grade CCSS for Writing and NGSS Lesson Plan on Physical Sciences

Crosscutting Concept	Patterns
Core Idea	Wave properties
Lesson Purpose	Comprehend the causes of waves
Focus Strategy	Note taking and graphic organizers
NGSS	
4-PS4-3. Generate and compare multiple solutions that use patterns to transfer information.	
CCSS	
W.4.8. Recall relevant information from experiences or gather relevant information from print and digital sources; take notes and categorize information, and provide a list of sources.	
W.4.9. Draw evidence from literary or informational texts to support analysis, reflection, and research.	
W.4.10. Write routinely over extended time frames (time for research, reflection, and revision) and shorter time frames (a single sitting or a day or two) for a range of discipline-specific tasks, purposes, and audiences.	

Source: Adapted from NGA & CCSSO, 2010a, p. 2, and Achieve, 2013a, p. 124.

Examining the Concepts and Language

Before Mr. Bernstein's fourth graders begin the process of composing an informational paragraph, he models how to think about composing a paragraph on science understandings. He begins by reading a content-based text aloud while conducting a think-aloud. He is preparing students to address the Next Generation Science Standard that asks them to "generate and compare multiple solutions that use patterns to transfer information" (4-PS4-3; Achieve, 2013a, p. 24).

Because he wants to demonstrate how he captures pertinent information in note form, he uses the document camera to display his notes as he records them. Students see and hear how an expert negotiates the text and simultaneously creates a usable record—the notes.

Modeling to Expand Learning

Here's how Mr. Bernstein uses a think-aloud to share his note-taking process:

"I'm going to read this section on waves from my text, because I know that I want to write a paragraph about waves in our world," he tells the class. "Here I go: 'Have you ever seen an ocean or lake wave move? Sometimes blowing wind can create waves. A bird sitting on the surface of the ocean will move up and down as the wave passes by. Waves have patterns of motion.'" He continues: "I wonder what that means? 'Waves have patterns of motion.' I remember last summer when my family went to the beach, we played in the ocean waves, and I could feel when a wave passed by. It lifted me up a little and let me back down as it passed. Maybe that's what they are talking about here—waves make materials, like water, move in different ways. I'll have to keep reading so I can learn more about this, but first, because I think this is important, I'm going to put this in my notes. . . . Now I'll continue to read. 'There are water waves, sound waves, and light waves in our world. Different waves move in different ways.' I know I need to get this down—waves can be found as sound, as light, and in water. Sound and light are caused by energy. I remember when we talked about that. I really like the picture on this page. It helps me to understand how waves move through water, air, and space. I'm going to make a little drawing of this in my notes" (figure 3.6).

Main Ideas	Details, Pictures, and Questions
Waves have motion. There are different kinds of waves. Waves look different.	Light Sound Water
Key Ideas (One to three sentences)	
There are different kinds of waves that move through different materials.	

Figure 3.6: Note-taking guide for waves.

After Mr. Bernstein finishes his text-based think-aloud and note taking, he shows students how he uses his notes to create a paragraph: "I'm going to review my notes and write one sentence that tells what my notes are about. I'll put my sentence at the bottom of my notes. Let's see. [*Mr. Bernstein rereads his notes aloud.*] After reading this, I think that a good sentence would be, 'There are different kinds of waves that move through different materials.' Now that I have my final summary sentence, I'm going to write a paragraph about this. I have a graphic organizer that will help me to do this."

At this point, Mr. Bernstein pulls out a graphic organizer specifically designed to guide students to write a paragraph. He knows that as his students later design their own graphic organizers, he'll be able to glimpse their growing understandings of the content. He shows how he organizes his information in response to the three questions on the organizer: (1) What are waves? (2) Where or when do we see waves? (3) Why should we know about waves?

Referring to his notes, Mr. Bernstein articulates the following ideas: "Looking at my notes, I think I can answer the first question, What are waves? Well, I wrote down that motion makes waves. I'll put that on the first line," he says. "I also know that energy forms waves. It said that in the book, but I'm not sure that I understand the word *energy*. I'm going to put that down, but I'll need to know more about that. Maybe I can use the Enchanted Learning science dictionary to look up *energy*. [*Mr. Bernstein shows how he looks up* energy *using the computer bookmark he has set up on all computers in the classroom; www.enchantedlearning .com/Dictionary.html.*] OK, I see that *energy* is needed for work. That helps a little, but I hope I'll learn more about this in class later. When I fill in my graphic organizer, I am recording short ideas. Later, I'll turn these ideas into complete sentences."

Figure 3.7 shows Mr. Bernstein's completed graphic organizer on waves.

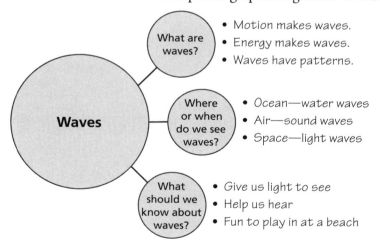

Figure 3.7: Graphic organizer on waves.

Mr. Bernstein continues his think-aloud to model how he responds to the graphic organizer questions. Once he's done, he discusses how he will compose a paragraph about waves: "I'm going to start with an interesting first sentence that explains what my paragraph is going to be about. 'Waves are found in many places in our world.' Now I'm going to refer to my graphic organizer. 'Motion makes waves. They carry energy.' I'm going to continue to look at my ideas on my graphic organizer for the second question. 'Waves can be found in the water. We see waves in the ocean and in lakes. Sound waves move through air, and light waves move through space.' Next, I'm moving on to the last question on my graphic organizer. Let's see if I can turn my ideas into sentences again. 'We should know about waves, because they affect our lives. They help us see as light waves and hear as sound waves. We can even enjoy waves at the beach when we play in the water. Waves are interesting and important.' That's it! I now have my paragraph."

Moving to Independence

Now that students have seen how Mr. Bernstein composes, they are ready to tackle the task of writing by themselves. Mr. Bernstein supports the students' building of new knowledge while tapping into prior knowledge by reading a poem about waves and beaches, "At the Sea-Side" by Robert Louis Stevenson (n.d.):

> When I was down beside the sea
> A wooden spade they gave to me
> To dig the sandy shore.
> My holes were empty like a cup.
> In every hole the sea came up
> Till it could come no more.

Upon prompting from Mr. Bernstein—"Tell your neighbor what the poem made you see in your mind"—students share the pictures they created in their heads.

Jaqui tells Jasmine, "I see water filling up holes that I've dug in the sand with a shovel."

Jasmine responds, "I see foam on a wave, especially after it's fallen over onto the beach."

Mr. Bernstein then directs students to work with their neighbor to record ideas on their note-taking guide, just as he had done.

Next he has them complete the graphic organizer. They now can add ideas from both sources—the book and the poem. Finally, students are ready to compose a paragraph with their partners. As pairs of students talk about what to write, Mr. Bernstein invites them to review what they learned and to use this information to support their writing. Even as students move toward independence in writing scientific descriptions, arguments, experiments, and conclusions, teachers may need to continue to offer support (Grant, Lapp, Fisher, Johnson, & Frey, 2012). With scaffolding and other forms of support, students like those in Mr. Bernstein's class will likely have the skills needed to confidently and competently compose.

Questions for Discussion or Reflection

1. Scientists use many types of note-taking guides and practices. What works well for you for note taking? How will you explain the value of this process to your students?

2. Mr. Bernstein uses multiple texts to support students' writing (informational text and poetry). What sources of information will you provide to students that might also support their information gathering?

3. How can note taking and graphic organizers support writing?

4. Which grade-level NGSS and CCSS does your instruction address?

Mr. Winter's Fifth-Grade Class

In Jon Winter's fifth-grade classroom, students explore content in many ways, including texts, diagrams and illustrations, podcasts, videos, and lectures. Ultimately, however, Mr. Winter wants his students to be able to write about their knowledge of science in an expert science style. Achieving this lofty goal does not come solely through Mr. Winter's strong desire for his students to be able to write like scientists. Quite conversely, it comes from intentional, diligent lesson planning and implementation that employs modeling by the teacher, use of language templates that include word and sentence frames to support the use of academic language, and lots of guided and collaborative practice offered to his enthusiastic students. Table 3.6 (page 110) demonstrates Mr. Winter's lesson plan.

Table 3.6: Fifth-Grade CCSS for Writing and NGSS Lesson Plan on Earth and Space Sciences

Crosscutting Concept	Energy and matter: Flows, cycles, and conservation
Core Ideas	Earth materials and systems
Lesson Purpose	Appreciate an inquiry-based investigation in an academic format
Focus Strategy	Collaborative guidesheet, language templates, and phrase cards
NGSS	
5-ESS2-1. Develop a model using an example to describe ways the geosphere, biosphere, hydrosphere, and/or atmosphere interact.	
CCSS	
• Writing standards:	
W.5.1. Write opinion pieces on topics or texts, supporting a point of view with reasons and information.	
W.5.2. Write informative/explanatory texts to examine a topic and convey ideas and information clearly.	

Source: Adapted from NGA & CCSSO, 2010a, p. 20, and Achieve, 2013a, p. 30.

Examining the Concepts and Language

To help students acquire the skills needed to write in a scientific way, Mr. Winter provides students with language templates—for example, a template for writing conclusions to laboratory experiments. As noted earlier in this chapter and in chapter 2, language frames support the oral or written sharing of a scientific word, phrase, sentence, or paragraph. Mr. Winter typically gives students language templates like the following to support them in making a claim, offering a counterclaim, searching for evidence, providing evidence, speculating, analyzing, evaluating, concluding, comparing and contrasting, and reaching consensus.

- "Our data show that _____." (Making a claim based on consensus involves collaborating, reflecting, synthesizing, and evaluating.)

- "Other researchers, such as _____, conclude that _____. This is in contrast to my findings, because _____." (Offering a counterclaim involves comparing and contrasting.)

- "In the future, I would like to further study _____, because _____." (Speculating involves analyzing and evaluating.)

- "Two key ideas I learned are _____ and _____." (Providing evidence involves analysis and summarizing.)

- "I am still wondering about _____, because _____." (Speculating involves analyzing, evaluating, and drawing conclusions.)

- "To investigate my prediction, I plan to _____, because this will help me understand _____." (Searching for evidence involves knowing, investigating skills, and applying.)

- "_____ puzzles me about these findings." (Speculation involves evaluation.)

- "First I thought that _____, but now I realize that _____, because _____." (Contrastive analysis involves knowing, analyzing, comparing, synthesizing, and speculation.)

- "From these data, which showed that _____, I conclude _____." (Providing evidence involves evaluation and synthesis.)

- "Your statements regarding _____ made me think that _____." (Drawing a conclusion involves applying and summarizing data.)

Language templates or sentence frames are intended to support students in collaboration and in translating their ideas into concise science-style talking and writing. Language frames also provide assessment insights for both the teacher and the student (Maloney & Simon, 2006).

Many elementary students are just emerging in their understanding of scientific concepts and the language needed to convey them. As the examples in the parentheses in the bulleted list illustrate, when preparing language frames for students, teachers need to consider the key science and language concepts they want to teach and assess and then create the frame accordingly. Teachers may also need to create related *phrase cards* and word banks that support students in conversing and writing about scientific concepts.

For example, a teacher helping students to consider the issue of junk food in school cafeterias might provide a phrase frame with two opposing options, both indicating that the claim is supported with evidence. Like other language frames, these are used to support students in gaining the skill of speaking and writing academic and scientific language:

"When I look at the evidence for _____, I can conclude that it is in support of my claim stating _____." (For example, "When I look at the evidence for the increase in health problems in young students, I can conclude that it is in support of my claim stating junk food should be banned in schools," or "When I look at the evidence for the principles of free choice, I can conclude that it is in support of my claim stating parents and students should be able to decide for themselves when selecting food in the cafeteria.")

Here's another example.

"First I thought that _____, but now I realize that _____, because _____."

For students who need more scaffolding for this phrase, teachers can provide a phrase card to show options for two different points of view. Both phrase options indicate that students will provide evidence to support their opinion: "zoos were harmful to animals"/"they are more helpful"/"the animals are cared for, and research is conducted to help other animals in the wild" or "zoos were the best way to help animals"/"there are other ways to protect animals"/"money can be put toward preservation efforts and funds for endangered animals."

At first, students may need such phrase cards for their argumentative writing; however, teachers can diminish or remove these scaffolds as students acquire proficiency.

Again, students can choose the option that best supports their thinking and their research. The phrase cards lead them toward a claim that evidence supports. Teachers may also provide phrase cards to provide students with options that represent all or most of the possible ways of thinking about the issue. They may also allow students to craft their own sentences in a way that best meshes with their claim. The frame and phrase cards are there to scaffold the learning, and any student who is ready to state his or her own claim and evidence logically and with academic phrasing should be permitted to do so.

Modeling to Expand Learning

Mr. Winter also has heat lamps and ice available. Students work with partners to devise a plan for experimentation. To guide this part of his lesson, Mr. Winter provides a collaborative guidesheet that scaffolds the inquiry process of thinking, planning, and investigating. (See figure 3.8.) This worksheet can also be found in reproducible form on page 206 and online.

At this point in the school year, Mr. Winter's students know how to use the collaborative guidesheet, but the first time the class utilized this tool, Mr. Winter

Area of Focus	My Ideas	My Partner's Ideas	Our Ideas (After Discussion)
Before the Investigation or Experiment			
What question do you want to study?			
What evidence do you want to look for in order to study your question?			
How will you record your evidence or data? For example, will you design a chart or table to hold your evidence?			
After the Investigation or Experiment			
What do your data tell you?			
How do your ideas connect with those of others in your class? How do your ideas connect with those of other scientists studying the same concepts?			
What are your conclusions? Record your conclusions by writing two or three paragraphs. Be sure your ideas are based on your evidence or data.			

Source: Grant et al., 2012.

Figure 3.8: Collaborative guidesheet template.

modeled it with another teacher, Paula Burton. They videotaped a discussion about how they might develop an inquiry plan of action to show to students who were just learning how to engage in collegial conversations centered on inquiry experimentation. For the model think-aloud shown at the start of the school year, Mr. Winter and Ms. Burton began by sharing how they would develop an experiment to determine why objects float or sink. On the video, Ms. Burton begins the conversation by questioning aloud, "Would a piece of wood float or sink? How about a cube of metal?" Mr. Winter replies, "I was wondering if the shape of a piece of paper affects how it floats or sinks. Why does a heavy boat float on top of the ocean?"

Using the template as a guide for their planning and writing, Mr. Winter and Ms. Burton modeled how to engage in partner talk that involves decision making, exchanges of ideas, and the language of negotiation. Because they scripted the target dialogue before they taped it, students heard the specific phrases of productive partner work. Students were exposed to language such as "I like your idea to investigate the types of objects that float, but I'm also interested in how shape affects floating and sinking" and comments like "Let's see if we can find a way to join our ideas together so that we can investigate questions that interest us both." Such dialogue shows students how to negotiate ideas to come to decisions that are agreeable to both parties. Without an opportunity to hear such conversations, students might not learn how to be productive partners or group participants.

Moving to Independence

Students work with partners to generate their own plans for experimentation using the collaborative guidesheet. Since Mr. Winter's students have practiced this skill several times this year, they are ready to jump right to it. Eduardo documents that he would like to investigate how temperature affects how much salt will dissolve in a liter of water. His partner, Priscilla, writes that she is interested in how much salt can be added to different amounts of water.

Using the protocol for inquiry planning noted on the collaborative guidesheet, Eduardo and Priscilla discuss their experiment ideas. At one point, Mr. Winter, who typically moves throughout the classroom during students' collegial discussions, leans in to help these two when they seem to be confused about how to combine their ideas to come up with one cohesive research question.

Eduardo states, "Priscilla, we could ask this question: 'Given three different amounts of water (half liter, one liter, and two liters), how much salt can be dissolved?' But how can we add in something about temperature? That's what I'm curious about."

Mr. Winter takes this moment to intervene and offer a prompt, "Is there a way to use Eduardo's plan to also look at temperature? Consider conducting a few different trials."

Priscilla responds with a question, "Could we do Eduardo's idea three times and use cold water, hot water, and warm water?" Mr. Winter nods his head in agreement and adds, "Now think about how you might create a data table to capture your data."

Mr. Winter's simple prompt is enough to spark a thought in the pair. The next step is to guide the students to document their ideas in several forms. First, after students note their ideas, Mr. Winter directs them to conduct experiments and collect and record data. Following this, students respond to the prompts in the rest of the collaborative guidesheet. This template strategically guides students to plan and document in writing an experiment based on ideas founded in background knowledge. After they conduct the experiment, they are guided to reflect in writing about their data in the same manner as a science researcher or engineer. Simply stated, students consider their data compared to others, including scientists, who have studied similar topics or issues. Students are learning to employ real-world practices that engineers and field scientists around the world use.

Questions for Discussion or Reflection

1. Mr. Winter's instruction—like that of many of the teachers in the scenarios in this chapter and in chapter 2—indicated that strong writers are also very proficient at using precise language to share their thinking. Think about yourself as a writer. What are you able to write well? How is your writing prowess in this area related to your understanding of related topical and academic language?

2. Science writing uses specific, precise language for analysis, comparison, synthesis, speculation, and evaluation. What language templates or phrase cards might you use to foster each of these aspects of science writing?

3. How could you use inquiry and experimentation as a foundation for science writing?

4. Which grade-level NGSS and CCSS does your instruction address?

Ms. Martin's Sixth-Grade Class

Because many of our real-world science issues are complex, having more than one perspective and complicated alternative solutions, we must provide ways for students to evaluate multiple sources of information so that they can synthesize ideas in a coherent, logical written form. Table 3.7 demonstrates Amy Martin's sixth-grade lesson plan.

Table 3.7: Sixth-Grade CCSS for Writing and NGSS Lesson Plan on Earth and Space Sciences

Crosscutting Concept	Stability and change
Core Ideas	Human impacts on Earth systems
Lesson Purpose	Explore the components of a real-world science issue
Focus Strategy	Frayer word cards, argumentative guidesheets, brainstorming map, and peer feedback guidesheet
NGSS	
MS-ESS3-3. Apply scientific principles to design a method for monitoring and minimizing a human impact on the environment.	
CCSS	
• Writing standards: W.6.1. Write arguments to support claims with clear reasons and relevant evidence. W.6.2. Write informative/explanatory texts to examine a topic and convey ideas, concepts, and information through the selection, organization, and analysis of relevant content. W.6.3. Write narratives to develop real or imagined experiences or events using effective technique, well-chosen details, and well-structured event sequences. W.6.4. Produce clear and coherent writing in which the development, organization, and style are appropriate to task, purpose, and audience.	

Source: Adapted from NGA & CCSSO, 2010a, pp. 42–43, and Achieve, 2013a, p. 61.

The decisions we make today have long-term effects on our futures. We want our nation's young people to become scientifically literate, informed citizens who are capable of making important decisions that will affect our planet. Weighing sides of an issue helps students develop the skills required for the critical evaluation of an issue.

Mike Schmoker and Gerald Graff (2011) praise the Common Core State Standards for English language arts/literacy as the "best English/language arts standards to date." Partly, this commendation arises from the emphasis on *argumentation*—a foundational element of the grade K–5 standards, that address the need for students to write and support their opinions with evidence. Discussing and debating ideas, reviewing supporting evidence, and composing a strong and convincing composition are at the heart of argument writing. We believe that it's never too early to start thinking and working on argument writing skills. As a matter of fact, most students have a bit of personal expertise when it comes to formulating an argument. At one time or another, every student has lobbied for an extra big piece of cake for dessert, argued why he or she should be able to get a new puppy, or asked to stay up late on a school night. While *making a case* is a natural part of our daily lives, the art of writing a powerful, compelling argument is not necessarily intuitive. It is, however, something that a knowledgeable and caring teacher can teach.

Examining the Concepts and Language

In Ms. Martin's class, sixth grader Ruthie is learning how to seek out reputable resources on the topic of space exploration. Ruthie's class has been studying planetary systems, including our solar system, as part of her study of the Next Generation Science Standard related to space systems: "Develop and use a model to describe the role of gravity in the motions within galaxies and the solar system" (Achieve, 2013a, p. 55). She learns about the *Apollo* missions and about some of the products and technologies that have emerged from the U.S. space program. Ms. Martin understands that many of her colleagues are leery of introducing the concept of *argument* in the classroom. She knows that the term *argument* is often connected to the concepts of *fighting, yelling, winning,* and *losing*. While these connotations may be commonplace in the media—just consider reality television and political debates—Ms. Martin's version of *argument* is rooted in research and academics as the process of creating a case in support of something and crafting the language for delivering it. Ms. Martin wants her students to investigate all aspects of a topic before they attempt to argue a positive. She wants them to be steeped in understanding and information before taking a position on a topic.

For the space unit, Ms. Martin wants students to consider the issue of funding continued space exploration. This study fits closely with the NGSS links among engineering, technology, science, and society: "Evaluate competing design solutions using a systematic process to determine how well they meet the criteria and constraints of the problem" (Achieve, 2013a, p. 63).

Ruthie and her classmates understand foundational concepts of space, including information about planetary systems and a little about the composition of stars and the sun. To further the study, Ms. Martin asks her students to read one opinion piece (Thangavelu, 2011) and view one news report (Is the Space Program Worth It? 2010):

- "Make Manned Space Flight Great Again" (http://lightyears.blogs.cnn .com/2011/11/18/opinion-make-manned-space-flight-great-again)

- Is the Space Program Worth It? [Video file]. 2010. Accessed at http:// abcnews.go.com/Technology/video/space -program-worth-11014480 on November 8, 2013.

Modeling to Support Learning

Because Ms. Martin knows that argumentative essays require students to make a claim, provide supporting evidence, state counterclaims, and summarize, she initially incorporates vocabulary instruction and modeling to ensure that students know what these terms mean. When discussing the term *claim*, Ms. Martin asks students to make a Frayer word card (figure 3.9) (Frayer, Frederick, & Klausmeier, 1969). Frayer word cards help foster a deeper understanding of a vocabulary term through the notation of a definition, characteristics, examples, and nonexamples in each of four quadrants of an index card.

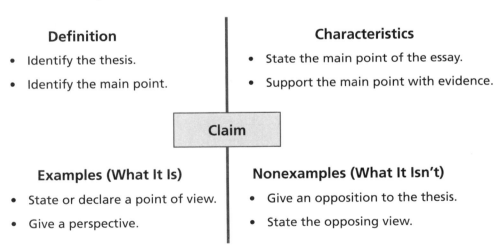

Figure 3.9: Frayer word card template for argumentative essays.

She also provides students with a guidesheet (figure 3.10) to support their argumentative essay writing and models how to use it. To get started, after reading the opinion piece and viewing the news video clip, Ms. Martin asks students to work in groups of three to brainstorm both ideas in favor of funding space exploration and ideas that oppose such funding.

Argumentative Essay Guidesheet

1. **Opening paragraph:** Describe the purpose of the essay.

   - Discuss the issue or problem, including background information.

   - State your claim or position.

   - Engage the reader with an interesting hook or thought.

2. **Paragraph two:** Present a piece of your supporting evidence.

   - State your evidence in the topic sentence.

   - Clarify and describe why the evidence supports your claim.

   - Discuss the counterclaims.

   - Summarize your evidence.

3. **Paragraphs three, four, five, and so on:** State your evidence in the topic sentence.

   - Clarify and describe why the evidence supports your claim.

   - Discuss the counterclaims.

   - Summarize your evidence.

4. **Concluding paragraph:** Summarize your points.

   - Restate your claim.

   - Restate your evidence in a condensed, simplified format.

   - End with an interesting thought, line, idea, or next question for study.

Figure 3.10: Guidesheet template for argumentative essays.

She also provides them with a brainstorming map specifically designed for argumentative essay writing (figure 3.11, page 120). Visit **go.solution-tree.com /commoncore** to find the guidesheet and map.

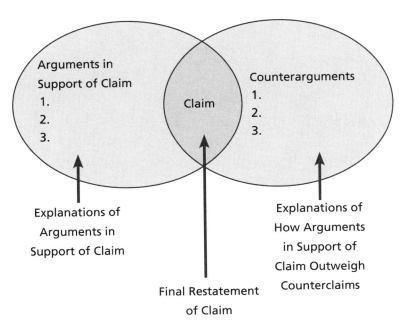

Figure 3.11: Brainstorming map for argumentative essays.

Moving to Independence

To use this tool, Ms. Martin has students work with a partner to list all the arguments they can think of in support of the claim. In this example, Ruthie and her partner Sam decide to support funding of space exploration. Based on Ms. Martin's previous examples of acceptable evidence to support an argument, Ruthie reminds Sam, "We can't just say we want to fund space exploration because we like the moon or because we want to travel to Mars. We need evidence from good sources. I know we're going to have to look for this evidence in newspapers and in news videos."

Sam adds, "I think that we should support private people funding space travel. Remember when Ms. Martin showed us Buzz Aldrin's blog? He thinks we might be going on vacation to Mars as early as 2059" (Erdman, 2009).

Ruthie rebuts, "Remember when we looked at the NASA website that told us how much it costs to run the space shuttle? I think it was between one and two billion dollars. That's so much money! What about all the poor people on this planet? What's more important: space travel or helping people in need on Earth?"

Sam counters, "Just think of all the technology that has come out of the space program. Smoke detectors came out of the space program research, and I know that most of us have them in our homes now. Maybe we can find a cheaper way to travel to space. Hybrid cars make it cheaper to drive on the freeway. Maybe we can develop a way to make space travel less expensive."

Ms. Martin's sixth graders are able to have this rich conversation because their previous study of the solar system entailed a look at blogs, video clips, and articles that explain how scientists have come to learn about space (for example, Conger, n.d.). They completed an activity in which they investigated the spectra of different gases when they looked at how to determine the composition of stars like the sun. They read about the technology that has come out of space research, and they have come to know that science is about examining issues and problems in a thorough, logical way in order to find answers or solutions. Ms. Martin guides students to build background knowledge and has worked with students to augment vocabulary comprehension. Now she is asking them to write in support of an issue, while still acknowledging other viewpoints. Ruthie and Sam's discussion indicates that they have enough knowledge to be able to fill in the circles on the brainstorming map that require a list of arguments and counterarguments.

The next step will involve the development of statements that connect the arguments to the claim. Ms. Martin shares an example of how to do this. She makes the claim, "Recycling should be required since it helps protect the environment." Most students nod in agreement as she makes this claim. Then, she prompts the students to talk with a partner about their answers to the following question, "How do you know recycling helps the environment?" She listens in as Shane tells Sara, "If we use fewer plastic bags there will be less CO_2 in the air."

Sara responds, "Also, we'd have fewer piles of soda cans in dumps if we recycled."

After the class shares for five minutes, Ms. Martin pulls the class together and comments on her observations. "I noticed that you talked about reasons why recycling keeps the environment clean. If you were writing an argumentative essay about this topic, you would have to state these reasons in your paper as evidence to support your claim."

To show how to discuss counterclaims, Ms. Martin asks students to talk to a partner about ideas that would oppose the claim that recycling helps the environment.

Tanya notes, "Most recycling bins have lots of stuff in them, including trash, like rotten banana peels, not just the cans or paper materials that should be in them. I don't think a recycling bin like that will help the environment. It's too hard for people to sort trash." Students continue to discuss this issue, and then Ms. Martin asks them to use counterclaims in their space paper.

Following this, Sam and Ruthie work together to compose their paper. They use their completed brainstorming map and argumentative essay guidesheet to jointly compose a draft version of their paper. Ms. Martin wants her students to be like scientists working to publish their research and experience the process of peer review, which entails reflecting on and learning from feedback. To facilitate this, she provides students with an opinion paper feedback guidesheet (available at **go.solution-tree.com/commoncore**) that directly correlates to the argumentative essay guidesheet. Students exchange papers with their partners and check each criterion the paper addresses in order to note accomplishment of that criterion. They also provide additional comments as necessary.

Students are then given the opportunity to revise their papers given the peer feedback. Ultimately, through Ms. Martin's activities, the class of sixth graders begins to understand the importance of background knowledge, evidence, and connections when it comes to solving science problems.

Questions for Discussion or Reflection

1. How will you guide students to consolidate ideas from multiple resources?

2. In your classroom, what role will partner conversations play in helping students to think through ideas in preparation for writing?

3. Which grade-level NGSS and CCSS does your instruction address?

Using Technology to Support Writing

Technology tools can also provide opportunities for students to compose science thoughts using written language. For example, teachers can use blogs like Blogger (www.blogger.com) and WordPress (http://wordpress.com) for students to reflect on science topics in writing. Clearly, blogs provide wonderful opportunities for students to write in an online setting. *National Geographic* has a blog that allows students to investigate topics ranging from recycling to deep-sea exploration (http://kidsblogs.nationalgeographic.com/blogs). Other options for online writing exist in the form of story writing. The website Storybird (www.storybird.com) provides illustrations that students can use to create a digital book. Storybird already has numerous science-related books on display, and students might find it even more intriguing to work with a partner to create their own science story. While it is still incumbent on the teacher to design and develop the lessons that will foster growth in science writing, using technology tools can provide a means for students to practice writing while using 21st century technology skills.

Optimizing Science Writing

When students write, they are expressing their thinking. While laboratory report writing is important, other forms of informational writing are essential as well (Prain & Hand, 1996). Students must learn how to document ideas as they develop inquiry investigations. They must know how to argue a point using a cohesive, logical format for writing. Finally, they must have opportunities to share knowledge through writing that comes from given perspectives.

The 21st century job market has, and will likely continue to have, opportunities rooted in science. They may range from technology-based positions to jobs in the medical profession to areas of research and development that we can't even imagine yet. If our K–6 students are going to be prepared to tackle the future, they must have the skills necessary to become competent, skilled science writers. They may need to craft a coherent but brief memo to a colleague in a medical office, or they may need to document a research report for an engineering firm. In any case, science writing is a needed skill for 21st century citizens who will need to know how to express their thoughts about the environment, their world, and their careers. It is incumbent on elementary educators to guide students to document their thoughts in writing and to provide them with the tools and the opportunities to engage in science writing.

CHAPTER 4

Learning to Read Like a Scientist

Although the Common Core State Standards offer a framework of expectations in each area of the English language arts—language, speaking and listening, writing, and reading—these become very integrated as students engage in experiences that promote the understanding of ideas, generation of information, reflection on a hypothesis or related data, and communication about scientific topics. It is also important to note that while the standards provide a guide designed to ensure that all students attain the same bases of understanding, this will not happen without the support of very skilled teachers and the involvement of families and a wider community that places value on learning science.

As noted in chapter 1, one of the six major shifts that will occur in elementary classrooms as a result of CCSS implementation will be the increase in time students spend engaged with informational texts. In many schools, students currently spend very limited amounts of time learning and reading social studies and science texts (Dorph et al., 2007; Mathis & Boyd, 2009). The balance between fiction and informational text will shift to 50 percent and 50 percent by fourth grade, 45 percent and 55 percent by eighth grade, and 30 percent and 70 percent by twelfth grade (National Assessment Governing Board, 2008). This increase in the relative proportion of informational texts is intended to occur across all content areas and grades, with the responsibility being shared by all teachers. Since most elementary classrooms are self-contained, the responsibility for increasing the reading of informational texts will remain with the classroom teacher but involve all the content areas.

What You'll Learn in This Chapter

Being able to read proficiently depends on having the foundational skills needed to understand the alphabetic principle that speech sounds are mapped to letters and that words can be efficiently decoded to support fluent processing of a text. Many strategies, including repeated readings, reader's theater, and choral readings, offer continual practice as readers develop their accuracy, automaticity, prosody (intonation, rhythm, and emphasis), and fluency when reading. Thinking aloud during a shared reading or a read-aloud is also often done to model how a proficient reader thinks through a text. In addition to revisiting these practices, in this chapter we share reciprocal teaching, ReQuest, jigsaw, collaborative and close reading, and vocabulary practices. As with chapters 2 and 3, we cast each within the context of a grade-level scenario, which also offers an example for implementation in grades K–6. The scenarios illustrate that carefully reading increasingly complex texts occurs by expanding their knowledge of scientific topics and literacy skills.

What Are the Standards?

Being a proficient reader means that one is able to deeply comprehend the text with which he or she is interacting. With limited access to informational texts, some readers have become more proficient at reading literature. However, much reading in college and workplace situations demands a proficient understanding of informational texts. A. J. Stenner, Heather Koons, and Carl Swartz (2010) indicate that there is a 200 Lexile-point difference between the texts students are required to read in a four-year college and those being read by graduating high school seniors. Lexiles, which are noted in the CCSS in grade-level bands, measure quantifiable text features such as word length, frequency, and familiarity; sentence length; and text length and cohesion. While it appears that shorter texts, which contain one-syllable words, would be easier, this may not always be true, as seen in "The atom is a basic unit of matter." What must be also considered are qualitative factors that involve the meaning of the passage, its structure and language, and the knowledge needed by the reader. So as you can see, closing this existing gap must result from students being taught to read increasingly challenging texts throughout their school careers with the goal being that they will develop their proficiency and stamina when reading informational texts to ensure their success during high school and after. For additional information regarding text complexity, we suggest reading *Teaching Students to Read Like Detectives: Comprehending, Analyzing, and Discussing Texts* (Fisher, Frey, & Lapp, 2012a) and *Text Complexity: Raising Rigor in Reading* (Fisher, Frey, & Lapp, 2012b).

Ten Common Core Reading anchor standards support students learning to read increasingly challenging high-quality literary and informational texts (NGA & CCSSO, 2010a). The Reading anchor standards have four domains: (1) Key Ideas and Details, (2) Craft and Structure, (3) Integration of Knowledge and

Ideas, and (4) Range of Reading and Text Complexity. In addition to identifying standards within each domain, the CCSS note that developing skills with print concepts, phonological awareness, phonics and word recognition, and fluency are foundational to learning to read. Information regarding foundational skills for grades K–5 can be found on pp. 15–17 of the CCSS (NGA & CCSSO, 2010a). As students advance through the grades, addressing the Common Core anchor standards combined with high school grade-specific standards enables the identification of learning expectations. The anchor standards provide a broad base of learning that supports the specificity of the content standards. The standards do not identify the curriculum to be taught and were never intended to replace existing curriculum.

> The Standards define what all students are expected to know and be able to do, not how teachers should teach. . . . Furthermore, while the Standards make references to some particular forms of content, including mythology, foundational U.S. documents, and Shakespeare, they do not—indeed, cannot—enumerate all or even most of the content that students should learn. The Standards must therefore be complemented by a well-developed, content-rich curriculum consistent with the expectations laid out in this document. (NGA & CCSO, 2010a, p. 6)

The primary focus of the Reading standards is to share a set of expectations designed to support developing a reader's ability to understand text-based information across the subject areas. The anchor standards, which are specifically delineated across the grade levels, do not emphasize text-to-self and text-to-world connections. The first three anchor standards in the category of Key Ideas and Details are very applicable to reading science texts. When reading science texts, students must be able to explain sequences of events and relationships occurring during and after investigation. Being able to do so requires identifying key ideas and details.

Key Ideas and Details

1. Read closely to determine what the text says explicitly and to make logical inferences from it; cite specific textual evidence when writing or speaking to support conclusions drawn from the text. (CCRA.R.1)

2. Determine central ideas or themes of a text and analyze their development; summarize the key supporting details and ideas. (CCRA.R.2)

3. Analyze how and why individuals, events, or ideas develop
    and interact over the course of a text. (CCRA.R.3) (NGA &
    CCSSO, 2010a, p. 10)

Reading anchor standards four through six address the ways in which a text structures information. The author's use of language, features (like graphs and charts that support the sharing of the information), and style provide such insights. Anchor standards four through six signify the importance of focusing attention not just on what the text says or implies but also on how it works. Authors use words, syntax, organizational structure, cohesive devices, and so on to convey the ideas. Readers need to learn to pay attention to how the text works.

Reading a science text differs from reading a story with a consistent and familiar structure, characters, problem, and resolution. The structure of a science book may include more than one text structure and multiple features. For example, in order to comprehend the following paragraph, the reader has to identify a series of elements or events that cause a condition to happen. The reader also has to study the author's use of language to infer that the writer had bias.

> Several months ago, the nuclear power plant was shut down due to a defective steam generator. This was identified when a radiation leak led investigators to find a faulty generator tube. While some local activists have expressed concern over the design of the reactors, the plant continues to publicize the many safety features built into the design. A new reactor with that same design is now ready to be put into operation. The reactors in the nuclear generating station are large and reliable. Safety is of prime concern to those who manage and work at the plant. Because nuclear energy is almost completely free of emissions, it provides a better way to generate energy when compared to plants that burn fossil fuels. This means that nuclear energy has helped the community to become less plagued by smog than it would have been with a plant that uses coal. Radioactivity is always monitored around the plant and waste is disposed of in a proper manner. For these reasons, the replacement of the old reactor with a new one of the same design is a welcomed development in this situation. Hopefully, the negative voices of overreacting activists will soon be silenced so that the community will once again benefit from nuclear power.

Comprehending this passage involves closely analyzing both the author's perspective and his or her use of language to convey information and to stimulate thinking. As students progress through the grades, they are expected to understand text structures, features, and author craft and language choices well enough to contrast information across multiple texts.

Craft and Structure

4. Interpret words and phrases as they are used in a text, including determining technical, connotative, and figurative meanings, and analyze how specific word choices shape meaning or tone. (CCRA.R.4)

5. Analyze the structure of texts, including how specific sentences, paragraphs, and larger portions of the text (for example, a section, chapter, scene, or stanza) relate to each other and the whole. (CCRA.R.5)

6. Assess how point of view or purpose shapes the content and style of a text. (CCRA.R.6) (NGA & CCSSO, 2010a, p. 10)

Reading anchor standards seven through nine specify behaviors that involve integrating information and ideas in a single text, and eventually across multiple texts. When applied to a grade-by-grade sequence of standards, this understanding pertains to information being presented in various forms, including orally, visually, and digitally. This is especially pertinent when conducting a scientific investigation, because it is incumbent on the researcher to read and learn about all that is written on a topic prior to developing and conducting a study. Additionally, students need to know how to identify credible sources of information. Anchor standards seven through nine guide teachers in supporting students as they derive, synthesize, and analyze information from multiple resources so that they can skillfully utilize gleaned concepts, themes, and evidence in scientific work.

Integration of Knowledge and Ideas

7. Integrate and evaluate content presented in diverse media and formats—visually and quantitatively, as well as in words. (CCRA.R.7)

8. Delineate and evaluate the argument and specific claims in a text, including the validity of the reasoning as well as the relevance and sufficiency of the evidence. (CCRA.R.8)

9. Analyze how two or more texts address similar themes or topics in order to build knowledge or to compare the approaches the authors take. (CCRA.R.9) (NGA & CCSSO, 2010a, p. 10)

Reading anchor standard ten calls for applying one's skills as a reader to independently and proficiently read multiple types of texts whose complexity continues to increase.

Range of Reading and Level of Text Complexity

> 10. Read and comprehend complex literary and informational texts independently and proficiently. (CCRA.R.10) (NGA & CCSSO, 2010a, p.10)

Although the Reading anchor standards do not specifically call for a connection between a reader and a text, engagement (Brozo, Shiel, & Topping, 2007; Gambrell, 1996; Guthrie & Wigfield, 2000) and background knowledge (Biemans, Deel, & Simons, 2001; Lipson, 1982; Martin-Chang & Gould, 2008; McKeown, Beck, Sinatra, & Loxterman, 1992) significantly support a reader's comprehension. Instruction that addresses the standards by supporting students' scaffolding from their existing bases of knowledge and language will certainly support their developing understandings and independence as readers of science. No single factor alone enables deep comprehension, but these factors coupled with the learning and thinking skills of the Common Core will hopefully result in every student becoming a proficient reader of a wide array of information. This, however, cannot happen without very efficient instructional practice.

Evidence Supporting These Standards

Richard Venezsky's (1982) early suggestion that by sixth grade more than 75 percent of a student's reading should be informational serves as foreshadowing of one of the key shifts promoted by the CCSS that students read increasingly more informational texts across content areas as they move through the grades (table 4.1).

Table 4.1: Distribution of Literary and Informational Passages by Grade in the 2009 NAEP Reading Framework

Grade	Literary	Informational
4	50%	50%
8	45%	55%
12	30%	70%

Source: National Assessment Governing Board, 2008.

As students move from topic to topic, the types of reading materials they encounter include essays, experiments, position statements, speeches, manuals, lab procedures, journals, mathematics problems, websites, government documents, newspaper and magazine articles, and directions. Technology offers various ways to obtain information. While sources of information share some similar characteristics, they are no longer just paper based, and they each contain unique structures, language, devices, features, and conventions. Reading a wide array of sources is necessary in order to continue to expand one's knowledge base within a content area. Scientific knowledge is no exception. To be scientifically literate, students must know how to read science materials, especially those that appear in the popular press. If we expect students to continue to independently grow their content knowledge, they must be taught to read each text type they encounter.

Most teachers begin the study of a scientific topic with a very engaging investigation that invites inquiry and wondering. Students often begin to lose interest when having to read science textbooks or scholarly articles that contain unfamiliar, multisyllabic words and complex sentences that require extensive background knowledge to comprehend the language. Many students do not have the content language or base of knowledge needed to succeed. Without an alternative plan, students will develop limited interest and subsequently will learn little beyond the initial inquiry. To learn more about this issue, see CCSS ELA appendix A (NGA & CCSSO, 2010b).

Level of Knowledge

Students must also be taught how to support their own reading when they encounter scientific information in a format that is too difficult for them. We all struggle to learn new information when the task or text does not match our entry-level language, knowledge, and skill set. This does not mean that we cannot learn the information or eventually read the text. It just means that it is too difficult for us now given our present level of knowledge. A literate person knows how to move to less difficult resources or get help from an expert when this occurs.

What do you do when this happens to you? You just bought a new iPhone, iPad, or computer, and you're eager to use it. Or maybe you are trying to learn to use the kettlebells that all of your friends are talking about. Or you're trying to build a back deck on your home, compute your income tax, select an insurance carrier, or choose a health plan. What do you do if you don't have an expert by your side to guide you? Of course you find resources that provide information at an introductory level by going to the Internet and typing in the browser "Tips for using new iPad," for example, or "building a back deck." When we are new to a topic, we need less difficult texts and tasks. To help students with difficult science reading, teachers can provide an array of topically related materials that include picture and trade books, news articles, and scientific magazines. The National Science Teachers Association (www.nsta.org/publications/ostb) and the American Association for the Advancement of Science (www.project2061.org/publications /rsl/online) compile lists of science-related trade books and reading resources. As students peruse related picture books, they read the visuals, which support their developing base of knowledge. As they develop a base of knowledge and language, they are able to continually read more sophisticated texts.

Text Complexity

The ability to read increasingly complex texts ensures that students graduating from high school will have the skills to read college and workplace texts. This skill depends on foundational skills that include decoding and fluency and understanding the text vocabulary and syntax—the most significant predictors of complexity (Nelson, Perfetti, Liben, & Liben, 2012). With the appropriate instruction, students will graduate from high school ready to read all texts.

Students need to be taught to read increasingly challenging texts through instruction that illustrates what a proficient reader does when encountering complex meaning, vocabulary, and structures. This also requires teaching students to closely read a text by using text-dependent questions designed to promote a deepening comprehension of the disciplinary information. Students must learn to examine documentary knowledge in social studies, experimental evidence in science, and the author style, craft, and use of clues in literature. Accomplishing this goal bodes well in science, since the National Research Council (2012) notes that language and literacy are essential to understanding the complex nature of written and spoken science.

As noted in appendix A of the CCSS (NGA & CCSSO, 2010b), identifying a continuum of text complexity involves consideration of the quantitative and qualitative dimensions of a text and also the reader and task considerations.

Quantitative Dimensions

As we have mentioned, quantitative features like word length, frequency of occurrence, sentence length, and text cohesiveness are often assessed by readability or Lexile formulae. Teachers are fairly good at using their judgment to determine the quantitative level of text complexity. However, many easy-to-use formulas, including the Fry Readability Formula (Fry, 1977), the Lexile Framework for Reading (Lexile Analyzer, 2013), and Coh-Metrix (Graesser, McNamara, Louwerse, & Cai, 2004), offer additional support in analyzing the quantifiable features of complexity, including the length of sentences, the frequency and length of words, and the cohesiveness of the passage. Appendix A of the CCSS (NGA & CCSSO, 2010b) offers a Lexile table for ease of quantifying these text dimensions (table 4.2).

Table 4.2: Text Complexity Grade Bands and Associated Lexile Ranges

Text Complexity Grade Band in the Standards	Old Lexile Ranges	Lexile Ranges Aligned to College and Career Readiness (CCR) Expectations
K–1	N/A	N/A
2–3	450L–725L	420L–820L
4–5	645L–845L	740L–1010L
6–8	860L–1010L	925L–1185L
9–11	960L–1115L	1050L–1335L
11–CCR	1070L–1220L	1185L–1385L

Source: NGA & CCSSO, 2012.

Qualitative Dimensions

Qualitative dimensions include the four factors of (1) meaning or purpose, (2) text structure, (3) language conventionality, and (4) knowledge demands needed for comprehension. Matching readers and science texts involves knowing the learning characteristics of students and the qualitative dimensions of the passage in question. Notice that the following passage contains a single level of meaning, conventional language, a syntactically familiar sentence structure, and a simple cause-and-effect organizational structure that supports an easy conveyance of information:

> The theory of plate tectonics states that the crust of Earth is broken into large plates that can move. There are places where plates come together. There are areas where plates move apart. Finally, there are plates that slide past each other. Plate movement results in the formation of trenches, mountains, and even earthquake fault lines.

This text conveys singular concepts with simple text structures and minimal technical vocabulary and defines unfamiliar terms in a cursory manner, thus placing less demand on the reader. In contrast, the following text has deeper explanations of science phenomena and utilizes more precise technical and academic vocabulary to convey the mechanisms behind plate movement:

> The plates that make up Earth's lithosphere are driven by convection currents within the asthenosphere. Molten material in the asthenosphere rises up and cools, causing plates to move like people riding atop a conveyor belt. Most geologic activity results from this movement and occurs primarily where plates converge,

diverge, or slide past each other. Various geologic features form as a result of this movement. These include mountains, trenches, and fault zones.

This complex text provides deeper explanations of science phenomena and utilizes more precise technical and academic vocabulary to convey the mechanisms behind plate movement. The additional dimensions of complexity (meaning, language, and knowledge demands) are more sophisticated. For example, the information presented requires an understanding of technical terms, an understanding that convection currents are driven by density and temperature differences, and the inference that there are connections between what occurs within the Earth and what occurs at the surface plates—knowledge that is not common to those working outside the science professions.

Reader and Task Considerations

In addition to these very obvious features, text complexity also involves matching the reader and the task. Reader and task considerations involve motivation, experiences, and knowledge of the reader. Task considerations include the purpose, the complexity of the task, and questions being posed. Teachers can determine if a text is appropriate for a student at a given time and for a particular purpose in a number of ways: knowledge of the student's experiences with the topic; cognitive abilities, which include attention to task, memory, and ability to infer information; knowledge of vocabulary and comprehension skills; and motivation, which includes interest, appreciation for the power of reading, and self-efficacy as a reader. Once readers and texts are matched, teachers must support readers in increasing their levels of knowledge and skill as they ascend the grades.

Into the Classroom

Effective science instruction must include intentionally supporting inquiry and also students' comprehension of science texts. Michael Pressley and Peter Afflerbach (1995) note that in addition to utilizing one's prior knowledge and language to make sense of text, students automatically apply many of the following skills in order to ensure that comprehension occurs. A proficient reader does the following:

- Identifies a purpose that supports an achievable focus
- Interacts with the author by making predictions about the information being read
- Validates or invalidates the identified predictions while reading

- Applies multiple strategies including context clues to figure out unknown vocabulary
- Creates mental visuals to enable understanding and remembering
- Questions the text and him- or herself to connect prior and new information
- Synthesizes large chunks of information to support remembering
- Underlines, takes notes, and creates graphic representations as needed
- Rereads and monitors reading speed
- Segments complex ideas and language into smaller, more comprehensible ideas
- Reflects and revises knowledge as he or she gains new insights
- Analyzes and evaluates the truth or value of the information
- Summarizes to ensure remembering the major thesis
- Applies and expands existing bases of knowledge through further exploration

As you read this list, were you applying these strategies individually? Of course not. When reading, one does not use these skills individually; instead, as Michael Pressley, Ruth Wharton-McDonald, Jennifer Mistretta, and Marissa Echevaria (1998) note, strategies are bundled and used interchangeably to support meaning making. Many readers automatically learn to bundle and use multiple reading strategies. Others need to be specifically taught how to do so. Consider this science text:

> Groups of molecules evenly distributed within a mixture are called solutions. There are solutions that have high concentrations of molecules dissolved and some that have low concentrations of molecules. A solution may consist of a solid dissolved in another solid, like copper dissolved into silver. A solution may also be a liquid dissolved in a solid or in another liquid. Gasoline is comprised of a liquid dissolved in another liquid. Additionally, a solid could be a gas dissolved in a solid, a liquid, or another gas. Soda is composed of carbon dioxide gas dissolved in a liquid.

To comprehend this paragraph, a reader might take notes in order to categorize and document ideas. For instance, after reading the first time, the reader, seeking out more understanding, would likely reread and then take notes on the various types of possible solutions. He might even make a sketch or a graphic illustrating the various ways that solutions may be formed (figure 4.1). Then he might add a summary statement that captures the main points of the text. This kind of skilled reading involves the application of several bundled strategies, including rereading, making notes and graphics, and summarizing. There are numerous excellent texts (for example, Moss and Loh, 2011) that offer many instructional ideas designed to teach specific strategies.

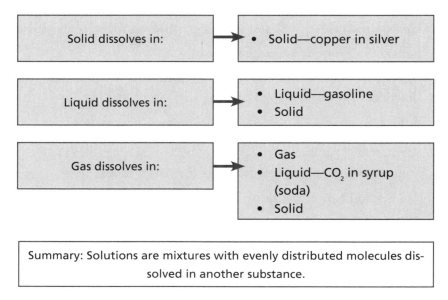

Figure 4.1: Ways in which solutions may be formed.

The NRC (2012) framework notes:

> Even when students have developed grade-level-appropriate reading skills, reading in science is often challenging to students for three reasons. First, the jargon of science texts is essentially unfamiliar; together with their often extensive use of, for example, the passive voice and complex sentence structure, many find these texts inaccessible. Second, science texts must be read so as to extract information accurately. Because the precise meaning of each word or clause may be important, such texts require a mode of reading that is quite different from reading a novel or even a newspaper. Third, science texts are multimodal, using a mix of words, diagrams, charts, symbols, and mathematics to communicate. Thus understanding science texts requires much more than simply knowing the meanings of technical terms. (p. 74)

In the following examples, we'll witness instruction that supports students becoming highly proficient readers of scientific information—instruction that prepares them to:

Read closely to determine what the text says explicitly and make logical inferences from it; cite specific textual evidence when writing or speaking to support conclusions drawn from the text. (CCRA.R.1) (NGA & CCSSO, 2010a, p. 10)

Read and comprehend complex literary and informational texts independently and proficiently. (CCRA.R.10) (NGA & CCSSO, 2010a, p. 10)

Mr. Hubbard's Kindergarten Class

Morgan loves science. Her kindergarten teacher, Geoff Hubbard, always makes it so interesting, and Morgan is always excited to learn about many things. Whatever the topic, the class always begins with an interactive investigation that invites personal inquiry and lots of questioning and conversation. Mr. Hubbard realizes that the main obstacles to learning science center on four issues: (1) lack of student engagement, (2) insufficient background knowledge and language, (3) texts that are too difficult, and (4) unintentional instruction.

To support students as they learn about weather, Mr. Hubbard not only exposes students to multiple books that have both illustrations and informational text but also shows them how an expert might approach such books. He does all this while strategically maintaining the perspective of a kindergartener, making it relatable and relevant to his young students. Table 4.3 (page 138) shows Mr. Hubbard's lesson plan.

Engaging Students in Scientific Practice

To begin developing his students' background knowledge and topically related language, Mr. Hubbard always involves his students in inquiry that is related to the scientific topic of study. In this study of weather, he asks them to look out the window and think about the weather. He says, "When you're looking outside, what clues tell you how to dress? What clues tell you what the weather is even when you're inside?"

After the students think about his questions and chat with a partner, Mr. Hubbard encourages them to draw pictures in their personal investigation journals (figure 4.2, page 139). Their drawings show what they know and wonder about his questions. A reproducible version of figure 4.2 can be found on page 207 and online.

While students share with their peers and work in their journals, Mr. Hubbard listens, observes, and talks with them. Mr. Hubbard's initial engaging questions

Table 4.3: Kindergarten CCSS for Reading and NGSS Lesson Plan on Earth and Space Sciences

Crosscutting Concept	Patterns and cause and effect
Core Idea	Weather and climate
Lesson Purpose	To see how weather changes over time
Focus Strategy	Personal investigation journal

NGSS

K-ESS2-1. Use and share observations of local weather conditions to describe patterns over time.

K-2-ETS1-1. Ask questions, make observations, and gather information about a situation people want to change to define a simple problem that can be solved through the development of a new or improved object or tool.

CCSS

• Reading standards:

RI.K.7. With prompting and support, describe the relationship between illustrations and the text in which they appear (e.g., what person, place, thing, or idea in the text an illustration depicts).

RI.K.10. Actively engage in group reading activities with purpose and understanding.

Source: Adapted from NGA & CCSSO, 2010a, pp. 11, and Achieve, 2013a, pp. 7, 16.

and activities serve as extrinsic or outside motivators to get the students initially involved with the topic.

While students are engaged in the exploration of a scientific question or hypothesis, teachers have the perfect opportunity to assess both their background and developing knowledge of the topic as they watch and listen to their performance. By listening to their wonderings, teachers can also determine the next questions or tasks that can get students excited and suggest deeper exploration to investigate or test a hypothesis. In real-world settings, these wonderings are often the questions that lead scientists to inquiry-based investigations. Very reciprocal in nature, extrinsic motivators, such as questions for inquiry, support the initial building of background knowledge and language that enables subsequent intrinsically motivated exploration. As a result, students' language and knowledge deepen, and their motivation to continue an investigation becomes more personal.

My Questions	My Observations	My Predictions	My Investigation	My Data	My Analysis	My New Questions
How do you know it will rain?	It's raining.	It will keep raining.	Will it rain for long?	See if it rains all day.	Cloudy skies mean rain.	When will it get sunny?

Figure 4.2: Sample personal investigation journal entry.

Deepening Scientific Language and Knowledge

Teachers like Mr. Hubbard realize that they can prompt their students' attention to scientific study through the motivating questions they initially ask, the problems they pose, the surprise inquiry events they stage, and the texts they share. They realize that in order to teach students, they must first be engaged.

On this particular day, Morgan shares with a partner that she wonders where the sun goes when it rains and what makes a puddle dry up even when it isn't sunny. Her friend isn't sure about the sun but thinks air has something to do with the puddle. As students build a base of common experience, knowledge, and language through their explorations of the weather and climate, a core idea of the NGSS, Mr. Hubbard listens in while supporting and pushing their thinking (Achieve, 2013a). He asks Morgan and her partner to consider what makes a wet towel dry when it's inside the house or what causes a paper towel to dry after being wet. They decide to dampen a sponge and observe it during the day to see what really happens to it. As Mr. Hubbard listens, he says, "Great thinking! Your observations of the sponge might give you the clues you need to answer your question about a puddle. Be sure to jot down some notes to share."

Moving Toward Independence as a Scientific Thinker

By reflecting on students' thinking through preliminary interactions, Mr. Hubbard is able to initially assess students' ranges of knowledge as they respond to the initial question and participate in their first investigative activity. Notice that he asks the question, and then as the students chat, he listens to their conversation. Everyone is participating, which allows him to make a quick assessment of everyone's base of knowledge and language. This works much better than asking one question and receiving a response from only one student while the others sit quietly, often not attending. One-to-one question-response interactions provide an assessment of only the responding student. An initial assessment like Mr. Hubbard's occurs as the teacher observes the performance of each student while that student is engaged in initial inquiry and chatting with a partner. As partners discuss and write information and wonderings in their investigation journals, the teacher is able to do a quick, cursory assessment of everyone. This information identifies the range of scaffolds that will be needed to ensure that all students learn the language and concepts they need in order to support their grade-level learning. Teachers like Mr. Hubbard realize this is not the end of formative assessment; it is just the beginning. They use consistent, subsequent observation of student performance to gather information about each student's developing understanding.

After supporting partners begin explorations, Mr. Hubbard always asks them to share their thoughts and drawings with the whole class. In this way, they record data for further analysis, just like real scientists. As they explain their findings and wonderings, Mr. Hubbard uses a document camera to post their thoughts. Together, they categorize the ideas into statements to tell what they saw, heard, or smelled as clues to the day's weather.

As the students share their statements, Mr. Hubbard listens to their language and assesses whether or not they understand the lesson purpose and how to accomplish it. He offers scientific terms for their observations. For example, when Morgan and her partner talk about water drying up, he says, "Yes, water does evaporate, and yes, you are correct that something, some variable, causes this." It is during this whole-class sharing, as students document their thinking, that he is able to support their growing understanding of the lesson purpose and its use of topically related language. He often reminds them that they are learning the language scientists use to investigate and share information.

Mr. Hubbard often chooses books like *Flash, Crash, Rumble, and Roll* (Branley, 1964), a book detailing the occurrence of thunder and lightning in a way that is clear to a kindergartener. He also likes *Down Comes the Rain* (Branley, 1963) and *Clouds* (Rockwell, 2008). Mr. Hubbard often shares short video clips from BrainPOP (www.brainpop.com) or Science Kids (www.sciencekids.co.nz) that allow students to see the weather phenomena they are discussing. He'll even occasionally do a read-aloud of a news article like "Germy Weather" (Ornes, 2011) or another news story found on Science News for Kids (www.sciencenewsforkids.org).

For this particular lesson, after the whole class shares, Mr. Hubbard invites students to look at books with great pictures. Some books students share during weather study include *Weather Forecasting* (Gibbons, 1987), *The Cloud Book* (dePaola, 1985), and *The Kids' Book of Weather Forecasting* (Breen & Friestad, 2008).

Even when Morgan and her friends can't read all of the words, they "read" all of the pictures and illustrations. They love exploring books that help answer their questions. When they finish browsing through the books, Mr. Hubbard encourages them to again talk with a partner about all of the new information they are learning and any new questions they have. As they talk, they add more pictures or words to their personal investigation journals to show the new information they learned. Morgan likes the books he chooses, because they introduce her to so many interesting topics about her world.

Reading and Thinking Aloud

After another whole-class discussion, Mr. Hubbard reads aloud to the students. Like others, he believes that reading aloud exposes them to topical language and concepts and offers an excellent way to develop both listening comprehension and attention to the visual aspects of a text (Beck & McKeown, 2001; Hoffman, Roser, & Battle, 1993). Reading for both visual and spoken details is very important to comprehending science.

When Mr. Hubbard reads aloud, he places the text on the document camera so that he can also reference visual details and important words with the students. When previewing, he explicitly thinks aloud regarding the vocabulary related directly to the topic. He calls these words the *topical vocabulary*, or the vocabulary of a content area. For example, some of the topical vocabulary words that might be related to the study of weather include *clouds*, *tornadoes*, *humidity*, and *precipitation*.

He also identifies the interesting ways language is used to convey information—for example, how it describes a problem and solution, a sequential pattern, a series, or a unique description. An example of a sentence that he would stop and think about is "Cirrus, stratus, and cumulus cloud formations often indicate the various weather patterns that can be expected." While reading this sentence, Mr. Hubbard pauses to think aloud: "Cirrus, stratus, and cumulus—I think the author is saying that there are three cloud groups and when they appear in the sky it means that we can expect a certain kind of weather. *Various* means different, so each type of cloud formation or shape must mean that I can expect a different kind of weather when I see each formation."

His thinking aloud in this manner is intended to suggest to the students that in order to be successful readers, they must have a comprehensive understanding of the academic style of the language used to convey information in the text. Developing this proficiency involves not just understanding the vocabulary words but also understanding how these words are placed in sentences to constitute a particular discourse structure. In addition to the language students share at home, they need to become familiar with the unique ways language is used to convey ideas and information in science, social studies, and math. Teachers can share examples of this each time they read and think aloud with their students.

As evidenced by the scientific experiences shared in this kindergarten classroom, Mr. Hubbard's primary goal is to motivate and engage his students in tasks that promote scientific inquiry and engineering practices. Additionally, he is addressing the science content by asking students to observe local weather, document what they see, and determine patterns.

> ## Questions for Discussion or Reflection
>
> 1. How can you assess individual student learning? What will you do to push students' thinking further? What will you do to help students clarify misconceptions or confusion?
>
> 2. How can you incorporate student journals into your science curriculum?
>
> 3. Mr. Hubbard asked students to investigate multiple texts to gain insights. How will you support students in accessing more than one text on a topic?
>
> 4. What resources (trade books, multimedia, and so on) will you use to support student learning?
>
> 5. How can these resources promote inquiry thinking?
>
> 6. Which grade-level NGSS and CCSS does your instruction address?

Ms. Owens's First-Grade Class

Cynthia Owens knows that first graders like to ask questions. "When do we have lunch?" "Can you help me spell the word *yesterday*?" "Do I put my last name on my paper, too?" She capitalizes on this by showing them the connection between science and questioning (table 4.4, page 144, shows her lesson plan). To facilitate this, Ms. Owens uses ReQuest.

Supporting Comprehension With ReQuest

Designed by Tony Manzo (1969), ReQuest is an instructional routine that illustrates the power of creating text-based questions as a way to support meaning making. As with any other routine that utilizes a bundling of strategies to support independent meaning making, the teacher should model the strategy first. Teachers often illustrate the power of ReQuest while conducting a think-aloud during a shared reading. Once the students understand the routine, they are able to attempt it as partners, individuals, or small groups.

To begin, the teacher selects the target text and chunks it into sections. These are often the same sections designated by the subheadings within the text. When introducing the segment as a think-aloud, the teacher acting as the expert reads and also thinks aloud, usually questioning him- or herself about some confusing vocabulary as the students read along. Each student may have a copy, or the teacher can share one copy via a document camera.

Table 4.4: First-Grade CCSS for Reading and NGSS Lesson Plan on Physical Sciences

Crosscutting Concept	Cause and effect
Core Ideas	Wave properties
Lesson Purpose	To see how light moves through different objects
Focus Strategy	ReQuest
NGSS	
1-PS4-3. Plan and conduct an investigation to determine the effect of placing objects made with different materials in the path of a beam of light. K-2-ETS1-1. Ask questions, make observations, and gather information about a situation people want to change to define a simple problem that can be solved through the development of a new or improved object or tool.	
CCSS	
• Reading standards: RI.1.1. Ask and answer questions about key details in a text. R.I.1.4. Ask and answer questions to help determine or clarify the meaning of words and phrases in a text.	

Source: Adapted from NGA & CCSSO, 2010a, p. 13, and Achieve, 2013a, pp. 9, 16.

After finishing the segment and thinking aloud, the teacher invites the students to reread and think about the text themselves so that they can compile questions related to it. The students next act as questioners and ask the teacher two or three questions about the segment just read. The teacher cannot look back at the text to answer, but must first try to recall the answer. The students (questioners) check the text segment to make sure that the teacher gave the correct response. If the answer is beyond the scope of the segment just read, the respondent (the teacher) lists it so that the class can find the answer through another source. ReQuest thus involves a bundling of cognitive strategies on the part of questioner and respondent.

As the questioners who develop text-based questions, the students must examine the textual information, make personal connections and clarify them, create questions, and return to the text to verify the appropriateness of the response. As the respondent, the teacher must engage in very careful reading that supports synthesizing and sharing of the information as responses to questions. Eventually the teacher turns over the role of respondent to students in the class. Students can work in partnerships, with one being the questioner and the other the respondent.

Promoting Scientific Inquiry With ReQuest

Ms. Owens is preparing her students to address the Next Generation Science Standard that requires them to "plan and conduct an investigation to determine the effect of placing objects made with different materials in the path of a beam of light" (1-PS4-3; Achieve, 2013a, p. 9). In order to do this, students need to develop the proficiency to ask relevant science questions along with an understanding of waves and light. When using ReQuest, Ms. Owens pulls out her laminated Questioner and Respondent Task Cards and distributes them. Half of the students get the Questioner cards, and the other half receive the Respondent cards (figure 4.3).

Respondent	Questioner
1. Read a chunk of text. Think of two questions to ask your partner.	1. Read a chunk of text. Think of two questions your partner might ask you.
2. Ask your partner to answer each of your questions.	2. Without looking at the text, try to answer each of your partner's questions.
3. Provide a hint if your partner needs one.	3. If you need help, ask your partner for a hint.
4. If your partner needs more help, show him or her the answer in the text.	4. If you need more help, ask your partner to show you the answer in the text.

Figure 4.3: ReQuest questioner and respondent task cards.

Questioners are then paired with Respondents. Using the text *Light: Shadows, Mirrors, and Rainbows* by Natalie M. Rosinsky (2003), students play the role of the questioner, and Ms. Owens is the respondent. She reads the first six pages aloud for students to hear and typically chooses books that have clearly labeled illustrations so that her striving readers are better able to negotiate meaning. Additionally, she provides partner talk time before students share questions with her. Ms. Owens next asks for the first question. Throwing a confident hand in the air, Sherry inquires, "How does light move?"

Ms. Owens responds, "Well, I remember that in the sentences I read it said that light streams out as rays. Is that how it moves, Sherry? As rays?"

Sherry, hoping to stump the teacher, but still delighted that Ms. Owens got it, nods her head to indicate yes. Next, Juan shares his question, "Ellie and I have a good one. Can light go through a glass?" While this is not a text-dependent question with an explicit answer in the text, Ms. Owens concurs that it is a good one.

"Juan, I like your question. It shows that you and Ellie are really thinking about how light interacts and acts in the real world. I remember the picture of the boy in the book. The light couldn't go through the boy, but maybe light can go through a glass, since a glass is made up of different material. What do you think, Juan?"

Juan, now not sure of the correct answer, says, "I don't know."

Responding quickly, Ms. Owens asks, "How could we find out?"

Without hesitation, Juan says, "Let's try it."

Ms. Owens grabs a flashlight from her desk drawer and asks Juan to help her. Juan stands up and is given a glass beaker. Then Ms. Owens shines the light beam through the beaker, asking, "Does it look like light can go through the glass beaker?" In unison, all students shout, "Yes!"

Following this, Ms. Owens asks students to work with their predesignated table partners to continue the process of ReQuest. As they finish the reading, she explains, "You will be using all the important things you just learned about light to plan an investigation with your partner. I want you to think of how you could check to see what light does when different materials are put in its beam. I have lots of materials you can use. Remember, scientists always write down what they learn. Think of how you will record your ideas."

Juan and Ellie talk together and come up with a plan to test a mirror, a tennis ball, a triangular piece of glasslike material (they will soon learn this is a prism), a book, and a piece of foil. Ellie grabs a flashlight as Juan holds up the tiny mirror. The light strikes the mirror and seems to stop, but two students next to Ellie notice that the beam from her light is on the front side of the mirror, as a reflection. "This is funny," notes Amed. "How is the light on the mirror?" Students continue testing. Ellie starts to make notes on her paper. She draws a beam hitting the mirror and a white spot on the wall. She next tries shining the beam on a book. Then she correspondingly sketches the light striking the book. She shows it stopping when it hits the book.

In order for students to be able to formulate testable questions, they need at least a bit of background knowledge to serve as a springboard to their inquiry. As students start to learn more about a science topic by reading, they naturally begin to express curiosity and consequently are more eager and adept at formulating questions.

Questions for Discussion or Reflection

1. Ms. Owens used a science-based trade book to implement ReQuest. What topics will you focus on using ReQuest? What texts might you select?

2. Ms. Owens's students developed text-based questions and questions that went beyond the text in scope. How will you support students in asking both kinds of questions?

3. Which grade-level NGSS and CCSS does your instruction address?

Mrs. Newman's Second-Grade Class

An understanding of the processes that shape Earth requires an examination of multiple types of informational resources. Because Lenore Newman wants her students to learn about both fast and slow Earth events, her students must engage in careful examinations of multiple resources, from photographs to videos to informational texts. The Earth events examined in this second-grade classroom include volcanic eruptions, earthquakes, landslides, and erosion (table 4.5, page 148, shows her lesson plan). When Mrs. Newman asks her students to read about several of these Earth events, she employs close reading. To learn about landslides, students are reading a few pages from *Landslides* (Zuehlke, 2009).

Effective teachers realize that in order for their students to be able to comprehend the many text styles and structures in their academic worlds, they must be able to self-regulate their use of cognitive strategies such as predicting, inferring, visualizing, questioning, clarifying, and monitoring. To do so, they must have a thorough knowledge of the subject and an understanding of the language of the text (Fang, Schleppegrell, & Cox, 2006; Halliday, 1987; Halliday & Matthiessen, 2004). Understanding the language of the text means knowing how the vocabulary and the language structures are used to convey information. Students learn this as a result of intentionally planned instruction that is:

> embedded in the actual text assigned and should reflect the interactive, constructive aspects of making sense of text and of effective explicit instruction. The selected strategy should be modeled by the teacher, practiced by the students with guidance from the teacher, used in controlled situations by students with assigned text, and transferred in other reading assignments and texts by the students. (Yore, 2004, p. 88)

Table 4.5: Second-Grade CCSS for Reading and NGSS Lesson Plan on Physical Sciences

Crosscutting Concept	Stability and change
Core Ideas	The history of planet Earth
Lesson Purpose	To determine which Earth processes are fast events and which are slow events
Focus Strategy	Close reading
NGSS	
2-ESS1-1. Make observations from media to construct an evidence-based account that Earth events can occur quickly or slowly.	
CCSS	
• Reading standards:	
RI.2.2. Identify the main topic of a multiparagraph text as well as the focus of specific paragraphs within the text.	
RI.2.4. Determine the meaning of words and phrases in a text relevant to a *grade 2 topic or subject area.*	
RI.2.5. Know and use various text features (for example, captions, bold print, subheadings, glossaries, indexes, electronic menus, icons) to locate key facts or information in a text efficiently.	
RI.2.8. Describe how reasons support specific points the author makes in a text.	

Source: Adapted from NGA & CCSSO, 2010a, p. 13, and Achieve, 2013a, p. 19.

As a result, students learn the discourse features, or the forms and functions of expository academic text language, thus enabling their successful functioning within each content area.

Sharing a Plan of Intentional Instruction

In an attempt to develop students' independence as readers, teachers often explicitly model for them how to prepare themselves *before* starting their actual reading, how to monitor and support comprehension *during* reading, how to evaluate their growing knowledge, and, *after* the reading, how to plan the next steps in their learning. These behaviors are based on the work of Sandra Kujawa and Lynne Huske (1995), whose insights have helped us get inside the minds of proficient readers to understand how, regardless of the content, they prepare to read, monitor their understanding as they read, and then reflect, assess, and evaluate what they have learned from the reading.

Teaching the Process of Close Reading

In order to prepare students to closely read a science text, teachers need to explain the process and convey that closely reading a sentence, a passage, or a text involves rereading the selection in order to go beyond the initial understanding to deepen one's understanding of the workings of the text, including the information, the language, and the author's purpose or message. The intent of initially engaging students in learning the process of a close reading is to teach them to pay attention to how the text works. Before asking students to engage in closely reading a science text, it is important to model and support their learning. It is also important to share that they have many skills they can use to enrich their comprehension, and close text reading is one of these.

Modeling how to dig deeply into a text for an initial purpose and then returning more than once to gain deeper and deeper understandings is a process you may need to share each time your students encounter a new genre. Once you have modeled the process of closely reading a science passage, students will understand what they are being asked to do when they are assigned a science passage that requires a close reading. Once students learn the process of close reading, they will be able to do so independently, without extensive frontloading. The scenarios in the following sections are intended to show how to explain and model a close reading of a science passage. Frontloading information or modeling should not continue once the students understand the process. At that point, step to the side and allow them to closely read subsequent text passages without your extensive frontloading.

Using Text-Dependent Questions to Promote Deepening Analysis

Sending students into a complex text multiple times, each with an explicit purpose, causes them to address not just what the text says or implies, but how it works. Questions that send students back to the text for rereading should cause them to analyze the word choices, syntax, organizational structure, and cohesive devices authors use to convey the ideas. Answers to questions teachers pose throughout the close reading should be *text dependent*, which means that in order for the reader to answer the question, he or she has to comprehend the information the author is sharing as well as the language, style, and structure the author has used to convey the information. Text-dependent questions require that the reader extract information directly from the text being read. They involve a literal interpretation but should also require students to infer and synthesize implied information not literally stated. Answering text-dependent questions should require the reader to address multiple dimensions of the text

(Fisher & Frey, 2012; Frey & Fisher, 2013). Figure 4.4 shows the progression of text-dependent questions.

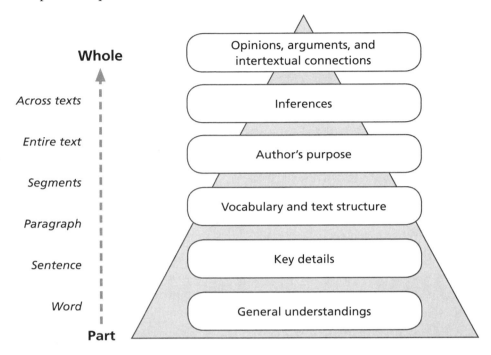

Source: Fisher & Frey, 2012

Figure 4.4: Progression of text-dependent questions.

Questions requiring a general understanding of the textual information might ask the readers to synthesize information from the text in order to describe a sequence of information the author has shared. In science, when reading about the topic of phase changes, for example, a general understanding would include asking a question like "What happens when a solid, like ice, is warmed to its melting point?" or "What happens when a liquid, like water, is cooled to its freezing point?"—questions that call for understanding the sequence of changes that occur when matter is cooled or heated.

A key detail question asks the reader to identify critical text details that support a deep understanding of the text. In science, as the reader reads a passage about the human digestive system, a question asking for identification of key details might be "How does peristalsis aid the process of digestion?"

Vocabulary and text-structure questions support the reader in making inferences in order to better understand the author's use of word choice and organizational features. When reading a science passage on the topic of light, a question about vocabulary that would alert the reader to the importance of the precision of word choice might be "Why does the author use the term *reflection* to describe the behavior of light when you look in a mirror?" The question would guide students not only to express the concept that they are viewing their reflected image but also to consider the behavior of a light ray as it strikes the mirror and bounces off.

Questions addressing an author's purpose help the reader to understand the effect the author is attempting to have on the reader. A question that asks the reader to identify whose voice is present in a health-related headline is very important, because students daily read and hear much hype regarding products being marketed. When students are reading headlines such as "Energy Drinks Promote Edge" or "Energy Drinks to Jumpstart Your Game," questions like "Who is making the claim?" and "What facts are presented to support the claim?" invite them to critically analyze who is sharing the information and what key details support that information.

Questions that cause students to make inferences while reading ask them to identify details in an informational text, arguments in a persuasive text, and shades of meaning in a literary text. In the previous energy drink headlines, a question like "What information in the text helps you to understand the author's reason for sharing this information?" would cause the reader to make an inference regarding intent.

Questions that move the reader to identify opinions, arguments, and intertextual connections invite using one's background knowledge from lived experiences and one's reading of other texts as a base of comparison with the information currently being read. "How true are the energy drink claims?" and "What supports your perspective?" are questions that invite the reader to make such connections. Although these examples pertain to the reading of science texts, teachers can ask similar questions as students read within other content areas and fictional texts.

Annotating the Text for Deeper Investigation

Teaching students the process of close reading also involves teaching them how to annotate the text. This means teaching students to circle or underline words they find confusing, use question and exclamation marks to denote their questions or to indicate information they find surprising, draw arrows to make connections between and among points that signify relationships, and circle big ideas and write examples next to them. If an author is providing multiple arguments or details, teachers should explain that skilled readers often add numbers to track their ideas. Proficient readers also often rewrite a phrase that was initially confusing but one they stuck with long enough to figure out. Using similar annotations and closely reading science texts are skills that should be taught to students before they begin independently wrestling with scientific information during a close reading. Teaching annotation involves selecting a passage, modeling how to identify the key features, and then engaging students in guided instruction to support their independence in becoming proficient annotators. Figures 4.5 and 4.6 are examples of primary and intermediate grade annotation charts that teachers can modify and use to teach students how to annotate as they closely read a text.

Notice the arrow in the intermediate chart. The arrow identifies for students the focus of the annotation in which they are engaging and is moved as the focus is changed. Eventually, when students are able to annotate well, the arrow will be completely removed.

Additional annotating features can be added. For example, some teachers suggest including connecting arrows to show relationships among ideas discussed within a passage—for instance, if the passage says that there are many different Earth events. Connecting arrows can be drawn among the sections discussing the various types of event—erosion, earthquakes, volcanic eruptions, landslides, and so on. This is a way of marking up the text to document thinking as a reader reads the text.

In Mrs. Newman's class, when students read a text about mass movements, and about landslides in particular, they are given a general-knowledge question to address: "What is the author discussing in this text?" As they read, they mark up the text by noting their questions on the photocopy, highlighting main ideas—especially as they pertain to the general knowledge, text-dependent question, and documenting

Figure 4.5. Primary grade annotation chart.

wonderings. Neicey highlights "Rock, dirt, and debris slid down the mountain." Charles puts a question mark near the word *debris*. Gloria puts three exclamation points near the description of a landslide event in the Philippines in 2003. Once they are done reading, Mrs. Newman asks students to talk with their table partners about the text-dependent question, "What is the author discussing in this text?" Neicey tells Charles that the text is about land that falls down. Charles agrees, saying, "It happens fast sometimes."

For the next reading, Mrs. Newman wants students to address a vocabulary question. She tells students, "Sometimes science words are explained by examples. If I wanted to explain what snow is like, I might describe how it forms in clouds when the air is cold and how it falls to the ground because of gravity." Mrs. Newman now asks students to address this text-dependent question: "How does the author explain what landslides are and how they occur?" Mrs. Newman asks students to reread and suggests that they could answer this question by underlining where they see the word *landslide*. Gloria moves through the text underlining these sentences: "A landslide buried homes and trees. Some landslides move slowly. Other landslides move very fast."

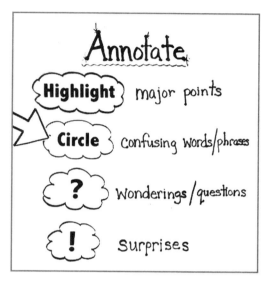

Figure 4.6: Intermediate grade annotation chart.

After the second reading, students are again asked to talk to table partners. Gloria tells Xiao that she thinks the author means that a landslide causes rocks to fall. Xiao adds, "It says that landslides happen where there are mountains and hills and there's lots of rain. I wonder why there needs to be rain?" Listening in on the conversation, Mrs. Newman acknowledges that students are acquiring the concept that debris falls due to gravitational pull during a landslide. She is satisfied that students are developing a formative understanding of the process but notes that she'll need to clarify a few ideas about wet sediment and about the role that earthquakes and human action can play in landslides.

For the final reading, Mrs. Newman wants to challenge students to connect this text to a photo and caption from a mass movement event described in another text. She asks them to compare and contrast what they see in the photo (La

Conchita, a coastal area of southern California) and what they read in the text by providing this question: "What aspects of Earth events seen in the photo are described in the text?" As she rereads, Neicey makes a note in the margin of the text near the sentence "Big rocks pile up near the bottom after the rocks fall." Near the sentence "It starts to slide downhill," she writes "Rocks fell off. Mess at bottom."

When students are given the chance to discuss their ideas, Charles tells Neicey, "I think this is a mass movement in the picture. I see lots of big rocks at the bottom of the tall rock. I think they fell down really quick."

Neicey, agreeing, says, "That means it's a fast Earth event." Text-dependent questions offered for consecutive readings give students a reason to go back into the text to dig deeper. Clearly, Neicey, Charles, Gloria, and Xiao have developed a deeper understanding of mass movement through this process. They continue using other texts that document slowly occurring Earth events so that they can build a body of knowledge that allows them to address the standard "Use information from several sources to provide evidence that Earth events can occur quickly or slowly" (2-ESS1-1; Achieve, 2013a, p. 15).

In the next scenario, notice how Shanita Juarez, a third-grade teacher, shares the importance of attending to both the vocabulary and the way the language is used during a unit of study about birds and their habitats. Knowing the language of the subject supports comprehension.

Questions for Discussion or Reflection

1. Mrs. Newman developed text-dependent questions that could be used to drive students back into the text multiple times. Consider an informational text that you might use to implement close reading. What text-dependent questions will you ask?

2. What supports might you employ to teach annotation during close reading?

3. Which grade-level NGSS and CCSS does your instruction address?

Ms. Juarez's Third-Grade Class

Shanita Juarez knows that many students have prior knowledge about the life cycle of organisms—birth, growth, reproduction, and death. Some of her students have pets, like puppies or kittens, that they have seen grow up. In class, students have even had the opportunity to watch their pet caterpillar eat leaves, build a cocoon, and emerge as a butterfly. To capitalize on this knowledge and to address NGSS 3-LS1-1, Ms. Juarez shows how to "develop models to describe that organisms have unique and diverse life cycles but all have in common birth, growth, reproduction, and death" (Achieve, 2013a, p. 2). Table 4.6 shows her lesson plan.

Table 4.6: Third-Grade CCSS for Reading and NGSS Lesson Plan on Physical Sciences

Crosscutting Concept	Patterns
Core Idea	Growth and development of organisms
Lesson Purpose	To identify common elements of the life cycle of organisms
Focus Strategy	Think-aloud
NGSS	3-LS1-1. Develop models to describe that organisms have unique and diverse life cycles but all have in common birth, growth, reproduction, and death.
CCSS	• Reading standards: R.I.3.3. Describe the relationship between a series of historical events, scientific ideas or concepts, or steps in technical procedures in a text, using language that pertains to time, sequence, and cause/effect. R.I.3.4. Determine the meaning of general academic and domain-specific words and phrases in a text relevant to a *grade 3 topic or subject area*. RI.3.7. Use information gained from illustrations (e.g., maps, photographs) and the words in a text to demonstrate understanding of the text (e.g., where, when, why, and how key events occur).

Source: Adapted from NGA & CCSSO, 2010a, p. 14, and Achieve, 2013a, p. 206.

Thinking Aloud to Support Reading Comprehension

Ms. Juarez articulates her thinking as she reads a text. She is, in a metacognitive way, showing students how she tackles a text so that she can make connections to herself and to content she's learned in school. Ms. Juarez uses "I" statements when she thinks aloud. She says phrases like "When I read this I think . . ." and "I remember when I saw . . ." and "I think I need to reread this part." Students gain insight into how a proficient reader can tackle complex texts by drawing on prior knowledge and by using skills like rereading or looking at word parts to figure out the meaning of unknown terms. She unlocks the mystery of reading tough texts so that her students can practice and acquire such skills themselves.

As Ms. Juarez previews the text *Night of the Pufflings* (McMillan, 1997), she looks at the front cover and says, "Hmmm, the title says *Night of the Pufflings*. The picture shows a little bird in a girl's arms. I'm predicting that the little bird is a puffling, and maybe something happened to it, because people usually do not hold birds in this way."

Continuing to read the text, she draws attention to other topically related vocabulary words, such as *burrows*, *village*, and *moonbeams*, that she thinks the students may not know well enough to comprehend or use in their spoken and written languages. While thinking aloud about the meaning of each of these words, she highlights them in yellow as a way to illustrate that she is explicitly attending to each. Additionally, she calls students' attention to the unique ways in which the author shares ideas through language phrases that are not everyday speech. While reading, Ms. Juarez says, "'In the darkness of the night'—wow, that's an interesting way of saying 'late at night.'" And when she reads the phrase "wing-flapping trip from the high cliffs," she says, "I am trying to picture what the author means when he says 'wing-flapping trip from the high cliffs.' I picture this as the pufflings are starting their flight from the high cliffs. I like how the author doesn't say 'pufflings' but instead says 'wing-flapping,' because he knows that since this text is about pufflings, readers can infer or figure out that he is talking about the pufflings' flight."

Ms. Juarez reads another page, "'Most of the birds splash-land safely in the sea below. But some get confused by the village lights—perhaps they think the lights are moonbeams reflecting on the water.'" Then she adds, "*Perhaps*—that's an interesting word. Remember that in addition to paying close attention to the words, good readers must also pay very careful attention to how the author uses the language. This is called *academic language*, which is more formal than the language we use at home or when we are chatting with our friends about topics that aren't connected to school. At school, when we share and in our books, the language is more formal, so don't let yourselves get confused by the way the words are used to share ideas. You'll want to try using these more formal patterns in your writing and partner conversations."

Modeling Fluent Reading

Through this think-aloud, students learn to negotiate meaning for difficult words. They become more proficient at identifying and noticing academic language. And they acquire content knowledge. As their background knowledge and vocabulary awareness grow with such reading, they become more able to tackle such texts and even more complex texts.

Questions for Discussion or Reflection

1. What aspects of a text will you notice when you think aloud for students?

2. Terms like *predict* and *hypothesize* are common academic terms in science texts. What other academic terms would you expect to see in science texts?

3. How does the think-aloud strategy connect to the NGSS and to the CCSS?

4. Which grade-level NgSS and CCSS does your instruction address?

Mrs. Johnson's Fourth-Grade Class

In Delia Johnson's class, students are investigating NGSS 4-PS3-4, "Apply scientific ideas to design, test, and refine a device that converts energy from one form to another" (Achieve, 2013a, p. 23). When addressing this standard, students are encouraged to design and develop plans for a device that will allow the conversion of energy from one form to another. More specifically, they are building solar ovens using their own designs. To be able to do this, they first must read about the conversion of solar energy to heat and about the possibilities for design. Mrs. Johnson guides students to accomplish this task using the Directed Reading and Thinking Activity (DR-TA) (Stauffer & Harrell, 1975). Table 4.7 (page 158) page shows her lesson plan.

Scaffolding the Process of Reading

DR-TA is a framework for reading that guides students to:

1. Respond to guiding questions that require the use of the structure of the text to predict upcoming content

2. Read to confirm or refute predictions, so that predictions may be acknowledged as accurate or revised according to newly acquired knowledge

3. Use predictions and revisions to participate in conversations centered on content

Table 4.7: Fourth-Grade CCSS for Reading and NGSS Lesson Plan on Physical Sciences

Crosscutting Concept	Energy and matter
Core Idea	Growth and development of organisms
Lesson Purpose	To design and construct a device that converts energy from one form to another
Focus Strategy	Think-aloud DR-TA

NGSS

4-PS3-4. Apply scientific ideas to design, test, and refine a device that converts energy from one form to another.

3-5-ETS1-1. Define a simple design problem reflecting a need or a want that includes specified criteria for success and constraints on materials, time, or cost.

CCSS

• Reading standards:

RI.4.3. Explain events, procedures, ideas, or concepts in a historical, scientific, or technical text, including what happened and why, based on specific information in the text.

RI.4.7. Interpret information presented visually, orally, or quantitatively (e.g., in charts, graphs, diagrams, time lines, animations, or interactive elements on Web pages) and explain how the information contributes to an understanding of the text in which it appears.

RI.4.9. Integrate information from two texts on the same topic in order to write or speak about the subject knowledgeably.

Source: Adapted from NGA & CCSSO, 2010a, p. 14, and Achieve, 2013a, pp. 23, 32.

For each chunk of text, students use the DR-TA protocol to guide their reading. Mrs. Johnson places her students in heterogeneous groups of three for this project (students with advanced knowledge, emerging learners, and possible English learners—all in the same group). The groups are responsible for using DR-TA to read three texts: a text about the conversion of solar energy to heat, another about a method for building a solar oven, and a third about a different method for building a solar oven.

The first article is chosen by Mrs. Johnson: "How Does a Solar Cooker Work?" (Discovery Channel, 2011). To prepare students to read a complex paragraph from this article, Mrs. Johnson has already employed several vocabulary strategies. Before students read, she reminds them that they should predict what the paragraph will be about. Students record these predictions on a sheet of notebook paper on which they have written the numbers 1, 2, and 3. The numbering correlates with the three DR-TA tasks. As he proceeds to look at the article, James predicts that it will be about how solar ovens capture energy from the sun to cook food. He notes this on his paper for number 1 and indicates that the word *solar* means "sun." He then reads the paragraph and enthusiastically indicates for number 2 that his prediction was correct. After James finishes reading, for number 3 he turns his chair to have a conversation with Solange about what he has learned. Knowing that the two will have to design a solar oven, Solange suggests that they use foil for the reflective panels—a concept mentioned in the text. James adds that mirrors might work, too.

Reading Multiple Texts to Build Background Knowledge That Supports Innovative Design

Mrs. Johnson provides multiple resources that provide information on building different kinds of solar ovens, from pizza box ovens to large cardboard box ovens. These include YouTube videos and various websites, including the following:

- New Mexico Solar Energy Association (www.nmsea.org)
- National Science Teachers Association (http://science.nsta.org)
- Solar Cookers International (www.solarcookers.org)
- Google (www.google.com)
- CBS News (www.cbsnews.com)

Visit **go.solution-tree.com/commoncore** for links to the webpages on these sites that accompany Mrs. Johnson's lesson.

Students use DR-TA protocol to examine at least two of the documents, images, or videos. After they acquire ideas for designing and constructing solar ovens, they proceed to sketch out their plans. Solange and James settle on a large cardboard box, with the inside and flaps lined with foil. Another pair, Mark and Robert, utilize nested wooden boxes, painted black inside and covered with glass. They add a plane mirror as their reflector to a top that is angled above the boxes. After design and construction are completed, students will utilize the ovens to make s'mores and will record temperature data. Group data will be shared with the whole class to enable an analysis of solar cooker effectiveness based on design elements.

Bringing Science and Engineering Together

When science and engineering practices are implemented in tandem, students use scientific concepts to construct explanations and to develop design solutions for real-world problems. Because energy use is a worldwide issue, an understanding of energy efficiency as it relates to effective design is essential. Students in Mrs. Johnson's class not only learn that thoughtful, well-tested design results in engineering solutions to relevant, real-world problems, but they also realize that success is often achieved through a review of failures. When students design a solar oven that doesn't toast the marshmallows for the s'mores, Mrs. Johnson encourages them to reflect in writing on the failure by noting what they think went wrong and how they might redesign the project to achieve success in the future. With this reflection, students can earn the same good grade as students who achieve success on their initial project. Through this method of reflection, Mrs. Johnson is encouraging the true spirit of engineering—a field that promotes the construction of multiple prototypes and ongoing reflection as a part of the ultimate design for a device, machine, or gadget.

Questions for Discussion or Reflection

1. What aspects of DR-TA do you think relate to the CCSS?

2. How does students' engagement in engineering practices strengthen their scientific understandings?

3. When teaching this lesson, what additional real-world connections might Mrs. Johnson have made that would have supported her students' understanding of energy efficiency?

4. Which grade-level NGSS and CCSS does your instruction address?

Mr. Smith's Fifth-Grade Class

Before beginning his shared reading of *Cloudy With a Chance of Meatballs* (Barrett, 1978), Leon Smith, a fifth-grade teacher, explains to his students that whenever he reads a text he often reads either the whole text or a part of it very closely in order to fully understand the information, the language the author is using to share the information, the layout of the text, or how the parts of the text work together. He explains that he often has to reread a science text multiple times in order to deeply comprehend the information. Table 4.8 shows his lesson plan.

Figure 4.4 contains the image Mr. Smith shares as he explains the areas that he attends to when closely reading a text.

Table 4.8: Fifth-Grade CCSS for Reading and NGSS Lesson Plan on Physical Sciences

Crosscutting Concept	Cause and effect
Core Ideas	Chemical reactions
Lesson Purpose	To design experiments that answer questions about phase changes
Focus Strategy	Close reading
NGSS	
5-PS1-2. Measure and graph quantities to provide evidence that regardless of the type of change that occurs when heating, cooling, or mixing substances, the total weight of matter is conserved.	
3-5-ETS1-3. Plan and carry out fair tests in which variables are controlled and failure points are considered to identify aspects of a model or prototype that can be improved.	
CCSS	
• Reading standards:	
RI.5.3. Explain the relationships or interactions between two or more individuals, events, ideas, or concepts in a historical, scientific, or technical text based on specific information in the text.	
RI.5.5, Compare and contrast the overall structure (e.g., chronology, comparison, cause/effect, problem/solution) of events, ideas, concepts, or information in two or more texts.	
RI.5.8. Explain how an author uses reasons and evidence to support particular points in a text, identifying which reasons and evidence support which point(s).	

Source: Adapted from NGA & CCSSO, 2010a, p. 14, and Achieve, 2013a, pp. 28, 32.

close reading

– what claims does the author make?

– what evidence does the author use to support those claims?

– how is this document supposed to make me feel?

– what words or phrases does the author use to convince me that he/she is right?

– what information does the author leave out?

Source: Fisher & Frey, 2012.

Figure 4.7: Close reading texts.

Explaining How to Use All of One's Skills to Closely Read a Science Text

After discussing each area in the close-reading chart, Mr. Smith further explains that when he begins to read a text, including science books, he asks himself questions like "What do I already know about this topic?" or "What's my reason for reading this text?" He explains that he often has to reread the text several times in order to really understand it well. He says that this is a practice referred to as *close reading*. He shares that he often starts by writing notes and questions to show himself how much he knows and wonders about the topic. He also explains that as he reads, he annotates the text to identify his questions and discoveries. He reminds students of their previous practice with text annotating.

As Mr. Smith continues to model the process of close reading, he next places a copy of the text on the document camera and explains that when he closely reads a text he needs to understand how all parts of the text work together in order to help him better understand the author's message, language choices, and information. To do so, he shares that he may return to the text several times to repeat the reading. He explains that he made a copy of this text so that he could illustrate for his students how he annotates the text as he reads. He says that when he can't annotate right in the text he makes an annotation guide where he writes the page number and his thinking.

He further explains that close reading is one of many strategies that he uses to help him comprehend a text. He also initially examines a text by previewing all of the pictures, maps, graphs, charts, and other illustrations. When doing so, he asks himself, "What do I already know that I can connect to what I'm now seeing and reading?" He also explains that when he looks at the visuals, he tries to gain clues about the information the author is trying to share. He says that when scientists read and think about a topic they look for clues that will help them solve a puzzle. He notes that sometimes the puzzle is just to figure out what they know and do not know about the topic and then to figure out how to read and reread to add to what they know. As he looks through the text and reads it a bit, he asks himself, "What new ideas am I learning?" He highlights these since they are also the major ideas of the passage.

He explains that he also asks questions related to the text before, during, and after reading. Doing so allows him to understand if he is comprehending the information. If he is unable to comprehend, he has to select a less difficult text on the same topic or seek help from someone who has a better understanding of the topic. Often if the text seems too hard, he selects one on the same topic that has more illustrations because it's important to learn from the text, rather than feeling stumped or frustrated. He explains that building this knowledge helps him to be able to return to the initial text with enough knowledge and language to read it well.

Mr. Smith also says that talking with others who are interested in the topic gives him new information and also an opportunity to use scientific language. He tells the students that although they are amateur scientists, they should think about how a real scientist might investigate a topic as they wonder about it and investigate it through their experiments and their reading.

Paying Attention to Language

Once Mr. Smith finishes examining the text, he reminds students that paying attention to the author's use of language is a part of how he understands a text. He has chosen *Cloudy With a Chance of Meatballs* (Barrett, 1978) to illustrate how the author uses language to draw comparisons as a way to illustrate a concept. When reading the description of Main Street in Chewandswallow in the book, Mr. Smith says, "I really like how the author describes Main Street because she makes it seem so real. It's like our downtown. Then she named the city Chewandswallow, which is pretty absurd. This comparison between real and absurd gives me a clue that she might use many similar comparisons throughout the book to help me think about science. I'm going to draw circles around Main Street and Chewandswallow and write *contrast* in the margin. This will help me remember that the author is using comparisons as a technique in writing this text. These comparisons are *metaphors*, which compare something that is familiar with something that is unfamiliar."

After reading a little further, Mr. Smith says, "Each time the author describes a weather condition, I really think it's clever how she substitutes a certain familiar food for what would have been the weather element. She uses these comparisons throughout. For example, when she talks about the liquids that rained, it makes me think about how rain really looks because I have to compare it to soup and juice. I'm going to circle this comparison too. As I read further, see if you can also get pictures of the real weather conditions in your mind as you think about the food comparisons or metaphors the author uses."

Guiding Instruction to Scaffold Learning

After orally reading a few more pages, he invites the students to silently read their copies, circle the comparisons they see, and highlight the exact language the author uses to cause them to think about metaphorical images. After reading and annotating, students partner share the language, weather conditions, and visuals the author uses to cause them to identify their selected metaphors.

As he listens to his students' partner conversations, Mr. Smith hears Anthony say that he wonders why the author compared green peas and mashed potatoes with snow. Although Anthony has highlighted green peas, mashed potatoes, and snow and circled them to show a metaphorical comparison, it's obvious to Mr. Smith that he's having some trouble trying to picture and understand the comparison.

First reinforcing that Anthony has indeed identified a metaphor, Mr. Smith asks him to jot down his question in the margin regarding why the author has compared green peas and mashed potatoes to snow. Then, using a combination of cues and prompts designed to scaffold Anthony's understanding (Fisher & Frey, 2008a), Mr. Smith gestures toward a chart in the room that contains photos of various snow formations over time. While verbally cuing Anthony to look at the photo of fresh snow, he prompts him to compare it with another photo showing the changes in appearance after a few days. He says, "Notice how the snow formations—the texture, size, and shape of individual grains or flakes—look different in the photos." Prompting further, he says, "Remember that the temperature still affects the snow once it is on the ground."

Anthony replies, "Oh yeah, it melts a little, and then some chunks refreeze, which makes it not look so smooth. I see why it would look like it has lumpy peas stuck in mashed potatoes. I can write that freezing, then melting, then refreezing changes how snow looks—it gets lumpy. This answers my question."

This cognitive prompt pushed Anthony to think about his existing knowledge of the physical changes that occur to snow because of temperature and chemical changes. This interaction supported Anthony in activating his existing knowledge and using it to understand new information.

As Mr. Smith listens and observes the thinking of other students, he offers additional prompts and cues, asks questions, and re-explains information through what Nancy Frey and Douglas Fisher (2010) call a teacher's strategic moves to bridge or scaffold existing and new understandings.

Although Mr. Smith uses a fictional text to show metaphorical language, he explains to the students that paying close attention to the author's choice of language is a skill that is very commonly used in science. He shares that DNA is often described as a *building block of life* or a *blueprint*. Gas molecules are sometimes likened to billiard balls moving and colliding with each other. While it's clear to those who already have an understanding of these terms that we use metaphors to help make abstract concepts more concrete and relatable, students will need teacher guidance to initially conceptualize the power that the author's language choices have over the reader's comprehension. This particular text is used to build a foundation for the study of phase changes using the relatable and familiar concepts of the phase changes of water as exemplified through different types of precipitation (rain, snow, and so on). From this, students will progress to a consideration of changes that occur when heating, cooling, or mixing substances. Because *water* is a familiar substance in all of its states (solid, liquid, and gas), it is a logical choice when building background knowledge in this area of science study. Students will eventually move toward an understanding of the conservation of mass when heating, cooling, or mixing substances.

Questioning After Reading

Continuing, Mr. Smith asks himself questions and again shares his thinking. He says, "One question I always ask after reading is, 'Was I able to learn something from this text?' If not, I ask, 'Why not?' In this book, I was able to think a lot about real weather conditions by comparing them to similar food falling from the sky.

"I also like to ask myself, 'Is the text too hard or too easy?' For me, this book didn't have really hard words, but I did have to stop and reread to really visualize each example. All of the visuals made it pretty friendly. The illustrator really helped me.

"I also ask myself, 'Is there some additional information I'd like to know about this topic?' I like the pictures of the fog, and I really wonder what causes fog. I'm going to make a note in my annotations that I'd like to know that.

"My final question is 'Where can I find information about my new wondering?'—in this case, the causes of fog. I think I'll start by looking at the weather books in our library to see if one has this information. I could also ask a librarian or check Google."

To provide students with practice with close reading, Mr. Smith next invites the students to select one of the books about phase changes or properties of matter or to read the section from their science books that would help them to gain new facts to answer their initial wonderings, new ideas, or new wonderings related to how matter changes. Mr. Smith encourages them to annotate their texts while reading.

In her science text, Daniella reads that evaporation occurs when water changes from a liquid form to a gas form. She knows that water from the faucet is in the liquid form, but she didn't know until she read in her textbook that steam coming out of a teapot on the stove is actually water in gas form. She highlights this information, adds a question mark, and writes a question in the margin: "How does liquid water actually change into steam?" She will investigate this wondering during the class's next exploration of the scientific topic of weather.

Supporting Independent Learning

In many classrooms when students finish reading and annotating, they are then often invited to collaboratively share with other students. Collaboration offers students a time to elaborate on their thinking as they work together on real-world applications of their newly acquired and developing language and information. The knowledge that students build from their reading is then drawn on as they develop laboratory experiments that address the questions they are creating themselves. Mr. Smith prompts students to brainstorm questions they have after reading about phase changes and matter.

Fifth graders Daniella and Frank are wondering about the mass of a wet sponge and the mass of the same sponge after it dries out. They conduct a few trials in which they soak a sponge and find the mass using an electronic scale. They then let it dry out and remass it. As Daniella and Frank share with an expanded group of five their findings about how a soaked sponge dried up during the course of the day and how it changed mass, Mr. Smith encourages them to think about what factors might cause evaporation. While chatting, they decide to again wet two sponges but this time to place one outside and another under a lamp. They determine mass for both sponges after soaking with water and after they dry out. Daniella and her peers think that by adding additional conditions to their experiment, they might be able to better show what causes a puddle to dry up and to determine why the mass changes when the sponges dry out. As is characteristic of the NGSS, concepts originally explored in earlier grades (for example, evaporation as a part of a weather study in kindergarten) are expanded on as students progress in grade level. This is a hallmark of the NGSS—a way to deepen content knowledge beyond superficial, shallow concepts. In this particular case, fifth graders are moving toward an understanding of conservation of mass when matter is heated, cooled, or mixed.

Mr. Smith asks this group to think about comparing temperature under the lamp with the temperature outside. The students agree that it is warmer under the lamp, and Daniella predicts that the sponge will dry up more quickly under it. Mr. Smith, through his questioning, leads students to think about the relationship between air temperature and evaporation. He knows that if students understood that warmer air can hold more water vapor, they would be more apt to comprehend ideas related to condensation and vaporization when they get to science in upper grades. Frank wonders why the wet sponges always have more mass than the dry ones. Daniella tells him that it's because the water is gone. Mr.

Smith makes a mental note to offer a prompt that directs students to consider where the water goes when it leaves the sponge.

As Mr. Smith moves around the room, he notices that another group has a plan to go outside with a small ice cube that the students have massed on the balance. This group wants to observe if mass changes after the ice cube melts. Once the students finish their collaborative work, Mr. Smith invites each student independently to continue to dig deeper into the current topic of study or return to a previous topic he or she might be simultaneously investigating.

Daniella and Frank are still curious about evaporation and mass so they decide to fill one pie pan with a half-inch of dirt soaked in water and another with just a half-inch of plain water. They place each pan on the scale to determine its mass and then put both pans under a heat lamp and observe them every ten minutes. Both students draw pictures of the pans at ten-minute intervals as a way to record their observations. They also put them both on the balance to record mass at these intervals. Mr. Smith appreciates the fact that Daniella and Frank are curious about how water soaking into a surface might affect evaporation rate. He knows that he can move them toward an understanding of the concept that even when materials are mixed, mass remains constant.

These students were working on the crosscutting concept cause-and-effect relationships as noted in the NGSS (Achieve, 2013a, p. 38). Opportunities for collaborative and independent work provide intrinsically motivated study and make scientific investigation seem like a real-life activity.

Questions for Discussion or Reflection

1. Mr. Smith used fiction to introduce the process of closely reading and annotating a text. How will you help students ask questions as they closely read a science text?

2. How can metacognitive questioning help students to tackle challenging texts?

3. Why do you think it's important to teach students to annotate as they read?

4. Mr. Smith read *Cloudy With a Chance of Meatballs* with his students. Then he allowed them to choose other texts to read. How does this kind of wide reading—reading an array of books within a content area—support inquiry and investigation?

5. Which grade-level NGSS and CCSS does your instruction address?

Ms. Cruz's Sixth-Grade Class

In the following sixth-grade classroom example, Maria Cruz has selected a science text on the topic of *producers, consumers, and decomposers*. Table 4.9 shows her lesson plan.

Table 4.9: Sixth-Grade CCSS for Reading and NGSS Lesson Plan on Physical Sciences

Crosscutting Concept	Energy and matter
Core Ideas	Organization for matter and energy flow in organisms
	Cycle of matter and energy transfer in ecosystems
Lesson Purpose	To ask questions about how matter is cycled and how energy flows from living and nonliving organisms through an ecosystem
Focus Strategy	Reciprocal teaching
NGSS	
MS-LS2-3. Develop a model to describe the cycling of matter and flow of energy among living and nonliving parts of an ecosystem.	
CCSS	
• Reading standards:	
RI.6.1. Cite textual evidence to support analysis of what the text says explicitly as well as inferences drawn from the text.	
RI.6.2. Determine a theme or central idea of a text and how it is conveyed through particular details; provide a summary of the text distinct from personal opinions or judgments.	

Source: Adapted from NGA & CCSSO, 2010a, p. 39, and Achieve, 2013a, p. 50.

As she shares the reading, she stops to think aloud about the characteristics and roles of each of these types of organisms and plans to note patterns and cause-and-effect relationships as per NGSS MS-LS2-3, "Develop a model to describe the cycling of matter and flow of energy among living and nonliving parts of an ecosystem" (Achieve, 2013a, p. 63). She articulates her thoughts, "I know that producers must make something because *producing* is about creating something new. It sounds like they produce their own food. Plants use photosynthesis to do this. *Consumers* must eat or take in something. I think that I'm a consumer because I eat vegetables and meat, but I don't make my own food. I'm not sure what *decomposers* do, but I hope I can read more to find out."

This thinking aloud draws the students' close attention to the text. When she concludes the segment of reading, Ms. Cruz covers the text and asks the students to compose a question based on what was just read. Students can be asked to write individual questions, or they can partner share developing the questions. Ms. Cruz uses a combination of these approaches because she wants all students to have a chance to write a question, but she also values the power of collaboration. Sample sixth-grade questions are: How do plants make their own food? What are the different kinds of foods that consumers eat? How do decomposers break down plant and animal material?

Together the students return to the text and try to determine answers to their own questions. Sixth-graders Marisol, Heather, and Kelly wonder how decomposers break down plant material and how they "eat" it. To answer their question, they employ reciprocal teaching—a way for students to discuss text together and a way to create and answer questions. Ms. Cruz provides them with a text that details the behaviors of decomposers and the process of decomposition.

Using Reciprocal Teaching

Reciprocal teaching is a tool for instruction that provides an opportunity for a small group of students, usually four, to read and discuss a text in a structured and organized manner. As groups of four students reciprocally teach each other to read a science passage, teachers call on them to apply the strategies of (1) *questioning* the text as they ask each other literal and inferential questions about what they are reading, (2) *clarifying* a confusing point by checking the glossary together or consulting a less difficult source that will support their understanding of a word or a concept, (3) *summarizing* what they have learned, and using their base of knowledge to support (4) *predicting* what they can anticipate. Schools widely use this well-researched instructional routine (Palincsar & Brown, 1986).

Modeling to Support Learning

Just as with most other information that you want students to learn, you may need to begin by modeling the expected performance. You'll want to model and then practice each role separately. For example, with reciprocal teaching, after you have modeled each of the four roles, you may want to form a fishbowl in which four students perform the roles as the others watch. Follow this with a series of practice sessions that you support through guided instruction as you listen in and coach the groups until they can function independently.

To ensure that students have the language to support their initial conversations during practice, you may find it helpful to supply them with cue cards similar to those in figure 4.8 (page 170). These cues will support students in performing each role.

To make a PREDICTION I look for clues that will help me to:
- Bet
- Decide
- Conclude
- Determine what will happen or what I will learn next

When I SUMMARIZE, I think about:
- The main ideas, people, events, and words
- How to remember only these important facts

I CLARIFY and clear up confusion by:
- Rereading
- Slowing down my pace
- Determining which part is confusing me
- Looking closely at information in the graphs and charts
- Thinking about how the words sound and what they mean
- Reviewing my predictions to see if they still hold
- Seeking outside help

Figure 4.8: Sample cue cards.

The goal is that, eventually, each student will become skilled at performing each of the roles, because each represents a strategy of skilled readers.

By reviewing the text to determine answers to questions, students like Marisol, Heather, and Kelly are learning to attend to details and to synthesize ideas. This careful attention to each segment of the text supports the building of the background knowledge and language the students need to continue their successful engagement with the text. Many teachers like this instructional routine, because it can accommodate the whole class as well as small-group structures.

Questions for Discussion or Reflection

1. How will you model questioning for students?

2. What resources will you provide to promote questioning? Intriguing photos? Quotes from texts?

3. How do text-based questions connect to the CCSS and to the NGSS?

4. Which grade-level NGSS and CCSS does your instruction address?

Instructional Practice That Supports Scientific Investigation

The very intentional instruction the teachers in the scenarios in this chapter were implementing was designed to help students "become part of society's science conversations by using real-world applications of science in instruction and by inviting students to discuss and debate relevant and motivating content" (Grant & Lapp, 2011). They believe that in order to develop their students' critical scientific literacy abilities, they have to engage their interests and allow their motivation to spur their language and literacy learning, knowledge expansion, and refined skills of inquiry. They also know their students began an investigation with a range of language, ideas, and concepts about the topic. They understand that their students' levels of expertise are based on their prior experiences, not on their individual potential to learn science. They also believe "the most important single factor influencing learning is what the learner already knows; ascertain this and teach him accordingly" (Ausubel, 1968, p. 149). If teachers don't motivate students and begin with what they already know, the new content learning will be overwhelming. This is true as students learn in each of the content areas.

Students' ability to read, write, and think about literature adds to their comprehension of the content areas of math, science, and social studies. Acknowledging that everyone can learn and then continuously assessing students' bases of introductory and developing knowledge and language help teachers continually make decisions about the materials they select and the instruction they design. Such teachers consider the processes involved in comprehending a text, as well as the instructional routines that support students' reading and learning from myriad texts.

Throughout the remainder of this chapter we emphasize the relationship that must exist among vocabulary, reading with fluency, and comprehension as students encounter texts across the disciplines. While doing so, we will continually re-emphasize that in order to learn science well and to do so independently, students must be engaged, have appropriate bases of knowledge and language, be exposed to many texts they can closely read to learn, and be supported through intentional instruction in doing so.

Comprehending Science Texts

As we've noted throughout this chapter, the ability to comprehend and critically respond to a text is initially dependent on one's background knowledge and language about the topic. One's ability to decode and assign meaning to words with a level of fluency further supports comprehension. For detailed information regarding the process and the teaching of decoding, see Diane Lapp, James Flood, Cynthia Brock, and Douglas Fisher (2007) and D. S. Strickland (2011).

Fluency

Enjoy reading the following passage about electricity.

> There are two types of circuits. You can identify each by determining how many conducting paths are available. In a *series circuit*, there is one path. An electrochemical reaction in the battery causes energy to flow through the conducting path to the device that is receiving the energy. The device might be a lightbulb or a toaster. When the zinc rod of the battery comes in contact with the acid material inside the battery, the acid eats away at the zinc. This releases electrons that can move through the wire till they eventually combine with hydrogen on the carbon rod. This flow of electrons is electricity. In a *parallel circuit*, there is more than one conducting path. If a bulb burns out in a particular conducting path of a parallel circuit, it is possible for the remaining conducting paths to continue to carry electrical current from battery to bulbs.

Now that you've finished, please answer these questions.

1. What is the difference between parallel and series circuits?
2. What devices might be wired as parallel circuits?
3. Can you describe the path of energy flow in a circuit?

How well did you do? If readers have difficulty reading this passage, it may be because of insufficient background knowledge and language. Did you notice that because of your limited background knowledge and language you were also unable to read with much fluency? Even though you could decode the words, you were still unable to comprehend the passage. Proficient readers who are comprehending do so without much effort, because they have the background knowledge and language. They are not struggling. They are able to apply the strategies needed to move through the text while gaining increasing knowledge.

Being provided with or placed in a text that can be read fluently means that the reader can rapidly and efficiently use the context and syntax to automatically decode and understand the language. Karen Broaddus and Jo Worthy (2001) state, "In order to be truly fluent, a reader must comprehend and interpret text and read with appropriate timing, expressiveness, stress, and intonation" (p. 335). Fluency is enhanced when students are placed in texts that complement their growing independence as readers.

Comprehension may be jeopardized if the reader does not have the necessary base of knowledge or has to expend too much attention trying to decode or understand unfamiliar language. Once students are placed in texts that they can read fluently and are supported through shared readings with their teacher, repeated readings alone or with their peers, wide reading, and intentional instruction designed to teach them how to apply their reading strategies through word recognition, their fluency, bases of language and knowledge, and subsequent comprehension will increase.

The assessment in figure 4.9 provides a snapshot of what oral reading fluency looks like. Camille Blachowicz, Diane Sullivan, and Char Cieply (2001) offer one way to quickly assess the reader's fluency when reading a specific text. To determine if a student can read the classroom science text or any other topically related text, invite him or her to orally read for one minute. As the student reads, note any words miscalled or skipped. Subtract this number from the total number of words read, and you will be able to determine who can independently read each text. This knowledge will help you plan both homogeneous and heterogeneous reading groups. A reproducible form of figure 4.9 can be found on page 208 and online.

Student Name	Name of Text	Grade Level	Oral Reading Rate (Words per Minute)
Mike	*From Seed to Plant* (second grade text exemplar from the CCSS ELA, appendix B)	2	65
Anna	*From Seed to Plant*	2	70
William	*From Seed to Plant*	2	67

Figure 4.9: Snapshot of oral reading fluency.

Notice that all three of these students are reading the same text with approximately the same rate of fluency. A teacher could work with these three either individually or as a small group to develop their fluency so that it does not interfere with their comprehension. One strategy that works well to develop fluency is the Neurological Impress Method (Heckleman, 1966, 1969), which involves a teacher and student simultaneously reading a text. Over time the student imitates the fluency being modeled by the teacher. You may wish to view a YouTube video on this subject (search "Neurological Impress Method [N.I.M.]" or visit **go.solution-tree .com/commoncore**).

Now reread the following passage about electricity and notice if your comprehension is better.

> A circuit has a conducting path, usually made of wire, and is hooked up to a battery and a lightbulb, a toaster, or maybe even a hair dryer. This allows electricity to flow. There are two types of circuits. In a *series circuit*, there is one path. A chemical reaction in the battery causes energy to flow through the conducting path to the lightbulb, toaster, or hair dryer that is receiving the energy. Inside the battery, the chemical reaction produces charged particles called *electrons*. The electrons can move through the wire to a lightbulb or toaster. This flow of electrons is *electricity*. In a *parallel circuit*, there is more than one conducting path. If a bulb burns out in one path of a parallel circuit, the other paths could still carry electricity. Holiday lights are usually wired in parallel so that one burnt bulb doesn't cause all the lights in the strand to go out.

Were you able to comprehend more than you did the first time? If so, why is this? It's because it's your second reading, you are getting more familiar with the language and topic, and it's written at a level that complements an entry-level base of knowledge and language. Because you and the text are better matched, you are able to more fluently read the passage. You were making sense of the text and *growing* your conceptual and language bases of knowledge. When students make sense of text and grow their conceptual and language bases of knowledge, reading does not end. Rather, with the help of very skilled teachers, they have a starting point for science reading. The Common Core Reading standards emphasize the importance of the teacher in teaching students to read complex texts.

By emphasizing required achievements, the standards leave room for teachers, curriculum developers, and states to determine how those goals should be reached and what additional topics classroom instruction should address. Thus, the standards do not mandate such things as a particular writing process or the full range of metacognitive strategies that students may need to monitor and direct their thinking and learning. Teachers are thus free to provide students with whatever tools and knowledge their professional judgment and experience identify as most helpful for meeting the goals set out in the standards. While the NGSS provide more specific direction for teachers in terms of content, the specific ways in which content may be accessed are left to the instructor. Given this, science-based instruction rooted in the NGSS that draws on reading, writing, listening, and speaking, as noted in the CCSS, provides the perfect opportunity for students to negotiate meaning and internalize content. Such content delivery can be engaging and thought provoking and is an ideal springboard for problem solving, collaborative endeavors, and engineering design.

Vocabulary

The more language one understands and uses, the more information one comprehends when reading. This is certainly true when reading a science text. Many wonderful books offer in-depth examples regarding how to teach vocabulary in general. Two of those we recommend have been compiled by Isabel Beck, Margaret McKeown, and Linda Kucan (2008) and Danny Brassell (2011).

In the next section, we share the application of a few vocabulary practices that we find work well to develop the language needed to read science texts. We suggest using these after applying the following considerations for word selection (Fisher & Frey, 2008b):

- Is the selected word representative of a base word from which many others can be derived (such as *dilute*, *dilutes*, *diluted*, and *diluting*)? If so, it is highly useful.

- Is the word going to be repeated often in the text or in other learning experiences? If so, it has wide transportability and would be useful to know (*hypothesize*, *prediction*).

- Is the word best taught through analyzing the context in which it appears? (For example, "An *atom* is a small unit of matter. It is composed of electrons, protons, and neutrons.")

- Is the word best taught through analyzing the affixes (prefixes and suffixes) of its structure (*reorganizing*, *postdating*)?

- Is the word a burden on the cognitive load of the student? The answer is yes if too many words or too many difficult words are being presented at once.

To make these decisions, you would need to have assessed the background knowledge of the students.

Once teachers have selected the words, one efficient way to support vocabulary instruction is to ask students to assess their own knowledge of the words that they will encounter in the science materials they will be reading as they explore a particular topic. Figure 4.10 shows a self-assessment chart containing the targeted words for study as students explore the topic of weather. A blank reproducible form of this figure may be found on page 209 and online. A student's responses help identify the vocabulary words that need to be taught and learned.

Vocabulary Term	Know Definition	Know an Example	Don't Know Either Yet	Definition	Example
Clouds	X			Fluffy, white puff balls that float in the sky	
Precipitation		X			Rain
Evaporation		X			Boiling water on the stove
Condensation			X		
Weather		X			Rain, snow, hot, cold, sunny, cloudy

Figure 4.10: Sample self-assessment chart.

Using this measure before beginning a topic of study helps to introduce the student to the targeted words. You may also want to administer it at the end to allow the student to see all the language that he or she has learned. This also provides one additional summative evaluation assessment.

If you believe the students may know a word but not know how to read it, you may want to read each word to them and then pause while they add their responses. There may be science words such as *electric, magnetic, force,* or *temperature* that they have heard but cannot yet pronounce. Also, invite students to add illustrations to support their definitions and examples. Remind them that scientists often add visuals to their charts. As students complete their assessments, encourage them to understand that there are degrees of knowing a word.

Some other words within topics that you might choose to have students self-assess include the following:

- Grade K
    - Physical science—*color, size, shape,* and *weight*
    - Life science—*stem, leaf, root, wing,* and *leg*
    - Earth and space science—*land, air, water, mountain, ocean, river,* and *valley*
- Grade 1
    - Physical science—*solid, liquid, gas,* and *property*
    - Life science—*plant, animal, shelter,* and *environment*
    - Earth and space science—*sun, thermometer, observation,* and *season*
- Grade 2
    - Physical science—*force, push, pull,* and *motion*
    - Life science—*offspring, reproduce,* and *organism*
    - Earth and space science—*rock, weathering, texture,* and *property*
- Grade 3
    - Physical science—*energy, heat, sound, light, wave,* and *electric current*
    - Life science—*structure, function, growth, reproduction, survival,* and *change*
    - Earth and space science—*stars, moon, lunar cycle, planets,* and *orbit*
- Grade 4
    - Physical science—*battery, bulb, wire, series circuit,* and *parallel circuit*

- Life science—*energy, matter, consumer, producer, decomposer,* and *ecosystem*
- Earth and space science—*igneous, sedimentary, metamorphic, mineral,* and *property*
- Grade 5
    - Physical science—*chemical reaction, reactant, product, atom,* and *property*
    - Life science—*multicellular, heart, lungs, digestive system, respiration,* and *waste*
    - Earth and space science—*evaporation, condensation, water vapor, forecast, variables, atmosphere,* and *predict*
- Grade 6
    - Physical science—*reactivity, vibration, disturbance, solubility,* and *conductivity*
    - Life science—*reproduction, organ system, internal structure, external structure,* and *variation*
    - Earth and space science—*earthquake, volcano, midocean ridge, lithosphere, epicenter, transportation, deposition, erode, conduction, convection, radiation, pressure, photosynthesis, biotic, abiotic, resource, renewable,* and *nonrenewable*

Now let's consider a few additional instructional practices that support vocabulary learning and work well in the science classroom. We have already explored semantic feature analysis (page 90); a reproducible chart for use in semantic feature analysis can be found on page 210 and online. Next we look at content-area word walls and sentence frames, shades of meaning, word cards, and semantic maps.

Content-Area Word Walls and Sentence Frames

To ensure that students have easy access to science language, you should designate a place in your classroom to display the content words being studied. Just as students "read the room" during English language arts study, they should additionally read the science words during science study. If your space is limited, you can attach these words to coat hangers or hang them on a clothesline or wire in one part of the room (figure 4.11). Consider posting two word walls—one with academic words (like *investigate, hypothesize, cause,* and *effect*) and one with relevant technical science terms (like *evaporation, weather,* and *precipitation*). This will augment the understanding that there are two components to the language of science—(1) academic, scholarly language and (2) precise technical terms. Students need both to successfully read, write, and speak the language of science.

Students should have consistent interaction with the terms on the science word wall. Teachers should encourage them to use the words in their writing and language. Students and teachers should collaborate to create the word wall and share sentence frames that include terms and phrases commonly seen in science reading. We have also seen teachers in many of the scenarios throughout the text use language frames to support students' use of academic language in their conversations and writing language. Students can use these frames to support their partner conversations, such as the ones we explored in Mr. Hubbard's classroom (page 137).

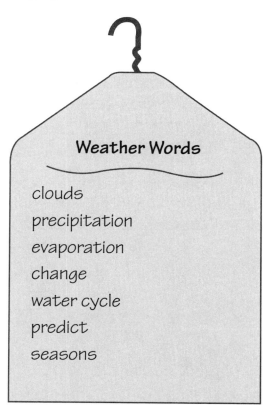

Figure 4.12 (page 180) shows how the words from the word wall can become sentence frames for second graders.

Figure 4.11: Sample word wall using a coat hanger.

Figure 4.13 (page 181) shows how the same words become more sophisticated in conversations in a grade 5 weather unit.

Shades of Meaning

Shades of meaning is another instructional practice that works well to support vocabulary learning (L. Goodman, 2004). This practice supports students in understanding the subtle differences among a set of conceptually related words. When reading or discussing science, subtle differences can make a significant difference. For example, a *light* wind moves at a speed of two to ten kilometers an hour. A *moderate* wind has a speed of thirteen to thirty kilometers an hour, and a *fresh* wind is between thirty-one and forty kilometers an hour. Clearly an understanding of the specific meanings of the terms *light*, *moderate*, and *fresh* is

Sentence Frames

Complete the sentence by adding your own ideas based on what you've learned in class.

Clouds are seen in _____.

Precipitation is seen as _____.

I've noticed **evaporation** when _____.

Water can change from ice to _____.

The **water cycle** shows us that water in a puddle can _____.

I **predict** that the weather tomorrow will be _____.

During the winter and fall **seasons** we see _____.

Figure 4.12: Sample grade 2 sentence frames for weather word wall.

critical. They each indicate a characteristic of wind, but their specific meanings and resultant implications are quite different.

Teachers invite students to talk about the differences in meaning among the words. To begin, list the target words on the board, then invite teams of three to five students to talk about the subtle differences and then to list their thinking along a continuum that shows the meaning variation. Have students show their thinking on colored paint strips with the strongest shade of color indicating the strongest definition of the word. If no paint strips are available, you can make a chart for students to complete. As shown in figure 4.14, the students can list their arrangement of terms in the left column and their definitions in the right. A third column allows them to add a graphic that they think describes their gradation.

Scientists tend to use very precise words to convey specific meaning about a concept or idea. This is a hallmark of science writing and discussions. Practicing

Sentence Frames

Complete the sentence by adding your own ideas based on what you've learned in class.

Clouds formed in the atmosphere indicate that _____.

Precipitation occurs when _____.

The process of **evaporation** occurs as _____.

Water can **change** from _____.

The **water cycle** shows how water _____.

Weather forecasters **predict** _____.

We notice **seasons** when _____.

Figure 4.13: Sample grade 5 sentence frames for weather word wall.

Term	What It Means	Graphic
Downpour	Very heavy rain	Heavy
Showers	Heavy but short rainstorm	
Rain	Water falling from the sky	↓
Drizzle	Low intensity, continuous rainfall	
Sprinkle	Very light rainfall	Light

Figure 4.14: Sample shades of meaning chart.

shades of meaning guides students to consider the exact meaning of a science term within the scope of other similar, yet different, words. Students gain a deeper knowledge of science vocabulary—one that will support both quality science writing and astute science conversations.

Word Cards

Focusing for a few minutes on a few selected words supports learning their meanings. After you, students, or both have selected the words, you can place them on a 5 × 7 blank card. The example shown in figure 4.15 uses the Frayer word card model, which contains the target word in the center, surrounded by a definition, an illustration, and examples and nonexamples. These may be written as words, as sentences, or a combination of both. A teacher should choose words that are needed for reading about the content. Words that can be determined through structural analysis or through examination of word parts are not good choices for word cards. Instead, teachers should select words that are challenging and essential to understanding the content. This will support reading comprehension. The important feature is that the cards are student created and that they support the student in remembering the meaning and using the word.

Other word cards can be created and then sorted into categories. Donald Bear, Marcia Invernizzi, Shane Templeton, and Francine Johnston (2007) refer to these as *closed sorts*, in which the teacher determines the categories that students will use to sort their cards; *open sorts*, in which the students determine the categories themselves and then sort cards; and *conceptual sorts*, which involve sorting according to a category. As students sort, teachers can easily assess their understanding of the information represented by the words or phrases being sorted. For example, after studying the periodic table, including concepts related to metals and nonmetals, in a fifth-grade class, the teacher might ask students to sort the following words into their appropriate categories of metals or nonmetals: *silver, gold, aluminum, hydrogen, oxygen, copper, sulfur,* and *nitrogen*.

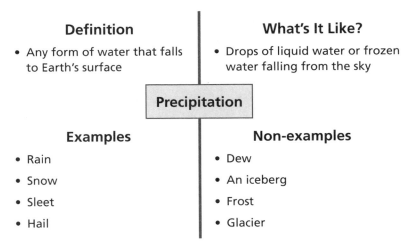

Figure 4.15: Sample Frayer word card.

Semantic Maps

Like the other vocabulary study activities we've shared, semantic maps support learning because they provide a visual dimension of the content (Robinson, 1998; Wood, Lapp, Flood, & Taylor, 2008). Students can be provided with either a partial or blank map, which they complete as they interact with the text. Doing so supports their close attention to the organization of concepts, facts, and details found in the text. Figure 4.16 is an example of a semantic map that was created as students studied the topic of precipitation, focusing on rain. See also the reproducible "Semantic Analysis Map" (page 211).

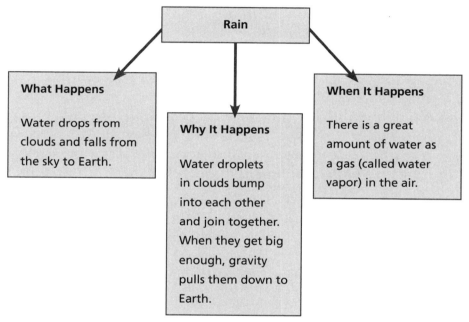

Figure 4.16: Sample semantic analysis map on rain.

As we previously mentioned, there are many wonderful books on the hows and whys of teaching vocabulary. Our intention here was to select a few vocabulary practices that you might use to assess students' knowledge of targeted words and support their learning them. These practices illustrate the importance of student involvement with the visual and oral dimensions of learning vocabulary. Because word knowledge directly influences what a learner comprehends when reading (Flood, Lapp, Mraz, & Wood, 2006), the time devoted to vocabulary instruction and learning must be very intentionally designed and shared in ways that support oracy, reading, and writing literacy across the content areas.

Being able to successfully comprehend myriad science sources means that the reader is able to fluidly and recursively process individual letters and their associated sounds, use this information to recognize and understand the words in the text, and then automatically move from word to full-text processing and comprehension. Applying these reading processes does not happen as a hierarchical arrangement. Rather, teachers combine, bundle, and apply them as needed. As we have discussed, intentional instruction that is based on a continuous assessment of students' strengths and needs supports each student in developing these processes. Intentional instruction occurs when teachers implement a plan that involves engaging students and supporting their explorations while modeling and guiding learning. The primary goal of intentional instruction is that students become collaborative yet independent in their continuing pursuits of knowledge.

Instructional Routines

We have shared many instructional routines such as ReQuest and reciprocal teaching that provide a context for students to blend literacy and science learning. A proficient reader of science is one who knows what to do when he or she experiences difficulty while reading. Such students know when to adjust their pace; when to pause to sound out a new word; and how to use context, word structure, or an alternative source to figure out the word that is interfering with their comprehension (Baker & Brown, 1984).

In all of the shared routines, students compare, summarize, and analyze information they are encountering as they read across science sources. They also predict and hypothesize possible solutions to both self- and text-initiated problems. Along the way, they gain the literacy skills needed to understand and communicate about the scientific phenomena they encounter daily.

Jigsaw is a grouping arrangement that accommodates the whole class reading multiple segments of one source or several topically related sources (Aronson, Stephen, Sikes, Blaney, & Snapp, 1978). Reading the identified text or texts occurs as students work in two group configurations: the *home group* and the *expert group*. Each student moves from the home group to an expert group. In this reconfiguration, students are referred to as experts, because they are studying one segment of the text, problem, issue, or other concern. After each expert group has achieved mastery, the students return to their home groups, and each member shares what he or she learned while in the expert groups. Before students participate in this routine, the teacher models the anticipated behaviors of each group.

To begin jigsaw, the teacher identifies a task. For example, a second-grade class might be studying about solids, liquids, and gases and what happens when they are heated, cooled, or mixed. This topic correlates with NGSS 2-PS1-4,

"Construct an argument with evidence that some changes caused by heating or cooling can be reversed and some cannot" (Achieve, 2013a, p. 13).

Students' tasks would be to identify the properties of each type of matter. For example, students might note, "Solids have a definite shape" or "Liquids can take on the shape of the container in which they are placed." Then, they would include a visual description of the structure of atoms for each type of matter. Students might say, "Solids have atoms that vibrate in place" or "Gases have atoms that can freely move past each other throughout the container." They will also tell what happens when each is heated, cooled, or mixed with another type of matter. It is common to expect statements like "Liquids, like water, change to solids when cooled."

This activity would involve six expert groups. Students in group one identify the properties of solids; group two looks at liquids; group three focuses on gases; group four notes what happens to solids when they are heated, cooled, and mixed; group five explores what happens to liquids when they are heated, cooled, and mixed; and group six examines what happens to gases when they are heated, cooled, and mixed. The science text may be the first source of information, but if some questions are still unanswered even after combing through the textbook, students would need to access other types of texts or media. Students might be directed to an online animation that shows how heating causes melting or to a trade book that looks at the crystalline structure of solids (Bayrock, 2007).

A fourth-grade class might be studying about energy as the students investigate NGSS 4-ESS3-1, "Obtain and combine information to describe that energy and fuels are derived from natural resources and their uses affect the environment" (Achieve, 2013a, p. 23). Their tasks would be to document how the following fuels are produced and how they can be used in the real world: oil, natural gas, and coal. Students will also investigate hydroelectric power, nuclear power, and wind power. A single group of students would become expert in one of these areas of energy and fuel as they explore the topic. Six expert groups could be formed—each with expertise in one area of the topic.

Next, the teacher identifies the appropriate section of the class science text. Since this is often the one text that all students share, it is very appropriate to begin with it. Since this source is often too difficult for some students to read, it is very fitting to have other related sources available for team members to share. You would identify these before the home groups meet. Then, if students are using one source, you should chunk it into subsections and number it. The number of students in a home group should match the number of subsections in the designated text. Simultaneously, students are clustered into home groups. You assign each member of the home group a number that corresponds with a subsection of the selected text segment. Groups should select a team leader who serves as the contact person. Again, if the science text as a first source of information doesn't have all the concepts that the students desire or need, other sources, including online sources like BrainPOP or the BBC science website, may be able to provide them. We have found that before the home group moves into the expert groups, it is important that the students preview the text together. This provides each home group member with a context of the entire text. This is very important, particularly when students are reading science material, and especially for those who will be reading a section of text that is not closer to the beginning. While previewing, we also encourage students in the home group to set expectations about what they are hoping to learn from each subsection. Often the leader of each group—a student who is identified by the teacher—can initiate identifying an initial expectation. Because of the range of home group expectations brought to the task, allowing time for initial home group previewing makes the conversations that occur in the expert groups much richer. To ensure that the students know how to function efficiently in the home groups, the teacher needs to model how to preview the text, set expectations, and convey the importance of each member's participation.

Once home groups have concluded previewing the text, you can form expert groups. An expert group has all of the students who had a particular number in the home group. For example all those who read section one become expert members of group one, those who read section two become expert members of group two, and so on. The numbers of home and expert groups always correspond, but the initial number may vary because of the length of a text being studied. If the students are reading multiple sources instead of subdividing one, home and expert groups operate in the same way. To recap, you select and number the sources; the home groups meet and number off according to which source each will read; you preview the activity and set some general purposes; and then the students move into expert groups.

Once in an expert group, each member reads his or her designated subsection or source. As a group, students then discuss it to ensure that they have mastered a rich and similar understanding. Each expert group also discusses how to share information with his or her home team so that it will be understood, remembered, and connected to the identified whole. The groups may decide to prepare a visual that supports their presentation of the information. Once the experts have completed their work, they return to their home teams, where each expert now presents to other home team members. As the teacher has previously modeled, the group leader should encourage home team members to question and clarify the information in order to formulate an understanding of the whole.

The role of every student is significant since understanding each segment or source is essential to developing a full understanding of the entire text and theme. Because each student is depending on the others to add information that completes the informational puzzle, all students listen very carefully, converse, question, clarify, and synthesize and summarize information along the way. Figure 4.17 provides a visual of the jigsaw routine.

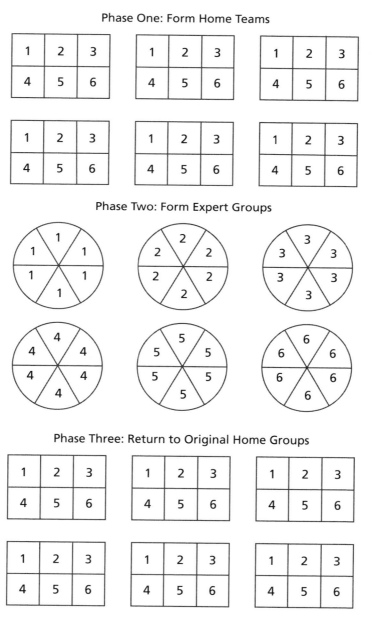

Figure 4.17: Jigsaw grouping.

Other classroom routines also promote the reading comprehension and social engagement of students as they explore a science topic through related sources. We have chosen to share reciprocal teaching, ReQuest, and jigsaw because of the numerous cognitive processes that students are called on to use while participating and their potential for developing the language of science through collaboration. Processes such as predicting, questioning, clarifying, synthesizing, and evaluating, which are consistently and continuously developed during these routines, are transportable to the next period of the school day when students encounter the reading of another content text. We have also shared these routines, as well as the other instructional practices in this chapter, because each offers a rich language and social component, which complements the social and collaborative nature of science exploration through engagement, examination, and communication while addressing the literacy focus of the CCSS. Additionally, these routines support content reading and experimentation because of the collaborative nature of the tasks. When students have the opportunity to read together, question each other, and discuss ideas, they are better equipped to delve deeply into the content of the NGSS.

Capitalizing on Students' Curiosities

From students' earliest years, their curiosity and creativity easily offer parents and teachers a natural starting place for scientific exploration. Questions like "Why do my fingers and toes wrinkle in water?" and "What makes my hair grow?" that young students often pose can be explored through picture books and conversations. Questions like these present the foundations for developing well-scaffolded scientific understanding through the grades. The result is that students develop a strong base of knowledge about core concepts, such as the structure, function, growth, and development of organisms, as noted in the NGSS (Achieve, 2013a).

The CCSS are scaffolded across grades to make obvious the incremental changes that should occur in literacy skill development in social studies, science, and technical subjects as students move through the grades. The design of the NGSS accommodates and extends this learning because the NGSS add the scientific specificity that identifies for teachers the topics and incremental changes in growth that must occur across the grades if individuals are to be considered scientifically literate. For example, the familiar topic of *force* is presented to kindergarteners as they learn about pushes and pulls. In third grade, students look at balanced and unbalanced forces and at electric and magnetic forces. In fifth grade, teachers guide instruction toward the topic of gravitational force. Throughout all of these grades the concept of force is explored with increasingly greater depth and is even revisited in middle and high school. Let's consider a lesson in kindergarten as students are taught "to compare the effects of different strengths or different directions of pushes and pulls on the motion of an object" (Achieve, 2013a, p. 5). They learn this by pushing and pulling toy cars and wagons and by accessing informational texts, like the book *Pushes and Pulls* by Claire Llewellyn (2003). Such informational text provides the springboard from which students discuss and share ideas about forces. Through such instruction, students not only address the NGSS, they also accomplish CCSS RL.K.10, which requires students in kindergarten to "actively engage in group reading activities with purpose and understanding" (NGA & CCSSO, 2010a, p. 11). The CCSS simply add the literacy dimension to the NGSS.

The outcome should be the acquisition of information that results in students having a well-developed understanding of identified NGSS scientific core concepts. These may include such topics as matter and its interactions, motion and stability, Earth's place in the universe, and Earth and human activity. While the examples in this chapter address many segments of the Common Core Reading anchor standards, the primary focus of the instruction is to develop students' reading skills well enough to enable them to "read and comprehend complex literary and informational texts independently and proficiently" (CCRA.R.10; NGA & CCSSO, 2010a, p. 10). The examples also illustrate how to integrate the NGSS scientific principles and practices as students engage in:

- Questioning
- Predicting and making claims
- Scrutinizing evidence
- Sharing reasoned arguments to defend their informational stances

Accomplishing the blending of literacy and scientific practice will happen over time as students become immersed each day in reading challenging yet engaging science materials and receiving instruction that supports their doing so.

CHAPTER 5

Empowering Students to Think Like Scientists

Purposeful instruction involves continually reviewing and revising a plan of action designed to accommodate growth in student learning. Alterations to instructional plans result from an ongoing assessment of each student's performance as related to predetermined goals that are aligned with state and national standards. Assessments of performance are collected as teachers listen to students' answers to questions and to their conversations with peers, read their written work, and observe multiple other forms of presentation of their thinking. While varied, students' performances offer teachers opportunities to assess what is being learned and what additional instruction needs to occur. Insightful teachers link learning, instruction, and assessment for each student.

Interest in the assessment of science performance among students in the United States continues to be of major concern since the publication of findings from the 2009 Programme for International Student Assessment (PISA; National Center for Education Statistics, 2009), which compared the performance in reading, math, and science literacy of fifteen-year-old students in the United States with students of the same age from sixty-five countries. When compared with students in the thirty-four member countries that represent the Organisation for Economic Co-operation and Development (OECD), findings indicate that U.S. students performed about average in reading, with a ranking of fourteenth; average in science, with a ranking of seventeenth; and below average in math, with a ranking of twenty-fifth. While these scores do show increases from PISA studies conducted in 2003 and 2006, the 2009 U.S. scores lagged behind other leading countries, such as South Korea, Singapore, China (Hong Kong and Shanghai), Finland, and Canada.

As alarming were the findings from the 2009 National Assessment of Educational Progress (NAEP) that concluded that only 34 percent of fourth graders, 30 percent of eighth graders, and 21 percent of twelfth graders were performing at or above the proficient level in science (National Assessment Governing Board, 2008). A small percentage (1–2 percent) at each grade scored at the advanced level, while large numbers of students at each grade level did not perform at the most basic level. Additionally, data from the *Nation's Report Card* (NAEP, 2011a) assessment indicate that understanding vocabulary significantly affects one's reading success. Fourth- and eighth-grade students with high scores on the vocabulary assessment performed above the seventy-fifth percentile in reading comprehension. This held true for twelfth graders on the 2009 assessment. These findings weigh heavily on educators as they attempt to engage students in collaborative conversations and scientific readings that require knowing and using the language of science and as they try to prepare them to live, work, and lead in a global economy.

Educators are feeling a sense of urgency about teaching science in ways that, over time, build the core concepts of science. The NGSS are a testament to this urgency, and fortunately, with the publication of these standards, educators have not only core ideas but also a sense of direction in terms of crosscutting concepts and science and engineering practices. Teachers must make scientific thinking visible—visible enough that all students will acquire the thinking, language, and skills that support scientific practice in their lives.

Sharing these concerns, the President's Council of Advisors on Science and Technology (2010) report begins:

> The success of the United States in the 21st century—its wealth and welfare—will depend on the ideas and skills of its population. These have always been the Nation's most important assets. As the world becomes increasingly technological, the value of these national assets will be determined in no small measure by the effectiveness of science, technology, engineering, and mathematics (STEM) education in the United States. STEM education will determine whether the United States will remain a leader among nations and whether we will be able to solve immense challenges in such areas as energy, health, environmental protection, and national security. It will help produce the capable and flexible workforce needed to compete in a global marketplace. It will ensure our society continues to make fundamental discoveries and to advance our understanding of ourselves, our planet, and the universe. It will generate the scientists, technologists, engineers, and mathematicians who will create the new ideas, new products, and entirely new industries of the 21st century. It will provide the technical skills and quantitative literacy needed for individuals to earn livable wages and make better decisions for themselves, their families,

and their communities. And it will strengthen our democracy by preparing all citizens to make informed choices in an increasingly technological world. (p. vii)

The next section of the report, "Troubling Signs," states:

Despite our historical record of achievement, the United States now lags behind other nations in STEM education at the elementary and secondary levels. International comparisons of our students' performance in science and mathematics consistently place the United States in the middle of the pack or lower. (pp. vii–viii)

The council, noting that many students determine early in their lives that they are not interested in pursuing careers in science and math, attribute the problem to a lack of clear standards:

What lies behind mediocre test scores and the pervasive lack of interest in STEM is also troubling. Some of the problem, to be sure, is attributable to schools that are failing systemically; this aspect of the problem must be addressed with systemic solutions. Yet even schools that are generally successful often fall short in STEM fields. Schools often lack teachers who know how to teach science and mathematics effectively, and who know and love their subject well enough to inspire their students. Teachers lack adequate support, including appropriate professional development as well as interesting and intriguing curricula. School systems lack tools for assessing progress and rewarding success. The Nation lacks clear, shared standards for science and math that would help all actors in the system set and achieve goals. (p. 4)

In its February 2012 report, the President's Council of Advisors on Science and Technology identifies what needs to happen in schools to better prepare U.S. students in science and technology. Although the report identifies five points that specifically address college education, we believe the first two points—(1) instructional practice should be research supported and (2) science learning should involve discovery learning—relate very significantly to the kind of instruction that should occur in K–6 classrooms. We believe that accomplishment of these two points can occur through instruction that involves teachers monitoring whether their instruction reflects the CCSS and NRC framework and whether that intention is felt by students and manifested in the resultant learning that takes place for every student. If so, a student should be able to succeed in acquiring scientific practices that thoroughly blend science (knowing) and engineering (doing science), thus meeting the instructional intentions of the NGSS, and will exhibit the characteristics of a scientifically literate person. As the CCSS note, a student who is scientifically literate:

- Demonstrates independence by comprehending and evaluating complex scientific texts with the intent being to "construct effective arguments and convey intricate or multifaceted information" (NGA & CCSSO, 2010a, p. 7)

- Builds strong content knowledge through research and study as he or she reads "purposefully and listen[s] attentively to gain both general knowledge and discipline-specific expertise" (NGA & CCSSO, 2010a, p. 7) that can be shared through speaking and writing

- Adapts his or her "communication to the varying demands of audience, task, purpose, and discipline" (NGA & CCSSO, 2010a, p. 7)

- Comprehends as well as critiques "the veracity of claims and the soundness of reasoning" (NGA & CCSSO, 2010a, p. 7)

- Uses "technology and digital media strategically and capably to support [his or her] communication goals" (NGA & CCSSO, 2010a, p. 7)

- Understands "other perspectives and cultures" (NGA & CCSSO, 2010a, p. 7) in order to work with and learn from a global network

The CCSS offer a parallel view of the characteristics that a scientifically literate person embodies, according to Sarah Michaels et al. (2008)—namely, the ability to (1) *understand* scientific explanations that are presented through many interconnected formats, (2) *generate* scientific evidence to think and talk about as new questions are continually identified, (3) *reflect* on one's accumulating knowledge and the validity of the evidence one is finding from investigation, and (4) interactively *communicate* one's thinking through evidence and argument.

As the instructional examples shared in chapters 2–4 indicate, we believe the best way to ensure that scientifically literate students are graduating from U.S. schools is to use these four broad characteristics to guide instruction from the very earliest stages of learning. Related formative assessments along the way should support teachers in knowing what instructional adjustments need to be made in order to guarantee that these characteristics become the foundations of each student's scientific practice. Through continuous assessment teachers are able to determine whether or not students are acquiring the information and skills they need to achieve predetermined goals and, if not, what changes need to be made to the instruction.

Formative Assessment: Reflecting to Feed Forward

Checking students' understanding often and systematically provides data about the learning that is occurring. Acting as snapshots of performance, a systematic collection of information helps the teacher assess the students' performance and the instructional techniques. Assessment information is then used to make decisions about the subsequent instruction, reteaching, and interventions that need to occur (Lapp et al., 2007). This decision-making process and consequent instruction are often referred to as *feeding forward* (Fisher & Frey, 2007).

Assessment information that provides data about learning for subsequent learning to occur is called formative assessment (Black, 1993; Ruiz-Primo & Furtak, 2006). Formative assessments can involve either formal or informal measures. Formal measures of formative assessment, which the teacher designs prior to beginning the instruction, occur in many formats, including quizzes, projects, and presentations. Informal formative assessments are not preplanned; they happen as the teacher listens to students' responses to questions or conversations during collaboration. This on-the-spot checking of understanding provides teachers with instant insights about how learning should be retaught in a new way or about what information they should teach next. Formative assessment data help teachers make informed decisions, but they also enable students to become self-assessors of their own growing banks of knowledge and skills as a way to support their individual paths to new understandings (Bransford, Brown, & Cocking, 1999; Donovan & Bransford, 2005; Fisher & Frey, 2007). In such a learning- and assessment-centered classroom, the teacher and students are continually assessing the knowledge, attitudes, beliefs, and skills being learned in order to support engagement with more challenging content and projects. Scientific practice relies on students learning to examine their ideas, premises, next questions of inquiry, and paths to their own learning over time.

By formatively assessing students' existing language and knowledge and viewing these as foundations for expansion, teachers can design very purposeful learning experiences. Also, by understanding students' preconceived ideas, teachers identify misconceptions that can be altered through well-planned instructional experiences. Instructional situations designed to scaffold learning allow time for shared dialogue or guided instruction between the teacher and students that move each student closer to learning independence. Guided instruction is the time in which teachers offer instructional prompts, cues, and questions as bridges enabling students to develop skills or concepts they do not yet independently understand or perform. Fisher and Frey (2008a) liken the instructional scaffolding that occurs during guided instruction to a detective who is watching closely for clues to support solving an investigation. Teachers who are engaging in formative assessment during guided instruction watch the learning moves of their students very closely so they can scaffold subsequent learning experiences that move each student closer to conceptual understanding and learning independence.

As exemplified by the scenarios in each chapter, learning independence is achieved through implementation of a recursive model of instruction that shifts the major responsibility from teachers motivating, questioning, modeling, guiding, coaching, and explicitly teaching to the students' independent pursuit of their learning. When this shift happens, students are able to assume primary ownership of their learning and become metacognitively aware of themselves as learners.

Formative assessments help teachers and students assess and monitor the development of one's metacognition. This involves an array of cognitive activities, including how one approaches a given learning task, how one questions, and how one monitors comprehension and attainment of the task, all while overseeing one's personal attainment of it and making alterations to the process as needed. In the assessment-centered classroom, where instruction and learning are continually scrutinized to ensure that students have every opportunity to learn scientific practice, these principles offer a foundation.

Snapshots of Classroom-Centered Formative Assessment

Effective teachers know that checking for understanding throughout instruction is critical, especially in science, a content area wrought with misconceptions and ripe for misinterpretation. Because the NGSS indicate that students should be able to ask questions; plan and carry out investigation; analyze and interpret data; obtain, evaluate, and communicate information; and construct explanations and design solutions, teachers need to engage in ongoing formative assessment to identify areas of need and strengthening in students and gaps in instruction. The CCSS ELA provide the mechanisms of reading, writing, speaking and listening, and language through which students can provide formative assessment data for their teachers to evaluate.

Let's observe a few teachers at work to better understand how formative assessment supports such scientific teaching and learning.

Knowing Where to Begin: Informal Formative Preassessment

The kindergarten students in Melissa Cunningham's class are studying the core concept of energy. As the students in groups of three conduct an experiment about sunlight and energy, Ms. Cunningham listens in to assess their levels of background knowledge and language. With this information, she will know how to support their study of the conservation of energy and energy transfer, a core disciplinary idea of the NGSS. Specifically, they are focusing on K-PS3-2: "Use tools and materials to design and build a structure that will reduce the warming effect of sunlight on an area" (Achieve, 2013a, p. 7). Sandi, a kindergartener sitting at a sunny table outside the cafeteria, notes, "The black cloth seems to heat up much more than the white one. I wonder why. They are both made of the same material."

Ms. Cunningham sees this as a perfect opportunity to capitalize on Sandi's curiosity, while simultaneously assessing her background knowledge. Ms. Cunningham uses strategic questions:

"Sandi, if it's not the material that's making the black cloth warm, what else could it be? Do you remember our story about heat and energy?"

Sandi immediately responds, "Oh yes, heat is a form of energy. Maybe the black cloth is getting more heat energy. I think the heat comes from the sun. It's always colder on a cloudy day." Noticing that Sandi is *obtaining, evaluating, and communicating information* (a NGSS science and engineering practice) and satisfied that she is on the right track to complete the lab and the upcoming picture book explorations, Ms. Cunningham moves along to listen in and assess the understanding of other students.

Knowing How to Reteach: Informal Formative Assessment

After thinking aloud about the structures and adaptations that animals have for survival, third-grade teacher Elijah Barnes listens in as students work in pairs to create a poster showing the structures three animals possess to survive in their habitats. Students are studying NGSS 3-LS4-3: "Construct an argument with evidence that in a particular habitat some organisms can survive well, some survive less well, and some cannot survive at all" (Achieve, 2013a, p. 19). Robert explains to his partner Elisa that the turtle's large shell serves as protection from predators. Elisa adds, "I love how bark bugs use camouflage to blend with the trunks of trees. I can barely tell they're there, and I'm sure no predator will be able to either."

Mr. Barnes pauses to offer a prompt, "Those are both great ideas, and they both relate to protection from predators. Can you think of other examples in which animals have certain features that help them find food or shelter?"

Elisa, thinking for a moment, cautiously replies, "Do you mean something like the long bill of the hummingbird, which you showed us in the textbook? Isn't it long so that the bird can get food from a flower easily?"

"Yes, that's exactly what I'm thinking about," replies Mr. Barnes. "You should add that one to your poster," he suggests as he walks away, satisfied that the students are now thinking about structures and adaptations in a broader, fuller sense.

Mr. Barnes's reason for offering questions, prompts, and cues is to assess his students' understanding of the concepts he has just modeled. As he circulates among the students, he is able to immediately ask questions and offer prompts to support students' continued learning.

Identifying the Next Steps: Formal Formative Assessment

In grade 6, Belinda Sanchez and her students have completed their study of the cause-and-effect relationship between resources and growth of individual organisms and the numbers of organisms in ecosystems during periods of abundant and scarce resources in order to address NGSS MS-LS2-1: "Analyze and interpret data to provide evidence for the effects of resource availability on organisms and populations of organisms in an ecosystem" (Achieve, 2013a, p. 29). She asks them to write a RAFT paragraph to illustrate their understanding of the relationship among organisms and the abundance of resources in an ecosystem. As the students do so, Ms. Sanchez discusses the scientific information they need to make their RAFTs clearer to their audiences.

David says he doesn't quite understand how populations are connected to resources. Ms. Sanchez suggests that David think about what squirrels eat. David thinks of the squirrels he saw near his house. "I think they eat acorns. Is that right?"

Ms. Sanchez confirms David's prediction and prompts, "Are squirrels the only ones who eat acorns?"

"Oh, that's easy," responds David. "Other animals eat acorns, too. I saw a bird try to steal an acorn from a squirrel."

Ms. Sanchez sees that David is making the connection now and allows him to continue his thinking. "Okay, I get it. If two animals want the same food, there might not be enough for both to survive. Only the animal that gets the food can survive." Now David has the facts he needs.

In addition to the students learning how to support their own learning, Ms. Sanchez is able to assess who understands the information well enough to begin studying the related concept regarding changes to physical or biological components of an ecosystem and how populations are affected. From their writing, she also identifies that Antonio, Grace, and Joel do not understand the flow of energy in an ecosystem. With this information she is able to engage them in an instructional intervention that involves looking at a video clip from *Nova* on energy flow in a coral reef ecosystem (PBS LearningMedia, 2007). Then students participate in partner talk in response to a discussion prompt.

As these scenarios suggest, teachers can successfully use different formative assessment techniques, whether formal or informal, to help both students and teachers make decisions about the next steps that should occur in learning and instruction. Use table 5.1 (page 200) to support making such decisions.

Understanding the Entwined Nature of Science and Literacy

Being literate in a content area presupposes that one is able to proficiently read, write, and converse (listen and speak) about the core concepts of a subject area (NGA & CCSSO, 2010a). Chapters 2–4 (pages 33–189) provide many examples of how to make the marriage between the English language arts and science a reality in your classroom. In the NGSS, science embodies "a set of practices and an accumulation of knowledge" (Achieve, 2013b, p. 1). The first two crosscutting concepts of the NGSS are fundamental to the nature of science: (1) patterns—observed patterns can be explained and (2) cause and effect—science investigates cause-and-effect relationships by seeking mechanisms that underlie them. Together with the other crosscutting concepts—(3) scale, proportion, and quantity, (4) systems and system models, (5) energy and matter, (6) structure and function, and (7) stability and change—they form the critical underpinnings of science instruction. Additionally, the need to reflect on both engineering and scientific practices—a key element of the implementation of the NGSS—is intended to deepen students' understanding of the nature of science (NRC, 2012). In essence, the intersection between the science practices, core ideas, and crosscutting concepts is intended to focus teachers and their students on "the regularities of laws, the importance of evidence, and the formulation of theories

Table 5.1: Making Informed Decisions About Learning and Teaching

Formal Measures	Next Steps for Those Who Understand	Next Steps for Those Who Don't Understand
RAFT about organisms and the abundance of resources in an ecosystem	Have students work with a partner to read about **changes to physical or biological components of an ecosystem and how populations are affected**, using ReQuest as a partner reading strategy.	Have these students watch the *Nova* video while completing a two-tabbed note guide, labeled with types of decomposers and what they do.
Energy activity	Have students brainstorm with a partner to list all the ways they use energy on a daily basis. Then read the book *Saving Energy (Help the Environment)* (Guillain, 2008). After reading, add more items to the list.	Share more examples illustrating how sunlight can be changed into heat (the interior of a car on a hot day, heating a swimming pool or lake in the summer, and so on). Read the book *Our Friend the Sun* (Palazzo, 1982) aloud to help students focus on the sun as a source of energy.
Animal structures and adaptations	In anticipation of a study of extinction, conduct a shared reading of an article about the skeleton of the dodo that was discovered in 2007. The dodo became extinct in the 1600s (Dodo, 2007).	Share pictures of various bird beaks, along with information about what the birds eat. Have students work with a partner to explain why the beak shape is best suited for the type of food that the animal eats (such as a woodpecker with a strong skeleton and beak to drill holes in wood in order to find insects, or an eagle with a strong, hooked beak to tear apart prey).

in science" (Achieve, 2013b, p. 4). With an emphasis on this intersection, students, like real scientists, can work to explain the world around them. Their curiosity, their need to solve relevant problems in the natural world, and their desire to innovate will be charged and recharged by a course of study that possesses the attributes that characterize the nature of science.

As suggested in the text scenarios, engaging students in learning activities like Four Corners, Picture It, inside/outside circles, and discussion webs provides them with opportunities to use the languages of science and school to communicate their thinking. As you listen to their conversations, you can assess their developing knowledge and also their use of language. Use the resource "Assessment of Student Oral Language Performance" (at **go.solution-tree.com/commoncore**).

Once the teacher identifies an area of need, he or she can determine an intervention. In this example, after writing their RAFT, students share and answer any questions their classmates ask.

Jimmy says, "A consumer is an autotroph." When questioned by his peers about his evidence, he is unsure. Ms. Sanchez checks "Not Proficient" in the "Understands science content" row and notes that an intervention is needed. Then, as a detailed intervention suggestion, she writes, "Does not understand the foundational vocabulary (meaning of autotroph and consumer). Use Frayer cards to support and further assess his word learning."

In addition to the many examples of formative writing assessment shared in chapter 3, you can use the reproducible rubric "Assessing the Strength of the Written Argument in Science" (**go.solution-tree.com/commoncore**) to assess student writing. Again, after identifying areas of need, the teacher can plan subsequent instruction.

A major outcome of reading instruction is that students become cognitively aware of their own strengths and needs and of how to support their personal acquisition of knowledge. In addition to the examples of formative assessment shared in chapter 4, the resource "Self-Assessment of Metacognition" (on reproducible page 212 and at **go.solution-tree.com/commoncore**) offers a self-assessment for students to measure their metacognition or understanding of how well they are comprehending the targeted information. Depending on your students' understanding of metacognition, you may need to read the items while explaining that metacognition involves thinking about how one thinks. Teachers can use RubiStar (http://rubistar.4teachers.org) to design rubrics that support both teacher and student assessments.

Using Assessment Data to Support Next Steps in Learning and Instruction

The following review of the formative assessments teachers used in the instructional scenarios shared in chapters 2–4 will illustrate the contractual relationship among teaching, learning, and assessment. These assessments also double as instructional routines. In an assessment-, learning-, and instruction-based classroom, these three elements—teaching, learning, and assessing—are all focused on students and are reciprocal and recursive. There is no specific beginning or end; these elements simply provide an interplay of information that illustrates students' progress toward the accomplishment of standards-supported goals.

Let's revisit a few of the shared instructional strategies and routines to understand how they can double as assessments. Reconsider these instructional routines and strategies as formative assessment measures through the eye of an instructional evaluator, and ask yourself the following questions:

- What is the lesson purpose?
- What scientific concepts are being addressed?
- What specific science ideas are being developed that support meaning making?
- What scientific practices do I want to see as a result of this instruction?
- What engineering practices do I want to see as a result of this instruction?
- What background information do my students need to help them understand the concepts?
- What levels of conceptual sophistication should I expect from my students?
- What science skills do the students need to develop?
- What scientific language do I want to incorporate?
- Do I fully understand all dimensions of the science concepts well enough to support student learning?
- What instructional strategies will help me to best teach these scientific concepts?
- What activities, inquiry investigations, or hands-on opportunities will support students' understanding?
- What additional realia, visual aids, or demonstrations will support my English learners?
- What ideas or skills can I anticipate will be difficult for my students?
- What possible interventions should I plan for students who may experience conceptual or language difficulties?
- What assessments will help me to know if my students have accomplished the identified science goals?

As you revisit the instructional examples, notice how teachers formatively assessed students during learning. The resource "Instructional Activities and Assessments That Support Learning and Communicating Like a Scientist" (**go .solution-tree.com/commoncore**) can be used to note the insights you gain about student performance when incorporating these collaborative instructional strategies into science instruction. This resource contains a list of all of the instructional activities in this book that double as assessments (see the book chapters and pages indicated for a fuller explanation of each activity). Use this table to record your findings when using these activities as assessments. In the third column (Feed Forward), note the next steps you would take to support the student's progress. (Feed Forward differs from feedback in that the teacher is not releasing all of the responsibility for next steps to the student but remains as a partner until the student's performance indicates he can function independently.)

As these examples indicate, formative assessments tightly tied to instructional goals can be a continual support for decision making about the next steps in teaching and learning. Teaching science means that the instructional practices being taught and assessed enable students to learn scientific ideas and crosscutting concepts. Learning science enables students to become scientifically literate individuals who are able to listen, converse, write, and read about scientific information.

Assessment must be responsive to the developing understandings of students. Diane Lapp, Douglas Fisher, James Flood, and Arturo Cabello (2001) highlight this relationship when they suggest that assessment should enable teachers to:

1. Diagnose individual needs

2. Inform instruction

3. Evaluate a program

4. Provide accountability information

In the classrooms we've showcased, we have seen teachers use a variety of techniques multiple times to assess what their students know as they provide instruction that makes science learning a continuous process. Their instruction was responsive to the actual learning that was occurring. The intent of each technique and strategy was to deepen and enrich each student's base of ideas and crosscutting science concepts.

These examples can enable you to operationalize science instruction that is responsive to your students' developing bases of knowledge and that will help them to be prepared for the uniqueness of their daily encounters. Being scientifically literate means functioning as a scientifically aware member within one's personal space and one's future workplace environment. It also means understanding that science is not a body of information to be memorized but rather a model of how to investigate, explore, and construct insights that lead to efficient decision making. According to the NRC (2012), author of *A Framework for K–12 Science Education*, the overarching goal of K–12 science education is:

> to ensure that by the end of 12th grade, *all* students have some appreciation of the beauty and wonder of science; possess sufficient knowledge of science and engineering to engage in public discussions on related issues; are careful consumers of scientific and technological information related to their everyday lives; are able to continue to learn about science outside school; and have the skills to enter careers of their choice, including (but not limited to) careers in science, engineering, and technology. (p. 16)

We believe that with the tools of literacy and the support of motivated, thoughtful teachers, our students will not only achieve these noteworthy goals but also become innovative leaders of our global society.

APPENDIX

Reproducibles

Visit **go.solution-tree.com/commoncore** to download the reproducibles in this book.

Collaborative Guidesheet

Use this collaborative guidesheet to scaffold the inquiry process of thinking, planning, and investigating.

Area of Focus	My Ideas	My Partner's Ideas	Our Ideas (After Discussion)
Before the Investigation or Experiment			
What question do you want to study?			
What evidence do you want to look for in order to study your question?			
How will you record your evidence or data? For example, will you design a chart or table to hold your evidence?			
After the Investigation or Experiment			
What do your data tell you?			
How do your ideas connect with those of others in your class? How do your ideas connect with those of other scientists studying the same concepts?			
What are your conclusions? Record your conclusions by writing two or three paragraphs. Be sure your ideas are based on your evidence or data.			

Source: Grant et al., 2012.

Personal Investigation Journal

Using pictures and words, students can note here the results of their study of a topic.

My Questions	My Observations	My Predictions	My Investigation	My Data	My Analysis	My New Questions

Oral Reading Fluency

To assess a reader's fluency when reading a specific text, invite him or her to orally read for one minute. As the student reads, note any words miscalled or skipped. Subtract this number from the total number of words read to get the oral reading rate. Use the key to determine the student's grade level. The data will help you plan both homogeneous and heterogeneous reading groups.

Key:

Grade Level	Oral Reading Rate (Words per Minute)
1	30–70
2	60–90
3	80–120
4	100–130
5	120–150

Student Name	Name of Text	Oral Reading Rate (Words per Minute)	Grade Level

Self-Assessment Chart

An efficient way to support vocabulary instruction is to ask students, using this chart, to assess their own knowledge of the words that they encounter as they explore a particular science topic.

Vocabulary Term	Know Definition	Know an Example	Don't Know Either Yet	Definition	Example

Semantic Feature Analysis Chart

Key Features of _____

Semantic Analysis Map

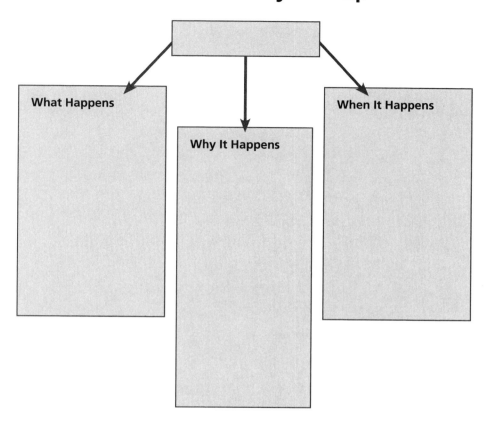

Self-Assessment of Metacognition

Students should read each of the statements contained in the assessment and place a + sign under the ones they perform well. Students should then reread the remaining statements, consider what they need to do to become more proficient, and note this in the sections labeled "Suggestions to Myself" and "My Plan of Action."

I attentively listen.	I ask appropriate questions.	I understand scientific concepts being shared.	I make connections among my ideas and those shared by others.	I consider evidence and research when making claims.	I offer thorough explanations.	I identify related areas for investigation.

Suggestions to Myself

My Plan of Action: How can I help myself understand this information better?

References and Resources

ABC News. (2010, June 25). *Is the space program worth it?* Accessed at http://abcnews.go.com/Technology/video/space-program-worth-11014480 on July 30, 2013.

Abell, S. K. (2006). Perspectives: On writing in science. *Science and Children, 44*(4), 60–61.

Achieve. (2012). *Standards for engineering, technology, and the applications of science.* Washington, DC: Author.

Achieve. (2013a). *Next generation science standards.* Washington, DC: Author.

Achieve. (2013b). *Next generation science standards—Appendix H.* Washington, DC: Author.

Adger, C. T., Snow, C. E., & Christian, D. (Eds.). (2002). *What teachers need to know about language.* Washington, DC: Center for Applied Linguistics and Delta Systems. Accessed at www.gse.harvard.edu/directory/faculty/faculty-detail/#ixzz2RhsRSNoD on June 17, 2013.

Aldrin, B. (2009). *Buzz Aldrin on Antarctica, the Titanic, and space exploration* [Web log post]. Accessed at http://blog.nationalgeographicexpeditions.com/2009/12/buzz-aldrin-on-antarctica-the-titanic-and-space-exploration on June 17, 2013.

Alvermann, D. E. (1991). The discussion web: A graphic aid for learning across the curriculum. *The Reading Teacher, 45,* 92–99.

Aronson, E., Stephen, C., Sikes, J., Blaney, N., & Snapp, M. (Eds.). (1978). *The jigsaw classroom.* Beverly Hills, CA: SAGE.

Ausubel, D. P. (1968). *Educational psychology: A cognitive view.* New York: Holt, Rinehart & Winston.

Baker, L., & Brown, A. L. (1984). Metacognitive skills and reading. In P. D. Pearson, R. Barr, M. L. Kamil, & P. Mosenthal (Eds.), *Handbook of reading research* (pp. 353–394). New York: Longman.

Barrett, J. (1978). *Cloudy with a chance of meatballs.* New York: Simon & Schuster.

Bayrock, F. (2007). *States of matter: A question and answer book.* New York: Capstone Press.

Bazerman, C. (1988). *Shaping written knowledge: The genre and activity of the experimental article in science.* Madison: University of Wisconsin Press.

Bear, D. R., Invernizzi, M., Templeton, S. R., & Johnston, F. (2007). *Words their way: Word study for phonics, vocabulary, and spelling instruction* (4th ed.). Upper Saddle River, NJ: Prentice Hall.

Beck, I. L., & McKeown, M. G. (2001). Text talk: Capturing the benefits of read-aloud experiences for young children. *The Reading Teacher, 55*(1), 10–20.

Beck, I. L., McKeown, M. G., & Kucan, L. (2008). *Creating robust vocabulary: Frequently asked questions and extended examples.* New York: Guilford Press.

Benko, S. L. (2012). Scaffolding: An ongoing process to support adolescent writing development. *Journal of Adolescent and Adult Literacy, 56*(4), 291–300.

Bianco, C. (n.d.). *How your heart works.* Accessed at http://science. howstuffworks.com/environmental/life/human-biology/heart.htm on April 12, 2013.

Biemans, H. J. A., Deel, O. R., & Simons, P. R. (2001). Differences between successful and less successful students while working with the CONTACT-2 strategy. *Learning and Instruction, 11*(4–5), 265–282.

Blachowicz, C. L. Z., Sullivan, D. M., & Cieply, C. (2001). Fluency snapshots: A quick screening tool for your classroom. *Reading Psychology, 22*(2), 95–109.

Black, P. J. (1993). Formative and summative assessment by teachers. *Studies in Science Education, 21*(1), 49–97.

Boothroyd, J. (2007). *Plants and the environment.* Minneapolis, MN: Lerner.

Branley, F. M. (1963). *Down comes the rain.* New York: HarperCollins.

Branley, F. M. (1964). *Flash, crash, rumble, and roll.* New York: HarperCollins.

Bransford, J. D., Brown, A. L., & Cocking, R. R. (1999). *How people learn: Brain, mind, experience, and school.* Washington, DC: National Academies Press.

Brassell, D. (2011). *Dare to differentiate: Vocabulary strategies for all students* (3rd ed.). New York: Guilford Press.

Breen, M., & Friestad, K. (2008). *The kids' book of weather forecasting.* New York: Williamson Books.

Broaddus, K., & Worthy, J. (2001). Fluency beyond the primary grades: From group performance to silent, independent reading. *The Reading Teacher, 55*(4), 334–343.

Brozo, W. G., Shiel, G., & Topping, K. (2007). Engagement in reading: Lessons learned from three PISA countries. *Journal of Adolescent and Adult Literacy, 51*(4), 304–315.

Bybee, R. W. (2011). Scientific and engineering practices in K–12 classrooms: Understanding *A Framework for K–12 Science Education. The Science Teacher, 78*(9), 34–40.

Chall, J. S. (1967). *Learning to read: The great debate: An inquiry into the science, art, and ideology of old and new methods of teaching children to read.* New York: McGraw-Hill.

Chall, J. S. (1983). *Stages of reading development.* New York: McGraw-Hill.

Cole, H. (1997). *Jack's garden.* New York: HarperCollins.

Conger, C. (n.d.). *10 NASA inventions you might use every day.* Accessed at http://dsc.discovery.com/tv-shows/curiosity/topics/ten-nasa-inventions.htm on June 17, 2013.

Cutler, L., & Graham, S. (2008). Primary grade writing instruction: A national survey. *Journal of Educational Psychology, 100*(4), 907–919.

dePaola, T. (1985). *The cloud book.* New York: Holiday House.

Discovery Channel. (2011). How does a solar cooker work? *Environmental Protection.* Accessed at http://curiosity.discovery.com/question/how-does -solar-cooker-work on August 1, 2013.

Dodo skeleton found on island, may yield extinct bird's DNA. (2007). *National Geographic.* Accessed at http://news.nationalgeographic.com /news/2007/07/070703-dodo.html on July 8, 2013.

Donovan, S., & Bransford, J. (2005). *How students learn science in the classroom.* Washington, DC: National Academies Press.

Dorph, R., Goldstein, D., Lee, S., Lepori, K., Schneider, S., & Venbateson, S. (2007). *The status of science education in the Bay Areas: Research brief.*

Unpublished manuscript, University of California, Berkeley, Lawrence Hall of Science.

Duschl, R. A., & Osborne, J. (2002). Supporting and promoting argumentation discourse in science education. *Studies in Science Education, 38,* 39–72.

Duschl, R. H., Schweingruber, H., & Shouse, A. (Eds.). (2007). *Taking science to school: Learning and teaching science in grades K–8.* Washington, DC: National Academies Press.

Eichinger, D., Anderson, C. W., Palincsar, A. S., & David, Y. M. (1991, April). *An illustration of the roles of content knowledge, scientific argument, and social norms in collaborative problem solving.* Paper presented at the annual meeting of the American Educational Research Association, Chicago.

Erdman, S. (2009, December 2). Buzz Aldrin on Antarctica, the Titanic, and space exploration [Web log post]. Accessed at http://blog.national geographicexpeditions.com/2009/12/buzz-aldrin-on-antarctica-the -titanic-and-space-exploration on July 30, 2013.

Fang, Z., Schleppegrell, M. J., & Cox, B. E. (2006). Understanding the language demands of schooling: Nouns in academic registers. *Journal of Literacy Research, 38*(3), 247–273.

Fearn, L., & Farnan, N. (2001). *Interactions: Teaching writing and the language arts.* New York: Houghton Mifflin.

Fisher, D., & Frey, N. (2007). *Checking for understanding: Formative assessment techniques for your classroom.* Alexandria, VA: Association for Supervision and Curriculum Development.

Fisher, D., & Frey, N. (2008a). *Better learning through structured teaching.* Alexandria, VA: Association for Supervision and Curriculum Development.

Fisher, D., & Frey, N. (2008b). *Word wise and content rich, grades 7–12: Five essential steps to teaching academic vocabulary.* Portsmouth, NH: Heinemann.

Fisher, D., & Frey, N. (2012, September). Text-dependent questions. *Principal Leadership,* 70–73.

Fisher, D., Frey, N., & Lapp, D. (2012a). *Teaching students to read like detectives: Comprehending, analyzing, and discussing texts.* Bloomington, IN: Solution Tree Press.

Fisher, D., Frey, N., & Lapp, D. (2012b). *Text complexity: Raising rigor in reading.* Newark, DE: International Reading Association.

Flavell, J. H. (1979). Metacognition and cognitive monitoring: A new area of cognitive-developmental inquiry. *American Psychologist, 34*(10), 906–911.

Flood, J., Lapp, D., Mraz, M., & Wood, K. (2006). Effective comprehension for the middle school classroom, part II. *Journal of the League of New England Middle Schools, 18*(1), 5–11.

Flower, L., & Hayes. J. R. (1981). A cognitive process theory of writing. *College Composition and Communication, 32*(4), 365–387.

Fowler, A. (2005). *What magnets can do.* New York: Children's Press.

Frayer, D. A., Frederick, W. D., & Klausmeier, H. J. (1969). *A schema for testing the level of concept mastery* (Working paper no. 16). Madison: Wisconsin Research and Development Center for Cognitive Learning.

Frey, N., & Fisher, D. (2010). Identifying instructional moves during guided learning. *The Reading Teacher, 64,* 84–95.

Frey, N., & Fisher, D. (2013). *Common Core English language arts in a PLC at work, grades 3–5.* Bloomington, IN: Solution Tree Press.

Fry, E. (1977). *Elementary reading instruction.* New York: McGraw-Hill.

Gambrell, L. B. (1996). Creating classroom cultures that foster reading motivation. *The Reading Teacher, 50*(1), 14–25.

Gerde, H. K., Bingham, G. E., & Wasik, B. A. (2012). Writing in early childhood classrooms: Guidance for best practices. *Early Childhood Education Journal, 40*(6), 351–359.

Gibbons, G. (1987). *Weather forecasting.* New York: Simon & Schuster.

Gibbons, G. (1993). *From seed to plant.* New York: Holiday House.

Gibbons, G. (1998). *The moon book.* New York: Holiday House.

Gibbons, P. (2002). *Scaffolding language, scaffolding learning: Teaching second language learners in the mainstream classroom.* Portsmouth, NH: Heinemann.

Gilbert, J., & Graham, S. (2010). Teaching writing to elementary students in grades 4–6: A national survey. *Elementary School Journal, 110*(4), 494–518.

Goodman, L. (2004). Shades of meaning: Relating and expanding word knowledge. In G. E. Tompkins & C. Blanchfield (Eds.), *Teaching vocabulary: 50 creative strategies, grades K–12* (pp. 85–87). Upper Saddle River, NJ: Merrill/Prentice Hall.

Goodman, P. (2004). *Animal classification.* London: Hodder Wayland Childrens.

Gore, A. (2012). *Our choice: A plan to solve the climate crisis*. New York: Push Pop Press. Accessed at http://pushpoppress.com/ourchoice/ on June 17, 2013.

Graesser, A. C., McNamara, D. S., Louwerse, M. M., & Cai, Z. (2004). Coh-metrix: Analysis of text on cohesion and language. *Behavior Research Methods, Instruments, and Computers, 36*(2), 193–202. Accessed at http://cohmetrix.memphis.edu/cohmetrixpr/cohmetrix3.html on May 20, 2013.

Grant, M., & Lapp, D. (2011). Teaching science literacy. *Educational Leadership, 68*(6). Accessed at www.ascd.org/publications/educational-leadership/mar11/vol68/num06/Teaching-Science-Literacy.aspx on February 20, 2013.

Grant, M., Lapp, D., Fisher, D., Johnson, K., & Frey, N. (2012). Purposeful instruction: Mixing up the "I," "We," and "You." *Journal of Adolescent and Adult Literacy, 56*(1), 45–55. Accessed at http://onlinelibrary.wiley.com/doi/10.1002/JAAL.00101/abstract on June 17, 2013.

Guillain, C. (2008). *Saving energy (Help the environment)*. Portsmouth, NH: Heinemann.

Guthrie, J., & Wigfield, A. (2000). Engagement and motivation in reading. In M. L. Kamil, P. Mosenthal, P. D. Pearson, & R. Barr (Eds.), *Handbook of reading research* (Vol. 3, pp. 403–422). Mahwah, NJ: Erlbaum.

Halliday, M. A. K. (1961). Categories of the theory of grammar. *Word, 17*(3).

Halliday, M. A. K. (1987). Spoken and written modes of meaning. In R. Horowitz & S. J. Samuels (Eds.), *Comprehending oral and written language* (pp. 55–82). New York: Academic Press.

Halliday, M. A. K. (1993). Toward a language-based theory of learning. *Linguistics and Education, 5*, 93–116.

Halliday, M., & Matthiessen, C. M. I. M. (2004). *An introduction to functional grammar* (3rd ed.). London: Arnold.

Hand, B., Prain, V., Lawrence, C., & Yore, L. D. (1999). A writing in science framework designed to enhance science literacy. *International Journal of Science Education, 21*(10), 1021–1035.

Hansen, R. S., & Hansen, K. (n.d.). *Quintessential careers: What do employers really want? Top skills and values employers seek from job-seekers*. Accessed at www.quintcareers.com/printable/job_skills_values.html on April 26, 2013.

Hart, B., & Risley, T. R. (1995). *Meaningful differences in the everyday experiences of young American children*. Baltimore: Brookes.

Hayes, J., & Flower, L. (1980). Identifying the organization of writing processes. In L. W. Gregg & E. Steinberg (Eds.), *Cognitive processes in writing* (pp. 3–30). Hillsdale, NJ: Erlbaum.

Heckelman, R. G. (1966). Using the neurological impress remedial reading technique. *Academic Therapy, 1*, 235–239, 250.

Heckelman, R. G. (1969). A neurological impress method of remedial reading instruction. *Academic Therapy, 5*, 277–282.

Heller, C. (2012, March 5). Neil deGrasse Tyson: How space exploration can make America great again. *The Atlantic*. Accessed at www.theatlantic.com /technology/archive/2012/03/neil-degrasse-tyson-how-space-exploration -can-make-america-great-again/253989/ on February 19, 2013.

Hoffman, J., Roser, N., & Battle, J. (1993). Reading aloud in classrooms: From the modal toward a "model." *The Reading Teacher, 46*(6), 496–503.

Jordan, H. J. (1960). *How a seed grows.* New York: HarperCollins.

Juel, C. (1988). Learning to read and write: A longitudinal study of 54 children from first through fourth grades. *Journal of Educational Psychology, 80*(4), 437–447.

Kagan, S. (1994). *Kagan cooperative learning.* San Clemente, CA: Kagan.

Kapur, A. (2010, August 26). A way of life swept away on a current. *The New York Times*. Accessed at www.nytimes.com/2010/08/27/world/asia/27iht -letter.html?_r=0 on March 29, 2013.

Kirkman, J. (2005). *Good style: Writing for science and technology* (2nd ed.). New York: Routledge.

Krashen, S. (2012). Developing academic language: Some hypotheses. *Journal of Foreign Language Teaching, 7*(2), 8–15.

Kuhn, D. (1991). *The skills of argument.* New York: Cambridge University Press.

Kujawa, S., & Huske, L. (1995). *The strategic teaching and reading project guidebook* (Rev. ed.). Oak Brook, IL: North Central Regional Educational Laboratory.

Lapp, D., Fisher, D., Flood, J., & Cabello, A. (2001). An integrated approach to the teaching and assessment of language arts. In S. R. Hurley & J. V. Tinajero (Eds.), *Literacy assessment of second language learners* (pp. 1–26). Boston: Allyn & Bacon.

Lapp, D., Fisher, D., & Wolsey, T. D. (2012). *Teachers' perceptions of their preparation for teaching writing*. Paper presented at the Literacy Research Association Conference, San Diego, CA.

Lapp, D., & Flood, J. (1985). The impact of writing instruction on teachers' attitudes and practices. In J. A. Niles (Ed.), *Proceedings of the thirty-fourth National Reading Conference on issues in literacy: A research perspective* (pp. 375–380). Chicago: National Reading Conference.

Lapp, D., Flood, J., Brock, C., & Fisher, D. (2007). *Teaching reading to every child* (4th ed.). Mahwah, NJ: Erlbaum.

Latour, B. (1987). *Science in action: How to follow scientists and engineers through society*. Cambridge, MA: Harvard University Press.

Lemke, J. L. (1990). *Talking science: Language, learning, and values*. Norwood, NJ: Ablex.

Lesaux, N. K., & Kieffer, M. J. (2010). Exploring sources of reading comprehension difficulties among language minority learners and their classmates in early adolescence. *American Educational Research Journal, 47*, 596–632.

Leutwyler, K. (2001, June 15). Scientists grow plants without sunlight or water. *Scientific American*. Accessed at www.scientificamerican.com/article.cfm?id=scientists-grow-plants-wi on March 28, 2013.

Lexile Analyzer. (2013). *MetaMetrics*. Accessed at ww.lexile.com/analyzer/ on May 20, 2013.

Lipson, M. Y. (1982). Learning new information from text: The role of prior knowledge and reading ability. *Journal of Reading Behavior, 14*(3), 243–261.

Llewellyn, C. (2003). *Push and pull (I know that)*. London: Franklin Watts.

Maloney, J., & Simon, S. (2006). Mapping children's discussions of evidence in science to assess collaboration and argumentation. *International Journal of Science Education, 28*(15), 1817–1841.

Manzo, A. V. (1969). ReQuest procedure. *Journal of Reading, 13*, 123–126.

Martin-Chang, S. Y., & Gould, O. N. (2008). Revisiting print exposure: Exploring differential links to vocabulary, comprehension and reading rate. *Journal of Research in Reading, 31*(3), 273–284.

Mathis, P., & Boyd, N. (2009). Who is teaching social studies? PreService teachers' reaction. *Social Studies Research and Practice, 4*(3), 76–85.

McKay, S. (2002). *About pets.* San Francisco: Treasure Bay.

McKeown, M. G., Beck, I. L., Sinatra, G. M., & Loxterman, J. A. (1992). The relative contribution of prior knowledge and coherent text to comprehension. *Reading Research Quarterly, 27*(1), 78–93.

McMillan, B. (1997). *Night of the Pufflings.* New York: Houghton Mifflin.

Mehan, H. (1979). *Learning lessons: Social organization in the classroom.* Cambridge, MA: Harvard University Press.

Michaels, S., Shouse, A. W., & Schweingruber, H. A. (2008). *Ready, set, science! Putting research to work in K–8 science classrooms.* Washington, DC: National Academies Press.

Minner, D. D., Levy, A. J., & Century, J. (2010). Inquiry-based science instruction—what is it and does it matter? Results from a research synthesis years 1984 to 2002. *Journal of Research in Science Teaching, 47*(4), 474–496.

Moss, B., & Loh, V. S. (2011). 35 strategies for guiding readers through informational texts. New York: Guilford Press.

Murray, D. M. (1972). Teach writing as a process not a product. *The Leaflet,* 11–14.

NASA. (n.d.). *Kennedy Space Center: Frequently asked questions.* Accessed at http://science.ksc.nasa.gov/pao/faq/faqanswers.htm on June 17, 2013.

National Assessment of Educational Progress. (2009). *The nation's report card: Reading 2009—National Assessment of Educational Progress at grades 4 and 8.* Washington, DC: U.S. Government Printing Office. Accessed at http://nationsreportcard.gov/reading_2009/reading_2009_report/ on June 17, 2013.

National Assessment of Educational Progress. (2011a). *The nation's report card: Science 2011—National Assessment of Educational Progress at grade 8.* Washington, DC: U.S. Department of Education. Accessed at http://nces.ed.gov/nationsreportcard/pdf/main2011/2012465.pdf on May 24, 2013.

National Assessment of Educational Progress. (2011b). *The nation's report card: Writing 2011—National Assessment of Educational Progress at grades 8 and 12.* Accessed at http://nationsreportcard.gov/writing_2011/writing_2011_report/ on July 15, 2013.

National Assessment of Educational Progress. (2012, August 30). *What does the NAEP writing assessment measure?* Accessed at http://nces.ed.gov/pubsearch/pubsinfo.asp?pubid=2012470 on July 15, 2013.

National Assessment Governing Board. (2008). *Reading framework for the 2009 National Assessment of Educational Progress.* Washington, DC: U.S. Government Printing Office.

National Assessment Governing Board. (2012). *The nation's report card releases Rresults from an innovative, interactive computer-based writing assessment.* Accessed at http://www.nagb.org/newsroom/naep-releases/2011 -writing.html on June 17, 2013.

National Center for Education Statistics. (2008). *The nation's report card: Writing 2007* (NCES 2008–468). Accessed at http://nces.ed.gov /nationsreportcard/pdf/main2007/2008468.pdf on June 17, 2013.

National Center for Education Statistics. (2009). *Highlights from PISA 2009: Performance of U.S. 15-year-old students in reading, mathematics, and science literacy in an international context.* Washington, DC: U.S. Department of Education. Accessed at http://nces.ed.gov/pubs2011/2011004.pdf on May 22, 2013.

National Center for Education Statistics. (2012). *The nation's report card: Vocabulary results from the 2009 and 2011 NAEP reading assessments* (NCES 2013-452). Washington, DC: Author.

National Governors Association Center for Best Practices & Council of Chief State School Officers. (2010a). *Common Core State Standards for English language arts and literacy in history/social studies, science, and technical subjects.* Washington, DC: Authors. Accessed at www.corestandards.org /assets/CCSSI_ELA%20Standards.pdf on January 6, 2013.

National Governors Association Center for Best Practices & Council of Chief State School Officers. (2010b). *Common Core State Standards for English language arts and literacy in history/social studies, science, and technical subjects—Appendix A: Research supporting key elements of the standards and glossary of key terms.* Washington, DC: Author. Accessed at www .corestandards.org/assets/Appendix_A.pdf on May 20, 2013.

National Governors Association Center for Best Practices & Council of Chief State School Officers. (2010c). *Common Core State Standards for English language arts and literacy in history/social studies, science, and technical subjects—Appendix B: Text exemplars and sample performance tasks.* Accessed at www.corestandards.org/assets/Appendix_B.pdf on May 20, 2013.

National Governors Association Center for Best Practices & Council of Chief State School Officers. (2010d). *Common Core State Standards for English language arts and literacy in history/social studies, science, and technical*

subjects—Appendix C: Samples of student writing. Accessed at www
.corestandards.org/assets/Appendix_C.pdf on May 20, 2013.

National Governors Association Center for Best Practices & Council of Chief
State School Officers. (2012). *Common Core State Standards for English
language arts and literacy in history/social studies, science, and technical
subjects—Appendix A: Supplemental information for appendix A of the
Common Core State Standards for English language arts and literacy: New
research on text complexity.* Accessed at www.corestandards.org/assets
/E0813_Appendix_A_New_Research_on_Text_Complexity.pdf on May
20, 2013.

National Research Council. (1996). *National science education standards:
Observe, interact, change, learn.* Washington, DC: National Academies
Press.

National Research Council. (2012). *A framework for K–12 science education:
Practices, crosscutting concepts, and core ideas.* Washington, DC: National
Academies Press.

National Research Council. (2013). *Next generation science standards.* Accessed
at www.nextgenscience.org/ on May 23, 2013.

National Science Teachers Association. (2000). *NSTA position statement: The
nature of science.* Accessed at www.nsta.org/about/positions/natureofscience
.aspx?print=true on February 19, 2013.

National Science Teachers Association. (2004). *NSTA position statement:
Scientific inquiry.* Accessed at www.nsta.org/about/positions/inquiry.aspx on
February 18, 2013.

National Writing Project. (2003). *National Writing Project statement on the
2002 NAEP writing report.* Accessed at www.nwp.org/cs/public/print
/resource/860 on June 17, 2013.

Nelson, J., Perfetti, C., Liben, D., & Liben, M. (2012). *Measures of
text difficulty: Testing their predictive value for grade levels and student
performance.* New York: Student Achievement Partners.

Noddings, N. (2006). *Critical lessons: What our schools should teach.* New York:
Cambridge University Press.

O'Donnell, A. M. (2006). The role of peers and group learning. In P. Alexander
& P. Winne (Eds.), *Handbook of educational psychology* (2nd ed., pp. 327–
348). Mahwah, NJ: Erlbaum.

Ogle, D. (1986). K-W-L: A teaching model that develops active reading of expository text. *The Reading Teacher, 39*(6), 564–570.

Ornes, S. (2011, June 15). *Germy weather: Bacteria high in the sky could be causing rain, snow, and hail.* Accessed at www.sciencenewsforkids .org/2011/06/germy-weather/ on May 20, 2013.

Osborne, J. E., Erduran, S., Simon, S., & Monk, M. (2001). Enhancing the quality of argument in school science. *School Science Review, 82*(301), 63–70.

Palazzo, J. (1982). *Our friend the sun: Now I know.* Mahwah. N.J: Troll Associates.

Palincsar, A. S., & Brown, A. L. (1986). Interactive teaching to promote independent learning from text. *The Reading Teacher, 39*(8), 771–777.

PBS LearningMedia. (2007). *Energy flow in the coral reef ecosystem* [Video file]. Accessed at www.pbslearning media.org/resource/hew06.sci.life.reg .foodweb/energy-flow-in-the-coral-reef-ecosystem on October 17, 2013.

Pittelman, S. D., Heimlich, J. E., Berglund, R. L., & French, M. P. (1991). *Semantic feature analysis: Classroom applications.* Newark, DE: International Reading Association.

Prain, V., & Hand, B. (1996). Writing for learning in secondary science: Rethinking practices. *Teaching and Teacher Education, 12*(6), 609–626.

President's Council of Advisors on Science and Technology. (2010). *Prepare and inspire: K–12 education is science, technology, engineering, and math (STEM) for America's future* (Report to the president). Accessed at www.whitehouse .gov/sites/default/files/microsites/ostp/pcast-stem-ed-final.pdf on May 23, 2013.

President's Council of Advisors on Science and Technology. (2012). *Engage to excel: Producing one million additional college graduates with degrees in science, technology, engineering, and mathematics* (Report to the president). Accessed at www.whitehouse.gov/sites/default/files/microsites/ostp/pcast -engage-to-excel-final_feb.pdf on May 23, 2013.

Pressley, M., & Afflerbach, P. (1995). *Verbal protocols of reading: The nature of constructively responsive reading.* Hillsdale, NJ: Erlbaum.

Pressley, M., Wharton-McDonald, R., Mistretta, J., & Echevaria, M. (1998). The nature of literacy instruction in ten grade-4/5 classrooms in upstate New York. *Scientific Studies of Reading, 2,* 159–191.

Reiser, B. J., Berland, L. K, & Kenyon, L. (2012). Engaging students in the scientific practices of explanation and argumentation. *Science Teacher, 74,* 34–39; *Science Scope, 35,* 6–11; *Science and Children, 49,* 8–13.

Resnick, L. (1995). From aptitude to effort: A new foundation for our schools. *Daedalus, 124*(4), 55–62.

Rijlaarsdam, G., & van den Bergh, H. (2006). Writing process theory: A functional dynamic approach. In C. A. MacArthur, S. Graham, & J. Fitzgerald (Eds.), *Handbook of writing research* (pp. 41–52). New York: Guilford Press.

Robinson, D. H. (1998). Graphic organizers as aids to text learning. *Reading Research and Instruction, 37*(2), 85–105.

Rockwell, A. F. (2008). *Clouds.* New York: HarperCollins.

Rosinsky, N. M. (2003). *Light: Shadows, mirrors, and rainbows.* Minneapolis, MN: Picture Window Books.

Ruiz-Primo, M. A., & Furtak, E. M. (2006). Exploring teachers' informal formative assessment practices and students' understanding in the context of scientific inquiry. *Journal of Research in Science Teaching, 44*(1), 57–84.

Rupley, W. H., & Slough, S. W. (2010). Building prior knowledge and vocabulary in science in the intermediate grades: Creating hooks for learning. *Literacy Research and Instruction, 49*(2), 99–112.

Saddler, B., & Graham, S. (2005). The effects of peer-assisted sentence-combining instruction on the writing performance of more and less skilled young writers. *Journal of Educational Psychology, 97*(1), 43–54.

Salahu-Din, D., Persky, H., & Miller, J. (2008). *Nation's report card: Writing 2007.* Washington, DC: National Center for Educational Statistics. Accessed at http://nces.ed.gov/nationsreportcard/pubs/main2007/2008468 .asp on February 19, 2013.

Santa, C., & Havens, L. (1995). Creating independence through student-owned strategies: Project CRISS. Dubuque, IA: Kendall Hunt.

Saville-Troike, M. (1984). What really matters in second language learning for academic achievement? *TESOL Quarterly, 18,* 199–219.

Schegloff, E. A. (2000). Overlapping talk and the organization of turn-taking for conversation. *Language in Society, 29,* 1–63.

Schmoker, M., & Graff, G. (2011). *More argument, fewer standards.* Accessed at http://mikeschmoker.com/more-argument.html on February 19, 2013.

Schwanenflugel, P. J., Meisinger, E., Wisenbakerm J. M., Kuhn, M. R., Strauss, G. P., & Morris, R. D. (2006). Becoming a fluent and automatic reader in the early elementary school years. *Reading Research Quarterly*, *41*(4), 496–522.

Shanahan, T., & Shanahan, C. (2008). Teaching disciplinary literacy to adolescents: Rethinking content-area literacy. *Harvard Educational Review*, *78*(1), 40–59.

Simon, S., Erduran, S., & Osborne, J. (2006). Learning to teach argumentation: Research and development in the science classroom. *International Journal of Science Education*, *28*(2–3), 235–260.

Stanovich, K. E. (1980). Toward an interactive-compensatory model of individual differences in the development of reading fluency. *Reading Research Quarterly*, *16*, 32–71.

Stanovich, K. E. (1986). Matthew effects in reading: Some consequences of individual differences in the acquisition of literacy. *Reading Research Quarterly*, *21*(4), 360–407.

Stauffer, R. G., & Harrell, M. M. (1975). Individualized reading-thinking activities. *The Reading Teacher*, *28*, 765–769.

Stenner, A. J., Koons, H., & Swartz, C. W. (2010). *Text complexity and developing expertise in reading*. Chapel Hill, NC: MetaMetrics.

Street, C., & Stang, K. (2008). Improving the teaching of writing across the curriculum: A model for teaching in-service secondary teachers to write. *Action in Teacher Education*, *30*(1), 37–49.

Strickland, D. S. (2011). *Teaching phonics today: Word study strategies through the grades* (2nd ed.). Newark, DE: International Reading Association.

Taboada, A., & Rutherford, V. (2011). Developing reading comprehension and academic vocabulary for English language learners through science content: A formative experiment. *Reading Psychology*, *32*(2), 113–157.

Thangavelu, M. (2011). *Opinion: Make manned space flight great again* [Web log post]. Accessed at http://lightyears.blogs.cnn.com/2011/11/18/opinion-make-manned-space-flight-great-again/ on June 17, 2013.

Venezky, R. L. (1982). The origins of the present day chasm between adult literacy needs and school literacy instruction. *Visible Language*, *16*, 113–136.

Wagner, A. (2012, May 30). *Neurological impress method* (N.I.M.) [Video file]. Accessed at www.youtube.com/watch?v=xhOGj6i8f8s on October 17, 2013.

Williams, K., Kurtek, K., & Sampson, V. (2011). The affective elements of science learning: A questionnaire to assess—and improve—student attitudes toward science. *The Science Teacher, 78*(1), 40–45.

Wong-Fillmore, L. (1985). Learning a second language: Chinese children in the American classroom. In J. Alatis & J. Staczek (Eds.), *Perspectives on bilingualism and bilingual education* (pp. 436–452). Washington, DC: Georgetown University Press.

Wood, K. D., Lapp, D., Flood, J., & Taylor, D. B. (2008). *Guiding readers through text: Strategy guides for new times* (2nd ed.). Newark, DE: International Reading Association.

Yore, L. D. (2000). Enhancing science literacy for all students with embedded reading instruction and writing-to-learn activities. *Journal of Deaf Studies and Deaf Education, 5*(1), 105–122.

Yore, L. (2004). Why do future scientists need to study the language arts? In E. W. Saul (Ed.), *Crossing borders in literacy and science instruction: Perspectives on theory and practice* (pp. 71–94). Newark, DE: International Reading Association.

Yore, L. D., Hand, B. M., & Florence, M. K. (2004). Scientists' views of science, models of writing, and science writing practices. *Journal of Research in Science Teaching, 41*, 338–369.

Zike, D. (2013). *Dinah Zike's reading and study skills foldables.* New York: McGraw-Hill. Accessed at http://teacherweb.com/fl/belleviewmiddleschool/mrsvnormand/foldables.pdf on June 17, 2013.

Zuehlke, J. (2009). *Landslides.* Minneapolis, MN: Lerner.

Index

What Principals Need to Know About Teaching and Learning Science
Eric C. Sheninger and Keith Devereaux
2nd Edition This accessible resource offers practical strategies for increasing student achievement in science and fostering a school environment that supports the science curriculum. With checklists, assessments, and reproducibles that you can share with stakeholders, discover how to improve science instruction and sustain a strong science program.
BKF544

Common Core English Language Arts in a PLC at Work™ series
Douglas Fisher, Nancy Frey, and Cynthia L. Uline
These teacher guides illustrate how to sustain successful implementation of the Common Core State Standards for English language arts in K–12 instruction, curriculum, assessment, and intervention practices within the powerful Professional Learning Communities at Work™ process.
Joint Publications With the International Reading Association
BKF578, BKF580, BKF582, BKF584, BKF586

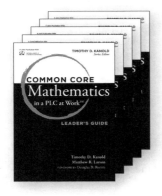

Common Core Mathematics in a PLC at Work™ Series
Edited by Timothy D. Kanold
These teacher guides illustrate how to sustain successful implementation of the Common Core State Standards for Mathematics. Discover what students should learn and how they should learn it at each grade level. Comprehensive and research-affirmed analysis tools and strategies will help you and your collaborative team develop and assess student demonstrations of deep conceptual understanding *and* procedural fluency.
Joint Publications With the National Council of Teachers of Mathematics
BKF559, BKF566, BKF568, BKF574, BKF561

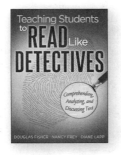

Teaching Students to Read Like Detectives
Douglas Fisher, Nancy Frey, and Diane Lapp
Prompt students to become the sophisticated readers, writers, and thinkers they need to be to achieve higher learning. Explore the important relationship between text, learner, and learning, and gain an array of methods to establish critical literacy in a discussion-based and reflective classroom.
BKF499

Solution Tree | Press
a division of
Solution Tree

Visit solution-tree.com or call 800.733.6786 to order.

Wait! Your professional development journey doesn't have to end with the last pages of this book.

We realize improving student learning doesn't happen overnight. And your school or district shouldn't be left to puzzle out all the details of this process alone.

No matter where you are on the journey, we're committed to helping you get to the next stage.

Take advantage of everything from **custom workshops** to **keynote presentations** and **interactive web and video conferencing**. We can even help you develop an action plan tailored to fit your specific needs.

Let's get the conversation started.

Call 888.763.9045 today.

solution-tree.com